Instructor's Manual and Test Bank to accompany
Arnold & Boggs:

INTERPERSONAL RELATIONSHIPS

Professional Communication Skills for Nurses

Fourth Edition

Kathleen Underman Boggs, PhD, FNP-C
Associate Professor
College of Health and Human Services
University of North Carolina at Charlotte
and Family Nurse Practitioner, Planned Parenthood NC West
Charlotte, North Carolina

Test Questions Written By

Barbara Harrison, RN, BScN, CPMHN(C)
Registered Nurse
Addiction and Mental Health Center
Montgomery General Hospital
Olney, Maryland

SAUNDERS
An Imprint of Elsevier Science
Philadelphia   London   New York   St. Louis   Sydney   Toronto

SAUNDERS
An Imprint of Elsevier Science
11830 Westline Industrial Drive
St. Louis, Missouri 63146

Vice President, Publishing Director: Sally Schrefer
Acquisitions Editor: Tom Wilhelm
Associate Developmental Editor: Jill Ferguson
Project Manager: Gayle May

Printed in the United States of America.

Last digit is the print number: 9 8 7 6 5 4 3 2 1

Introduction

The Prologue explains the use of class exercises and the experiential process as an established teaching-learning tool. The first section of the *Instructor's Manual* provides **teaching tips** for each exercise listed in the book, **suggested answers**, as well as some **teaching pitfalls** to avoid. **Additional exercises** are provided which can be used to enrich your class. The following section provides a **test bank** of suggested test questions, many of which have been used by the author.

A new feature in the fourth edition is the inclusion of **ethical dilemmas** in boxes, found in each of the textbook chapters. These situations are for the most part adapted from real-life dilemmas encountered in day-to-day nursing situations by the authors. The process for helping students think about each of these situations is fully explained in Chapter 3 *Clinical Judgment: Applying Critical Thinking and Ethical Decision Making*. Class discussion should generally follow the steps of critical thinking. Students need to base their decision about "What Would You Do?" on one of the principles of BioEthics listed in the text: *Autonomy*, *Beneficence*, or *Justice*, rather than on their personal values system. It is important to stress that there is no single correct answer! In many cases, resolution differs depending on which principle is used to guide thinking.

Prologue

TEACHING STRATEGIES INTRODUCTION

The 23 chapters presented in the Arnold and Boggs book are designed to provide the nurse with a comprehensive understanding of communication principles and of professional relationships. This information can be used to establish and maintain therapeutic relationships with clients and collegial relationships with members of the interdisciplinary health team. In presenting this content, the authors have integrated a generous number of learning exercises. Exercises are designed to provide opportunities for more active learner involvement in the teaching-learning process. When the term *student* is used this can apply equally to nurses in clinical practice as well as student nurses. Active participation and reflective analysis are essential components by which a student builds his or her *critical thinking* abilities (Bethune & Jackson, 1997). Use of these exercises provides the learner with preparatory practice needed to master essential communication skills that will be used daily throughout a nursing career. Case studies provide concrete examples to model application of specific concepts to enhance understanding.

Purpose

The *goal* of the experiential format is to enable a student to learn, grow, and develop new insights into concepts based on generalizations made from one's own activities in class. Personal behavioral changes congruent with professional role behavior are more likely to occur with participation. Exercises are designed to increase self-awareness and personal growth, impart new interactional skills, and provide opportunity to practice these new skills. This format not only allows for presentation of cognitive content but also strongly focuses on processing affective content and thus fosters synthesis of needed skills. Although this learning format is well-used in organizational management frameworks, it also has gained wide acceptance as a method for educating professionals, primarily through the use of selected, structured, game-like experiences (Pfeiffer and Goodstein, 1984).

Many instructors and students feel that the experiential learning format provides a more humanistic alternative to the traditional lecture-discussion format used in the majority of a nurse's educational process. Table 1 contrasts these two teaching modes. In the column describing the experiential mode, it can

Table 1. Teaching-Learning Differences Between Traditional Lecture Methods and Experiential Methods

	Traditional	Experiential
Information	Cognitive	Cognitive Affective Skill-oriented
Communication Direction	One-way: teacher to student-learner	Group focus: requires interaction among learners
Activity Mode	Passive listening, note taking	Active participation in structural "games"
Student View of the Topic	Usually initially viewed by student as directly relevant to role as nurses	Often, initially viewed by student as abstract, difficult to see as directly relevant
Use of Feelings	No consideration of feelings	Discussion of feelings seen as necessary and providing helpful information
Evaluation	Usually by paper-and-pencil testing	Ideally by behavioral changes
Major Focus	Teaching, transmission of didactic data	Learning, assimilation of behavioral content; no "right" answers

be noted that this innovative format deals with processing affective material and requires active participation of every class member. Ideally, the class is divided into small, interactive groups of fewer than 20 members for at least some of the exercises. Formation of groups provides opportunities for the development of group dynamics, which, in turn, provides data for analysis and discussion. Suggestions for managing large classes are offered in this *Instructor's Manual*.

Becoming actively involved in classroom exercises may be a new experience for some learners. Each structured exercise has a specific purpose. Some are designed to increase self-knowledge, whereas others focus on practicing one particular communication skill. The same learning process, however, is followed for all exercises. Doing the exercise is only the initial activity. Discussion of what was learned is a crucial component for developing critical thinking.

The experiential approach is ideally suited to the type of affective content presented in courses that emphasize development and maintenance of professional nursing relationships. Often such content is introduced in a fundamentals of nursing course and reinforced in later clinical courses, such as psychiatric nursing. In many of the integrated, concept-ori-ented curriculums, this type of content is taught in a professional communications course. Regardless of where the content is presented, mastery of communications skills is an essential aspect of client care. and is used throughout a nurse's career.

The Learning Process

Engaging in the exercises presented in the text provides all the class members with a shared base of experiences, thoughts, and feelings that can be described, explored, and analyzed. Examining this information through critical reflection allows the student to learn more about human relationships and communication principles. Figure 1 illustrates that both content and process are integral components in this format for mastering interpersonal relationship objectives.

Goodstein and Pfeiffer (1983) have identified five distinct steps in the experiential learning process. These have been adapted for nursing.

I.   Active involvement in an exercise
II.   Collegial sharing of experiences
III. Analysis and synthesis
IV.   Integration of experiences with theory
V.   Application to clinical practice

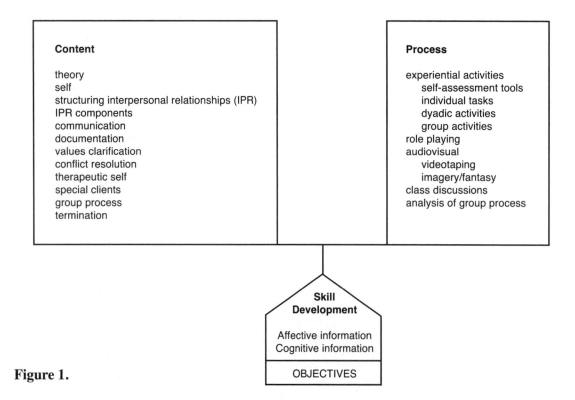

Content

theory
self
structuring interpersonal relationships (IPR)
IPR components
communication
documentation
values clarification
conflict resolution
therapeutic self
special clients
group process
termination

Process

experiential activities
    self-assessment tools
    individual tasks
    dyadic activities
    group activities
role playing
audiovisual
    videotaping
    imagery/fantasy
class discussions
analysis of group process

Skill Development

Affective information
Cognitive information

OBJECTIVES

Figure 1.

STRATEGIES FOR TEACHING AND LEARNING

I. Actively Become Involved in Doing Exercises

The basis of the experiential learning format includes participation in a structured, preplanned exercise about concepts being studied. The purpose of engaging students in this exercise is to provide a data base of thoughts and feelings that can be described, explored, and analyzed. Thus the content is personalized, relying on an individual's own immediate perceptions and experiences. There are both cognitive and affective components. Many of the exercises require multiple sensory and kinesthetic participation to maximize learning.

Exercises need to be preplanned. Goals and directions are listed so that they may be explicitly available to students prior to participation. Many of the exercises can be assigned as homework to be done just prior to class time.

II. Use Class Time for Sharing Self-Reflection

In the second step of the experiential learning process, individuals are expected to identify their affective reactions associated with participation in the exercise. Evaluative reflection upon one's learning experience is a crucial part of the critical thinking nurses use in clinical reasoning (Huston and Marquis, 1995; Lee and Ryan-Wenger, 1997). Collegial sharing of self-observations related to the exercise helps clarify what was learned, focusing on what each participant felt during the experience. This phase of the learning process should involve some distancing of students from their own feelings about personal performance. This distancing is accomplished by focusing on common feelings among group members. Participants may need assistance in separating themselves from the experience so that they may gain objectivity for the next step. In addition to a sharing of personal perceptions by individual students, this step and the next step in this learning process involve the use of feedback obtained from peers.

Feedback. *Feedback* is defined as the process by which a system (an individual or a group) gathers information about adequacy of functioning from others in the environment. This information or input from others in the environment allows the individual or group to evaluate whether there is disparity between ideal, desired functioning and actual behavior (Miller and Janosik, 1980). The focus is on individual personal growth. Feedback has been demonstrated to be an integral component in the development of social and interpersonal behavior. Homa and Cultice (1984) compared groups with and without feedback and found that minimal learning occurred in the nonfeedback group. They noted that more highly structured categories of subject material are more likely to be learned when feedback is provided. Of course, learning does occur in the absence of feedback, but such learning is less likely to be correlated with higher levels of performance.

Feedback from colleagues may reinforce the correctness of a given action or may allow a person to recognize the disparity between desired and actual effects of this action, thus stimulating change. Development of an effective therapeutic style of interaction with clients requires appropriate feedback so that health professionals have the opportunity to change some behaviors, decreasing the disparity between desired and actual behavior.

Within an experiential format, the offering of accurate feedback can be viewed as a professional responsibility, a commitment to assist in collegial growth. It needs to be perceived by students as a helping-oriented behavior.

Some controversy exists about the value of negative feedback. Many experienced educators feel that constructive feedback about ineffective communication or behavior is necessary for individual growth. Others, primarily behaviorists, feel that the main focus should be on reinforcing positive behaviors. In either event, feedback should be offered in such a fashion as to promote individual growth. Guidelines adapted from Hanson (1975) are provided here to facilitate students in giving constructive feedback.

RULES FOR GIVING FEEDBACK

1. Own and express your feelings directly. Example: "I feel. . . (angry)," rather than, "You make me. . . (angry)."
2. Specifically describe the observed behavior rather than attempt to interpret its meaning.
3. Be nonevaluative. Describe the actual result of the behavior rather than whether someone was bad or good.
4. Give immediate feedback. Focus on giving feedback as soon as possible within the group to tie it closely to the observed behavior.
5. Give constructive feedback, not destructive criticism. Comments should convey a sincere desire to help the person grow.

III. Analyze and Synthesize

Analysis is an essential component of the experiential process. It is important to develop some degree of insight into factors affecting the interactional process. Systematically examine common themes in the experience. Focus on how certain behaviors affected others and how the exercise affected group interaction. A useful tool in self-analysis is videotaping interactions or exercises. Burnard (1991, p. 145) offers the following assessment form:

ANALYSIS GUIDELINE FOR EVALUATING VIDEOTAPED INTERACTIONS

Assessment Form

1. Behavioral aspects of the interpersonal encounter
   - Did the person sit squarely in relation to the partner?
   - Did the person maintain an "open" position?
   - Did the person lean toward the other person?
   - Did the person maintain effective and appropriate eye contact?
   - Did the person appear to be relaxed?
2. Interpersonal interventions: What were the predominating interventions used? (Prescriptive, informative, confronting, cathartic, catalytic, or supportive?)
3. How did the person handle the stages of the encounter? (Introduction, Development, Closing)
4. How did the person demonstrate personal qualities? (Empathy, Concern, Openness)

IV. Integrate Content

The goal of step 4 involves facilitating the transfer of knowledge. Students often need assistance in correlating specific perceptions about isolated class activities with didactic content available in book chapters. Learning about self, interactions, and communication skills, for instance, needs to be related to the theoretical concepts relevant to the topic being discussed. Some class discussion may be helpful in making associations between behaviors exhibited during exercises and other class content, assigned readings, or prior life experiences. General communication principles applicable to client care may be derived from this type of analysis.

V. Apply to Clinical Practice

The final step in the experiential process involves utilization of knowledge and skills designed in class in the development of the professional role. The learner needs to be able to make a generalization from an isolated classroom experience to the larger world of professional nursing. This transfer of knowledge can be accomplished when students have a simultaneous opportunity to apply new knowledge in actual interactions with clients and colleagues. Using the student's own practice to recall and reflect on one's thinking process is ideal (Farrell and Bramadat, 1990). However, within class limitations, transfer of knowledge may be accomplished by examining case study applications or by speculating about how this new knowledge will be applied in similar future professional situations. The text in this book contains many case examples that may be useful in this step of the learning process.

It is of paramount importance that assistance be provided to students in their attempts to bridge the gap between classroom activities and applications to future role behaviors. If there is not an immediate opportunity to practice communication skills with clients, students can speculate aloud how this new knowledge could be applied in future encounters. Actual application of learning about use of communication skills within a therapeutic nurse–client relationship is a new experience for beginning practitioners and may be somewhat uncomfortable at first. For both beginning and experienced nurses, clinical experiences need to be reflected upon and examined.

REFERENCES

Bethune E and Jackling N (1997). Critical thinking skills: the role of prior experience. *Journal of Advanced Nursing* 26:1005-1012.

Burnard P (1991). Using video as a reflective tool in interpersonal skills training. *Nursing Education Today 11: 143-146.*

Farrell P and Bramadat IJ (1990). Paradigm case analysis and stimulated recall: strategies for developing clinical reasoning skills. *Chnical Nurse Specialist* 4:153-157.

Goodstein LD, Pfeiffer JW (eds.) (1983). *The 1983 Annual Report for Facilitators, Trainers and Consultants.* San Diego, University Associates Publishers.

Hanson PG (1975). Giving feedback: An interpersonal skill. In Jones JE, Pfeiffer JW (eds.) (1975). *The 1975 Annual Handbook for Group Facilitators.* La Jolla, University Associates Publishers.

Homa D, Cultice J (1984). Role of feedback, category size and stimulus distortions on the acquisition and utilization of ill defined categories. *Journal of Experimental Psychology* 10:83-94.

Huston CJ and Marques BL (1995). Seven steps to successful decision-making. *AJN* 95:65-68.

Lee JE and Ryan-Wenger N (1997). The think aloud seminar for teaching clinical reasoning. *Journal of Pediatric Health Care* 11:101-110.

Miller JR, Janosik EH (1980). *Family-Focused Care.* New York, McGraw-Hill.

Pfeiffer JW, Goodstein LD (eds.) (1984). *The 1984 Annual Report: Developing Human Resources.* San Diego, University Associates Publishers.

Contents

Chapter 4
Self-Concept in the Nurse–Client Relationship   10

PART II   THE NURSE–CLIENT RELATIONSHIP

Chapter 5
Structuring the Relationship   15

Chapter 6
Bridges and Barriers in the Therapeutic Relationship   19

Chapter 7
Role Relationship Patterns   23

Chapter 8
The Grief Experience: Life's Losses and Endings   25

PART III   THERAPEUTIC COMMUNICATION

Chapter 9
Communication Styles   27

Chapter 10
Developing Therapeutic Communication Skills in the Nurse–Client Relationship   29

Chapter 11
Intercultural Communication   34

Chapter 12
Communicating in Groups   36

PART IV   RESPONDING TO SPECIAL NEEDS

Chapter 17
Communicating with Clients Experiencing Communication Deficits   49

Chapter 18
Communicating with Children   51

Chapter 19
Communicating with Older Adults   54

Chapter 20
Communicating with Clients in Stressful Situations   57

Chapter 21
Communicating with Clients in Crisis   59

PART V   PROFESSIONAL ISSUES

Chapter 22
Communicating with Other Health Professionals   62

Chapter 23
Documentation in the Age of Computers   65

TEST BANK   67

Chapter 1

Theoretical Perspectives and Contemporary Issues

INTRODUCTION

Theory provides a basis for professional practice. Without its theoretical underpinnings, nursing could not be an independent profession. In this text, emphasis is placed on discussion of nursing theories, psychosocial theories, and developmental theories as they interface with communication concepts. Nursing has borrowed many concepts from other disciplines that can be useful in understanding how to develop and maintain professional relationships.

Arnold and Boggs, in Chapter 1 of their book, describe the development of knowledge in nursing, particularly as applied to communication within interpersonal relationships.

Exercises are designed to provide the student with experience in how to read and analyze new nursing knowledge.

There are eight exercises in this chapter of the text.

EXERCISE 1-1
Critiquing a Nursing Theory Article

Teaching Tip

This exercise may be submitted for a grade. It is recommended that students receive an outline of essential sections of a critique, such as those listed below:

1. Identify theorist.
2. Identify two concepts of the theory.
3. Give one example of how this theory was applied.
4. How relevant is this theory for clinical nursing practice?
5. Discuss how you might use this theory in your practice.

EXERCISE 1-2
Understanding the Meaning of Health as a Nursing Concept

Teaching Tip

A simple version of this exercise is just to have the class define "health." Use the blackboard to record brainstorming answers; then begin to seek commonalties, seek consensus (Delphi method), or use the questions in the text to stimulate discussion.

Sample Answers

In nursing, generally the correct answer would include ideas about health as a continuum; would be defined by the clients themselves; and would include concepts such as prevention, wellness, and rehabilitation.

EXERCISE 1-3
What Is Professional Nursing?

Teaching Tips

This exercise lends itself to brief **videotaped** interviews. Have three or four groups present their interviews in class by showing their video while classmates analyze content. Teachers should follow their institutional guidelines for videotaped subjects to "release" or give permission via signed documents. As an alternative, one of the authors has students post a summary of the small group's interview onto a class **Internet discussion room**. Students who are members of other work groups are then graded for reading and replying by entering comments about the content of the posted interview. Undergraduate students even as young as freshmen are easily able to master these Internet activities.

Then have students develop their own role philosophy. It is usually easier for beginning students to agree with or disagree with the comments made by the experienced nurse. Again, one author uses a class **Internet discussion room** for each student or group to post its philosophy. Students who are members of other work groups are then graded for reading and replying.

EXERCISE 1-4
Time Line

Even beginning-level students do well with this exercise. An alternative is have students interview someone outside the class and then try to evaluate which of Erikson's stages the person has mastered, writing up the evaluation in a few paragraphs.

Teaching Tip

The author divides the class into work groups of approximately six to eight members, again using a class **Internet discussion room** for each student group to post the common ideas expressed during their individual interviews. Students who are members of other work groups are then graded for reading and replying.

It can be helpful to provide a set of five or six questions as a guideline for the student to use during the interview.

EXERCISE 1-5
Completing the Life Cycle

Some of the most interesting class exercises have consisted of interviews with older adults, often a grandparent. Having the student ask about this person's most important life event often results in interesting, new information.

Teaching Tip

It can be helpful to provide a set of five or six questions as a guideline for the student to use in the interview helps (see examples). This exercise can be adapted to use in class **Internet discussion rooms.**

Suggested Interview Questions: The student begins interviewing an older adult by introducing self, explaining the purpose of the interview and that the identity of the interviewee is **confidential.** Then the student says:

1. Describe how you adjusted to retirement.
2. As you look back over your life, describe what has given you the most satisfaction. What would you do differently?

EXERCISE 1-6
Maslow's Hierarchy of Needs

This exercise is self-explanatory.

EXERCISE 1-7
Case Application of Maslow's Theory

Teaching Tip

Beginning-level students often have difficulty prioritizing nursing care. Maslow provides an easily understandable guide for choosing priority diagnoses and interventions.

Sample Answers

Priority I

Alteration in comfort related to myocardial function (infarction), as manifested by (as evidenced by) perspiration (diaphoresis), anxiety, and rubbing of the chest.

Rationale: Basic immediate biological needs appropriate at Maslow's first level, such as maintenance of cardiac function, take precedence over psychosocial needs.

Priority 2

Knowledge deficit related to lack of understanding of risk factors and discharge treatment protocols, as evidenced by selection of high-sodium diet foods and questions about medication administration (diuretics).

Rationale: Using Maslow's hierarchy, once basic biological and immediate safety needs are met, the client's care can begin to focus on psychosocial needs. Threats to self-esteem may be addressed. These may require long-term intervention. For example, Mr. Rogers might work with the nurse preparing him for discharge to regain some sense of what he can have control over.

EXERCISE 1-8
Differences Between Linear and Circular Models of Communication

This exercise is best used with more advanced students.

ADDITIONAL EXERCISES

EXERCISE 1-A
Communications Theory: Skills Inventory

Many people lack awareness of their own "style" of communication. Each textbook chapter is designed to develop or refine necessary communication skills. However, an initial step is to recognize one's own strengths and weaknesses. The following exercise can help.

Purpose: To increase awareness of one's own style.

Directions: Read each item and answer the question, "How satisfied am I with my communications skill in this situation?"

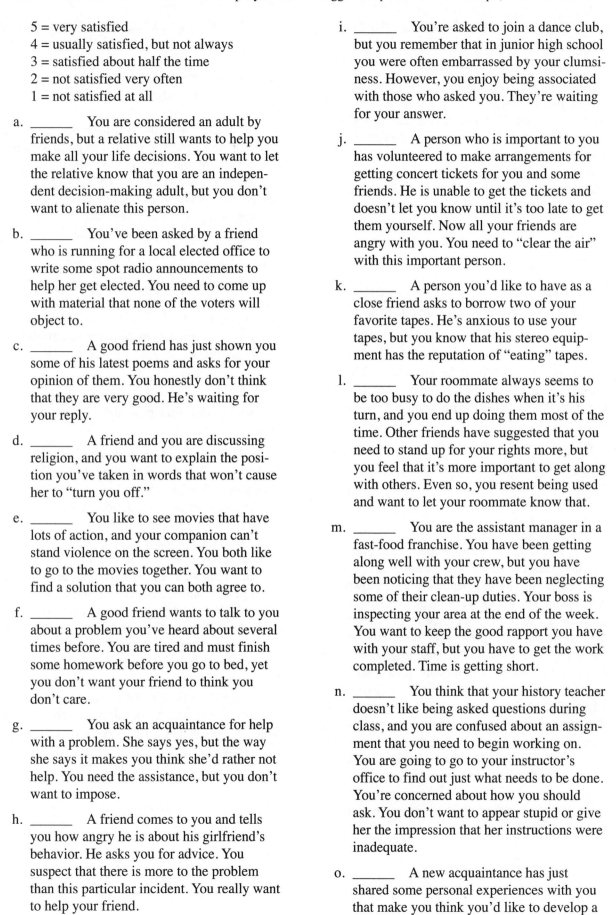

5 = very satisfied
4 = usually satisfied, but not always
3 = satisfied about half the time
2 = not satisfied very often
1 = not satisfied at all

a. _____ You are considered an adult by friends, but a relative still wants to help you make all your life decisions. You want to let the relative know that you are an independent decision-making adult, but you don't want to alienate this person.

b. _____ You've been asked by a friend who is running for a local elected office to write some spot radio announcements to help her get elected. You need to come up with material that none of the voters will object to.

c. _____ A good friend has just shown you some of his latest poems and asks for your opinion of them. You honestly don't think that they are very good. He's waiting for your reply.

d. _____ A friend and you are discussing religion, and you want to explain the position you've taken in words that won't cause her to "turn you off."

e. _____ You like to see movies that have lots of action, and your companion can't stand violence on the screen. You both like to go to the movies together. You want to find a solution that you can both agree to.

f. _____ A good friend wants to talk to you about a problem you've heard about several times before. You are tired and must finish some homework before you go to bed, yet you don't want your friend to think you don't care.

g. _____ You ask an acquaintance for help with a problem. She says yes, but the way she says it makes you think she'd rather not help. You need the assistance, but you don't want to impose.

h. _____ A friend comes to you and tells you how angry he is about his girlfriend's behavior. He asks you for advice. You suspect that there is more to the problem than this particular incident. You really want to help your friend.

i. _____ You're asked to join a dance club, but you remember that in junior high school you were often embarrassed by your clumsiness. However, you enjoy being associated with those who asked you. They're waiting for your answer.

j. _____ A person who is important to you has volunteered to make arrangements for getting concert tickets for you and some friends. He is unable to get the tickets and doesn't let you know until it's too late to get them yourself. Now all your friends are angry with you. You need to "clear the air" with this important person.

k. _____ A person you'd like to have as a close friend asks to borrow two of your favorite tapes. He's anxious to use your tapes, but you know that his stereo equipment has the reputation of "eating" tapes.

l. _____ Your roommate always seems to be too busy to do the dishes when it's his turn, and you end up doing them most of the time. Other friends have suggested that you need to stand up for your rights more, but you feel that it's more important to get along with others. Even so, you resent being used and want to let your roommate know that.

m. _____ You are the assistant manager in a fast-food franchise. You have been getting along well with your crew, but you have been noticing that they have been neglecting some of their clean-up duties. Your boss is inspecting your area at the end of the week. You want to keep the good rapport you have with your staff, but you have to get the work completed. Time is getting short.

n. _____ You think that your history teacher doesn't like being asked questions during class, and you are confused about an assignment that you need to begin working on. You are going to go to your instructor's office to find out just what needs to be done. You're concerned about how you should ask. You don't want to appear stupid or give her the impression that her instructions were inadequate.

o. _____ A new acquaintance has just shared some personal experiences with you that make you think you'd like to develop a closer relationship. You, too, have experienced some of the same things but have never revealed these very personal feelings.

Now that you have finished, total up the numbers you've placed beside all 15 items. If you've scored between *68* and *75*, you can conclude that you are highly satisfied with the way you are equipped to deal with these situations. A score of *58* to *67* suggests that you are usually satisfied with your communication behavior; a score of *45* to *57* suggests that you feel dissatisfied with your communication skills nearly half the time. The lower your score, the less satisfied you are and the more need for improvement is indicated.

EXERCISE 1-B

Application of Theory to a Clinical Example

Purpose: To introduce students to the idea that the assessment section of the nursing database can vary, depending on which theorist is used. More advanced students can use it to help synthesize their understanding of nurse theorists and nursing process.

Directions: Have students select a nursing theorist and develop a one-page admission assessment form using concepts from that theory.

Sample Answers

Example I

1.   The nurse collecting these data and using Orem's point of view might assess areas in which Ms. Smith can act independently as her own self-care agent. For example, perhaps obtaining equipment designed for glucose monitoring by the partially sighted would allow Ms. Smith to monitor her own blood levels reliably. As the nurse assesses more information about dietary noncompliance, he or she might discover that this behavior is due to a knowledge deficit about substitution of food groups. Thus, the nurse might determine that the appropriate action should be supportive-educative and arrange to spend time teaching Ms. Smith. On the other hand, if Ms. Smith is unable to cook balanced meals, the nurse might conclude that the needed nursing role is partially compensatory and perhaps might arrange for a referral to Meals on Wheels.

2.   Using Betty Neuman's model, the nurse might assess the dietary problem by collecting data about possible stressors. Perhaps an easily identifiable extrapersonal stressor is discovered to be a lack of money to buy the foods recommended on Ms. Smith's diet.

In examining Ms. Smith's difficulty in monitoring her glucose level, the nurse might assess basic vision strength and discover that the diabetes is a stressor that has altered Ms. Smith's vision sufficiently to warrant an eye examination. The nurse operates in the secondary prevention mode in performing early symptom identification.

Teaching Tip

For the novice learner, pick one more simple concept such as health teaching/health promotion for a well client. Select a few theorists to illustrate to the class how each might view health from a slightly different viewpoint.

Example 2

A young adult smokes a pack of cigarettes every day.

1.   The nurse collecting data and using Orem's point of view might ask questions to determine how this person functions as his or her own self-care agent in other areas of health practices, such as exercise and so on.

2.   Using Betty Neuman's framework, the nurse might assess whether this person is still in a primary preventive mode; that is, whether the individual has developed any smoking-related symptoms.

In teaching advanced practice students, our graduate students have used an elaborate version of this exercise to promote synthesis of concepts studied in their nursing theory course. In the clinical courses of their master's curriculum, they have successfully applied theory to clinical practice by selecting a theorist and, as a group, by developing a theory-based client assessment tool to organize the assessment part of their nursing care.

Chapter 2

Professional Guides to Action in Interpersonal Relationships

INTRODUCTION

This chapter describes standards of nursing practice. Many additional professional practice standards have been developed by specialty organizations. At a minimum, beginning-level students need to know that practice standards exist and where to find them so that they may be used as a reference for professional practice.

A new feature is the ethical dilemma cases presented in boxes (see Chapter 3). If you wish to begin introducing this concept during this chapter, try the situation below.

There are two exercises in this chapter of the text.

EXERCISE 2-1

Applying the Code of Ethics for Nurses to Professional or Clinical Situations

Teaching Tip

Beginning-level students usually have some difficulty in thinking of ethical dilemmas. Several videotapes are available that can be used as triggers for discussion. The Internet features a great number of case situations (see electronic references in Chapter 3). As an alternative, a student might interview an experienced nurse to identify a potential ethical dilemma.

Class or group discussion of this topic seems to require some guidance from the instructor to help students differentiate legal from ethical problems.

EXERCISE 2-2

Writing Nursing Diagnoses

Sample Answers

a. Alteration in thought processes related to (physiological) head injury, as evidenced by disorientation, or Self-care deficit related to musculoskeletal impairment, as evidenced by inability to feed oneself or bathe.

b. Knowledge deficit related to inability to understand English, as evidenced by an inability to repeat preoperative instructions, or Verbal communication impairment related to Chinese as primary language, as evidenced by inability to read operative consent form.

ADDITIONAL EXERCISES

EXERCISE 2-A

Development of Goals Based on Professional Standards

Purpose: To promote application of professional standards for more advanced-level students using an in-class activity. This type of synthesis is somewhat difficult for some students.

Directions: Students in small groups are asked to brainstorm and to develop a list of health goals for clients for 5 years from now. For example, when pediatric nurses were asked to develop such as list, they examined professional standards for health promotion and developed a list of client goals. Goal 1 stated that 100% of infants by age 1 year would be vaccinated through an immunization program by home health care nurses. Similarly, obstetrical nurses examined their standards and developed a list of goals. Goal 1 stated that 100% of all pregnant adolescents enrolled in county schools would receive adequate prenatal care by nurses in school-based clinics.

As an alternative, have students download the *Healthy People 2010* goals, and comment on what their role will be in implementing these goals (www.healthypeople.gov).

EXERCISE 2-B

Understanding the Usefulness of the Nursing Process

Purpose: To help students understand the utility of the nursing process in providing nursing care.

Directions: Divide the class into an even number of small groups. Each group writes a case situation with both physical and psychosocial aspects. Trade cases so that another group is developing diagnoses.

Discussion: Share each case with the large class and discuss additional diagnoses.

5

Chapter 3

Clinical Judgment: Applying Critical Thinking and Ethical Decision Making

INTRODUCTION

A nurse's ability to make correct clinical judgments has a profound effect on the quality of care given to a client. The process of learning to think critically is a skill that can be learned as a student rather than relying on learning while on the job.

The author has identified **10 steps in the Critical Thinking Process**. You are currently teaching some of these as steps in the **Nursing Process**, so you know students can be taught this process, practicing applying them in clinical labs or in class by critiquing videotaped interviews of experienced nurses. It is to be noted, however, that the experienced nurse is constantly scanning information and reassessing the client situation rather than following the steps in a linear fashion.

Value-laden issues such as abortion, decisions not to resuscitate clients, and patient rights stir feelings in nurses that can be destructive to the professional relationship if they remain unrecognized. Student nurses are often surprised at how strong a value orientation they actually possess on certain issues. The learning exercises in the book allow students an opportunity to examine different values in a reflective manner in a nonstressful classroom situation. Class discussion should focus on the *intensity* of values held and on speculation about how personal values affect client care situations rather than having the class discuss the merits of one position or another.

Eventually, every nurse becomes involved in a situation in which there is an ethical dilemma. Although often such a dilemma often falls to the agency or the physician to resolve, staff nurses encounter many ethical care problems. Use the ethical dilemmas located in each Ethics Box as practice cases. Have students use one of the principles of bioethics in their case decision making.

There are 10 exercises in this chapter of the text.

EXERCISE 3-1
Autonomy

Assign this exercise as homework with some class discussion. Try to have students speak from reference rather than merely express their personal opinion.

EXERCISE 3-2
Beneficence

Have students prepare by downloading one of the many cases available on the Internet. Refer to the list of electronic references supplied at the end of the text chapter.

EXERCISE 3-3
Justice

Have students prepare by downloading one of the many cases available on the Internet. Refer to the list of electronic references supplied at the end of the text chapter.

EXERCISE 3-4
Ethical Decision Making

Teaching Tip
Guide students to discuss methods used by nurses when their personal values conflict with professional responsibilities.

When an ethical dilemma is not resolvable, acceptable coping methods may include:

Answers
- Requesting reassignment to a different group of clients
- Trading a specific assignment with another staff member
- Assigning another care provider to do the direct care
- Requesting transfer to another unit

EXERCISE 3-5

Defining Values

Guide class discussion to avoid personalization, stereotyping, or any negative attributions by other students.

EXERCISE 3-6

Personal and Professional Value Descriptors

Pitfalls: Discussions of student's personal values are appropriate only insofar as they promote synthesis of content. Experienced instructors caution us about the need to avoid overanalysis of student values. Class discussions are focused on the concepts of value acquisition and the process of value clarification; they are not therapy sessions.

Teaching Tip

These exercises have no right answers; they should be done privately before class as a trigger to stimulate student thinking. Discussion may be directed toward identifying the source from which these values have been derived, such as family expectations, television programming, personal past experiences, and so forth.

EXERCISE 3-7

Range of Opinion

Teaching Tip

It is always helpful to practice before applying the value clarification process to actual clinical practice. This exercise will help to integrate all seven steps of the values clarification process into practical nursing applications.

EXERCISE 3-8

Professional Values Clarification

The items are intended to stimulate discussion and are best used prior to class. Emphasize that there are no incorrect answers.

EXERCISE 3-9

Professional Nurses' Values

The items are to be used to stimulate discussion.

EXERCISE 3-10

Interview of Expert Nurse

Students have conducted interviews using audiotapes or live guest speakers, but **videotaped interviews** seem to work best. The video is played in class, and the students analyze content. It is important to agree beforehand on refraining from negative criticism. The purpose is to have the student critically analyze the expert nurse's vignette for steps in critical thinking. Follow your agency policy regarding signed release forms.

ADDITIONAL EXERCISES

EXERCISE 3-A

Rights Questionnaire: Children's Rights

Maria, age 4, has recently experienced a second exacerbation of acute lymphocytic leukemia. She is receiving prednisone and an experimental drug intravenously. Nurses must check the rate of infusion every hour as well as administer other medication and monitor urinary output. For accurate monitoring of her therapeutic progress, Maria is scheduled for bone marrow aspirations every 3 days, which she finds extremely painful.

Maria complains of abdominal pain almost constantly in addition to the severe vomiting and diarrhea caused by the medication.

Maria is so fearful that she screams every time a nurse enters her room. Initially, her parents had been told that she had a 95% chance for recovery. With her second relapse, however, standard treatment protocols have failed to produce remission of her disease. Her chances of recovery were estimated at 10% or less, and this information was given to her parents. Since they heard this news, they have reduced their visits to 10 minutes once every other day. Maria frequently cries for her mother.

Questions for Discussion

1. What values should be communicated to parents about painful treatment procedures undertaken in the care of ill children?

Answers
- Information about purpose and benefits
- Measures that are being used to minimize pain

2. What verbal and nonverbal means of communication could be used by staff to reassure Maria about care that will be less painful?

Answers
- Honesty about what will and won't hurt

- Removing Maria from her room to a treatment room for all painful procedures so that she can feel safe in her bed

3.   How does the change in prognosis affect your feelings about performing invasive, painful procedures?

Answer
- Students answer individually

4.   You are asked to restrain Maria for her next bone marrow aspiration. Discuss possible ways to prepare Maria for this procedure to reduce her anxiety.

Answer
- Therapeutic play after the last procedure

5.   A coworker expresses anger to you about Maria's parents' absence. Identify some therapeutic communication responses you might use in your conversation with this coworker. What interventions might you use with the parents?

Answers
- Acknowledge validity of feelings
- Explore origin of strong feelings; that is, the coworker's own values
- Discuss need for positive intervention with parents
- Provide affective support and encourage verbalization of feelings

EXERCISE 3-B
Acquiring Professional Values

Purpose: To help students explore their professional values.

Directions: Consider your answers to these questions:
1.   What are some other professional values of nursing that I might expect to acquire when assuming the role of the professional nurse?
2.   How might I go about acquiring these values?

Answer
In addition to experiential exercises or case simulations, professional values are acquired by modeling instructors and staff nurses, participation in class discussions that stimulate self-reflection, participation in case discussions, and postconference review of client assignment.

Teaching Tip
The instructor may need to provide an overview of the nursing school curriculum showing where the curriculum addresses professional role development. Citing standards described in Chapter 2 or specialty practice standards also may help. Students can use clinical experiences to begin to identify the impact of professional role values on development.

EXERCISE 3-C
Removing Barriers to Action

Purpose: To give students practice in identifying and removing barriers to action. This exercise can be done as a homework assignment.

Directions: Write at the top of a piece of paper some action that you would like to take or a decision that you would like to make. It should be an action that you are having some difficulty taking or that you fear to take. Next, draw a line lengthwise down the middle of the paper. On the right-hand side of the paper, list all the perceived or real barriers that seem to be keeping you from acting. On the left-hand side of the paper, list steps that might be taken to help move or reduce each of the barriers. On the back of the paper, develop a plan of action for actually removing the barriers.

Sample Answer
Action: Quitting a part-time job

Removal steps	Barriers
1. Borrow $1,000 from Dad. Ask bank for loan. Seek scholarship. Apply for work-study program. Quit school for one semester to work full time.	Need tuition money
2. Get student association group insurance policy. Pay for own insurance.	Would lose health insurance
3. Sell car. Borrow $800 to pay off car loan.	Must make car payment

EXERCISE 3-D

Examining All Sides

Purpose: To demonstrate that there are many facets to every issue. How do you determine your position? What factors influence your thoughts and feelings? How will your choice be reflected in your behavior?

Directions: Discuss these questions with your peers in small groups. Then bring some of these issues to your clinical experience, and discuss options with staff nurses. Indicate your responses to the following statements in this manner:

SA = strongly agree
A = agree
U = undecided
D = disagree
SD = strongly disagree

1. _____ Clients have the right to participate in all decisions related to their health care.

2. _____ Continuing education should be mandatory for nurses.

3. _____ Clients should always be told the truth.

4. _____ Standards of nursing practice should be enforced by state examining boards.

5. _____ Nurses should be required to take relicensure examinations every 5 years.

6. _____ Clients have the right to obtain their health records upon request.

7. _____ Abortion should be legal.

8. _____ Badly deformed newborns should be allowed to die.

9. _____ There should be a law guaranteeing medical care for each person in this country.

Teaching Tips

This exercise deals with actual ethical issues confronted by nurses. Stress that although we as professionals hold differing opinions, there are no clearcut right or wrong answers to ethical dilemmas. As technology advances, nurses will be faced with an increasing number of situations in which no clear legal or ethical guidelines exist.

Creighton (1986, p. 254) writes that nursing's social value is concerned, first, with *knowing* the value being placed on systematic knowledge and intellect; second, with *doing* the value being placed on technical skill and trained capacity; and third, with *helping* the value being placed on putting nursing knowledge and skill to work in the service of others.

Chapter 4

Self-Concept in the Nurse–Client Relationship

INTRODUCTION

The content in this chapter is designed to investigate the components of self and to orient the learner to the purpose of the professional relationship. To be prepared to work in a professional capacity, students require a great deal of role socialization. Until entering the profession, many students have experienced only social relationships. Because the use of self is the most important tool in a therapeutic nurse–client relationship, each student must explore concepts related to self.

Experiential exercises are designed to help learners develop an increased sense of self-awareness through a structured examination of both the personal and the professional aspects of self. The exercises assist the learner in becoming more aware of concepts shared with others. Thus, a beginning sense of role socialization develops.

Occasionally, students may inadvertently reveal some intimate or embarrassing information. Because such students feel vulnerable, they may respond to the situation by withdrawing from future participation. Such behavior is typical and should be anticipated by instructors, who may choose to allow a temporary retreat. A better strategy for the instructor is to interrupt these students by asking them to refocus on the discussion question.

Another effective teaching strategy is to broaden the student's comment to encompass general experiences common to many class members. Peers are often reassuring, acknowledging similar thoughts, feelings, or life experience.

Several exercises can be done individually as homework before class to conserve time. It is suggested that only one or two exercises be done during one class period to avoid overload and diminished impact.

There are nine exercises in this chapter of the text.

EXERCISE 4-1
Who Am I?

Purpose: To help learners understand important data about the self-concepts in different interpersonal situations. This exercise may be done as a homework exercise but should be discussed in class.

Pitfalls: Answers to items such as:

My biggest fear is . . .
My biggest problem is . . .
My greatest concern is . . .
What I find hardest to deal with is . . .

are very revealing and should never be shared in class as personal statements.

Teaching Tips
The focus of the exercise centers on the process by which students identify characteristics about themselves. Discussion should focus on feelings incurred by students while they were in the process of deciding on their answers. Students often comment that the easiest items to answer are those requesting identification of negative or "worst" behaviors. Answers calling for a positive self-description may be more difficult for some individuals.

Depersonalize answers by searching for common themes. For example, place fears in categories, such as physical; psychological, dealing with self-esteem; and role-related, such as fear of receiving a failing grade. Emphasize common themes to the entire class.

Emphasize to the entire class that here we respect all opinions and never ridicule anyone's answers. If students laugh at or moan about someone's answer, the teacher must intervene with a statement about how we value the input and comment to the class about their reaction.

On a blackboard or overhead transparency, have the class respond to the discussion questions.

Questions for Discussion
1. What were the hardest items to answer?

2. In which area were learners most surprised about their answers?

3. What can one learn about oneself from doing this exercise?

4. Ask learners to speculate about how they could use this self-knowledge in professional interpersonal relationships with clients.

EXERCISE 4-2

Contributions of Life Experiences to Self-Concept

Purpose: To help identify some of the commonalties and diversity in life experiences present in a small group of students with the same major field of study.

Teaching Tips

1. To pair off students, go around the room, having students count 1, 2, etc. Pair 1s and 3s, 2s and 4s, and so forth, or have students turn to the person seated behind them. The intent is to place them with someone with whom they are not well acquainted.

2. Student A spends 5 minutes questioning student B to collect a biography of facts in student B's past life, collecting such information as age, ethnic background, marital status, place and date of birth, number of siblings, and unusual life experiences. The process is then reversed, and student B interviews student A.

3. Call on selected students to introduce the other to the class using the information gained from the interview.

For Discussion: Explore common themes regarding types of information chosen, whether initial impressions are different from perceptions after the interview, and how perceptions changed in light of the information shared.

To answer Question B (How do you think it might apply to nursing practice?), explain how therapeutic conversations often start off with some of the same demographic information the class just obtained.

EXERCISE 4-3

A Life of Integrity Through Imaging Possible Selves

This exercise can be done strictly as a homework assignment. The 60th birthday is a happier form of the funeral eulogy.

EXERCISE 4-4

Erikson's Stages of Psychosocial Development

Teaching Tip

Answers are negotiable. Life crises from previous stages may continue to be relived.

Answers

1. Identity
2. Generativity: may threaten one's role identity as "breadwinner"
3. Integrity
4. Generativity (may create problems with other relationships or intimacy)
5. Integrity: may result in crises at earlier stages: despair, self-absorption, isolation
6. Intimacy/generativity
7. Identity/intimacy (may lead to problems with self-image, isolation from peers)

EXERCISE 4-5

Correcting Cognitive Distortions

Answers

a. Self-talk
b. All or nothing
c. Fortune telling
d. Self-talk to avoid personalizing
e. Overgeneralizing
f. Acting on "ought to"
g. Awfulizing
h. Fortune telling
i. Overgeneralizing
j. Personalizing
k. All or nothing

EXERCISE 4-6

Clarifying Feelings

Teaching Tips

This exercise works better if students have experienced these problems. Common themes for some students are anger (initially at the nonfunctioning group member but later directed at the teacher who made the assignment), frustration, helplessness, and acceptance of the need to do that person's job for them.

In real-life class situations, we always use this type of class assignment. Experience has shown that to avoid the complaints of "it's not fair," it is helpful to explain the "hidden agenda" to the class; that is, this type of assignment not only results in a grade for an activity completed but also teaches valuable lessons in group process, negotiation skills, evaluation of group roles, and use of peer pressure. All of these skills are ones the professional nurse will need.

One strategy that has seemed useful in helping students overcome their response of helplessness is to allow the group to control the awarding of the grade; that is, have them turn in a list of group members who get the grade. Thus, it becomes a group decision if they believe "no work, no grade" for a member.

EXERCISE 4-7
Responding to Issues of Spiritual Distress

Teaching Tip
Avoid discussion of personal religious beliefs; focus class discussion instead on the appropriate role of a *professional nurse*.

EXERCISE 4-8
Social Support

Social support theory has identified three major types of support:

1. Material assistance (help with money, equipment, tangible goods)
2. Affective support (nurturance, emotional support)
3. Cognitive guidance (giving essential information)

To answer 4, focus on the role of the professional nurse in each of these areas: referrals to obtain equipment or financial assistance, conveying caring within the professional relationship, and teaching health education.

EXERCISE 4-9
Positive Affirmation: Contributions to Self-Esteem

This exercise is self-explanatory.

ADDITIONAL EXERCISES

EXERCISE 4-A
A Self-Characterization Exercise

Purpose: To help identify self-characteristics and to note the universality of self-descriptions as well as some differences in the ways individuals in a group might define the self.

Directions: This exercise works well when it is done in a large class. Answer the questions privately, but share general common themes. Alternatively, have students take a blank 9 x 11 inch piece of paper and fold it in half and half again, so that when it is opened, it is divided into four quarters. In the center where the folds intersect, have each student write the word "me"; then use the sections to list adjectives describing characteristics of themselves in the following four ways:

1. As your parents see you to be.
2. As your teachers (or friends) see you to be.
3. As the person you see yourself to actually be right now.
4. As the person you wish you were.

Questions for Discussion
Have students share only the positive adjectives. Have volunteers read some examples from each category. Go around the room quickly.
Ask the class:

1. Are there differences in your descriptions of self among parents, teachers, and self?
2. What are the differences between your actual self and your ideal self?

Discuss how students might use the knowledge gleaned from doing this exercise in therapeutic relationships with clients, such as the need to assess how the client sees himself or herself.

EXERCISE 4-B
Role Relations and Self-Concept

Purpose: To demonstrate the role of others in the formation of self-identity.

Directions
1. Think of a person or relationship that was most important in the development of your own personal evaluation of your competence—a relative, friend, teacher, neighbor, or child, for example.
2. Describe how that person's evaluation of you contributed to your opinion of yourself as a person.
3. In the group, share your impressions with your classmates.
4. Write on a board some of the ways in which the evaluations of others contribute to the way you feel about yourself today.

Questions for Discussion
1. What were some of the common variables that made appraisals of self by others more noteworthy?

2. In what ways were the appraisals by others congruent or incongruent with your own perception of self at the time?

3. What contributed to your acceptance of the evaluation as true and important in your development as a person?

4. In what ways do you think this exercise might help you understand self and others in nurse–client interactions?

Teaching Tip

Students may need some help in identifying common ways in which the evaluation of self-worth influences an individual's self-concept. Suggest that self-esteem may be positively influenced by justifiable praise for accomplishments or appearance, public recognition of goal achievements, and tangible rewards for cleverness or hard work. However, actions that decrease self-esteem may include absence of expected praise or rewards.

EXERCISE 4-C
Identifying Personal Strengths

Purpose: To help students identify the unique personal strengths that underlie accomplishments judged important to self.

Directions

1. Think of the one achievement you are most proud of.

2. List the strengths or personal actions that went into the accomplishment. "I was a good swim instructor," for instance, might be recast as personal strengths: "I was dependable, organized, persistent; I worked well with children, was able to inspire others, and was compassionate with slow learners."

3. Identify the interplay of physical, psychological, and psychosocial components that contributed to these strengths.

4. Share your experiences and observations with each other.

Questions for Discussion

1. How difficult was it for you to put down the strengths that showed the best part of your self in this exercise?

2. How many different aspects of self were you able to identify that you used in giving service to others?

3. What physical, emotional, and cultural or ethnic variables contributed?

4. Do you see any of these talents or strengths as "transferable" skills that you might use with clients in professional interpersonal relationships?

5. What did you learn about yourself that was new information from doing this exercise?

EXERCISE 4-D
Positive Strokes: Contributions to Self

Purpose: To help students experience the individualized components of self-worth.

Directions

This exercise may be done in a group or used as a homework assignment and later discussed in class.

1. List a positive stroke you received recently—something someone did or said that made you feel good about yourself.

2. List a negative stroke you received recently—something someone did or said that made you feel bad about yourself.

3. What have you done recently that you feel helped enhance someone else's self-esteem?

4. In class, write phrases on a chalkboard that capture the essence of the positive stroke.

5. Do the same for the negative stroke.

Questions for Discussion

1. In general, what kinds of actions help enhance self-esteem?

2. What are some things people do or fail to do that diminish self-esteem?

3. What are some specific things you might be able to do in a clinical setting that might help a client develop a sense of self-worth?

4. What did you learn about yourself from doing this exercise?

EXERCISE 4-E
Giving Positive Reinforcement

Purpose: To demonstrate the concept experientially while having some fun.

Equipment: Several bags of cotton balls

Directions: Distribute 10 cotton balls to each student.

Goal: To acquire as many cotton balls as possible.

Rules: Students circulate freely in classroom or during break. Each time a student talks with another person, he or she tries to say something to enhance that person's self-esteem, to give a compliment. If the student is successful in giving a positive stroke, the recipient awards him or her with a cotton ball (a "warm fuzzy"). Only one cotton ball can be collected from the same person. At the end of the time period, total up each learner's cotton balls.

Discussion: Discuss the relative importance of positive reinforcement in enhancing one's own self-esteem. Are external reinforcements just as important as internal assets in building a positive sense of self?

Pitfalls: Some students persist in treating these exercises as games rather than serious learning mechanisms. This may be due to a lack of clear understanding about class goals.

Common characteristics that affect student perceptions are:

1. *Neatness.* This quality includes cleanliness of clothes, length of hair, observable body hair, and type and cost of clothes.
2. *Facial expression.* Observable variations include presence of direct eye contact, frowns, smiles, wrinkled forehead, and the position of the lips or jaw.
3. *Body posture.* A closed palm or raised arm may signify a threat or anger; an open palm extended forward at waist level is a universal sign of friendliness. Body positions also signify attentiveness; for example, leaning forward is a sign of alertness.
4. *Attractiveness.* Physical characteristics can be identified that certain groups, according to variations in their culture, value as attractive or ugly, desirable or undesirable.
5. *Ethnic characteristics.* These may influence perceptions; for example, behaviors such as violence or laziness may be associated with skin color.
6. *Gender.* The individual's sex may affect perceptions held by others.
7. *Age.* Either the age of the observed individual or the age of the observer may affect attitudes.

Chapter 5

Structuring the Relationship

INTRODUCTION

Therapeutic relationships develop in a predictable sequence, although the unique contributions of client and nurse to the relationship determine the nature and depth of each professional encounter. The nurse's ability to develop an effective relationship is influenced by both parties' accurate perceptions of self as well as the duration of contact. Nursing students need to understand each phase and the types of interactions most likely to facilitate client movement through that phase.

In teaching this content, the nurse should emphasize the four phases of the relationship: preinteraction, orientation, working, and termination. Key concepts, specific tasks, and specific therapeutic and nontherapeutic response strategies are described in the text. Teaching emphasis should be focused on outcomes for each phase.

Learning exercises allow the student to practice skills associated with each phase. Spend a few minutes in class following each experiential exercise discussing which concept has been learned. The purpose of each exercise is to help students synthesize didactic content.

There are six exercises in this chapter of the text.

EXERCISE 5-1
Nonverbal Messages

Reflect on the pictures from the text, or cut out pictures from magazines as alternatives to this exercise.

EXERCISE 5-2
Recognizing Role Limitations in Self-Disclosure

Purpose: To help differentiate between a therapeutic use of self-disclosure and spontaneous self-revelation.

Directions: Have students list phrases that describe their personality, such as:

1. I am shy.
2. I get angry when criticized.
3. I'm nice.
4. I'm sexy.
5. I find it hard to handle conflicts. I'm interested in helping people.

Mark each descriptive phase with one of the following:

> x = too embarrassing or intimate to discuss in a group
>
> + = could discuss with a group of peers
>
> RN = this behavior characteristic might affect my ability to function in a therapeutic manner if disclosed.

Pitfalls: In self-disclosure exercises, students may inadvertently talk about feelings they had no intention of revealing.

Teaching Tip
Before beginning, suggest that students differentiate between what is appropriate to reveal in a counseling session and what is appropriate to discuss in a class such as this.

Additional Roles for Discussion
In a quicker version of this exercise, the following role relationships can be marked to signify roles in which an in-depth self-disclosure might be: [A] appropriate, [I] inappropriate, [M] mutually appropriate.

Teacher [I]–student [A] or [I]
Boy–girl [M]
Minister [I]–church member [A]
Supervisor [I]–clerk [I]
Husband–wife [M]
Nurse [I]–client [A]

Then discuss:

1. Which criteria were used to determine the appropriateness of self-disclosure?

2. How much variation is there in what each student would share with others in a group or clinical setting?
3. Were there any behaviors commonly agreed on that would never be shared with a client?
4. What interpersonal factors about the client would facilitate or impede self-disclosure by the nurse in the clinical setting?
5. What did you learn from doing this exercise that could be used in future encounters with clients?

EXERCISE 5-3
Introductions in the Nurse–Client Relationship

The introductory statement forms the basis for the rest of the relationship. Effective contact with a client helps build an atmosphere of trust and connectedness with the nurse.

The following statement is a good example of how one might engage the client in the first encounter: "Hello, Mr. Smith. I am Sally Parks, a nursing student. I will be taking care of you on this shift. During the day I may be asking you some questions about yourself that will help me to understand how I can best help you."

Teaching Tips
After the student identifies the who, what, when, and why in the statements, discuss the following:

1. What was the client's response to the introductory statement?

Answer: Receptive, nonreceptive, pleased, hostile

2. If different students experienced a variation in client responses, what variables might have contributed to this finding?

Answer: External factors such as visitors in room, pain, concern about procedure to be done, etc.

Adapted from Carkhuff RR [1983]. *The Art of Helping*, V, *Student Workbook*. Amherst, MA: Human Resource Development Press.

EXERCISE 5-4
Interpreting Nonverbal Cues

This exercise can be done on an Internet Web home page using the software program FrontPage.

EXERCISE 5-5
Establishing Mutual Goals

Answers: M = mutual goal   N = Nurse's goal   C = Client's goal

1 = M; 2 = N; 3 = M or N; 4 = N; 5 = M; 6 = C; 7 = M

EXERCISE 5-6
Selecting Alternative Strategies

Teaching Tip
To carry out this exercise, break the class into small groups of three or four students. Use the classroom chalkboard or an overhead transparency to compare priorities identified by each work group.

ADDITIONAL EXERCISES

EXERCISE 5-A
Data versus Inferences

Purpose: To develop skills in differentiating between behavioral acts and inferences.

Directions: Working individually or in pairs, indicate whether the following statements represent an objective behavioral observation or require the nurse to make an inference:

Answers (*in bold*)
1. The client appears sad. **Inference**
2. The client's hair is matted and dirty. **Objective observation**
3. The client is smiling. **Objective observation**
4. The client has a red face and complains loudly about dissatisfaction with hospitals. **Objective observation**
5. The client is confused. **Inference**
6. The client's eyes are puffy and red. **Objective observation**
7. The nurse smells alcohol on the client's breath. **Objective observation**
8. The child refuses to speak and hides behind mom's legs. **Objective observation**
9. The boy grimaces while receiving an injection. **Objective observation**
10. The client's husband is anxious about his wife's surgery. **Inference**

Variation: Have students reword each inference to make an objective observation, and vice versa.

EXERCISE 5-B

Confronting Incongruence in the Active Intervention

Phase

Purpose: To distinguish between congruence and incongruence. For this exercise, *congruence* refers to a match between *verbal* and *nonverbal* aspects of the same message. *Hidden* messages refer to an apparent dichotomy between *expressed* and *actual* meaning. *Conflicting* messages convey an opposing meaning to the one being expressed; that is, a hook or zinger is attached to a sentence that changes its meaning. *Mixed* messages convey two different messages. All of these can be considered as forms of *incongruence*.

Directions: This exercise may be done as a homework exercise. Read the situations below, and critique them for congruence, incongruence, hidden messages, conflicting messages, and mixed messages.

1.   A young teen dressing for her first date. Her mother walks close to inspect her daughter's face, saying, "You look so pretty, dear, but what are those blemishes on your face?"

Answer: Conflict between "pretty" and "blemishes."

2.   A student sits in the back of lecture hall and talks throughout class; later he approaches the teacher and says, "I found your lecture so interesting."

Answer: Incongruent nonverbal behavior.

3.   A nursing instructor advises a student to memorize norms for blood pressure in children because it is crucial to know them. During class, the instructor constantly refers to her notes to obtain this information herself.

Answer: Mixed message, "What's critical for you isn't as important for me."

4.   A nurse, engaged in demonstrating aseptic technique for wound care to client before discharge, touches the old dressing with sterile gloves several times during the demonstration.

Answer: Incongruency between saying it needs to be sterile and then breaking technique.

5.   A nurse enters Mr. J.'s room and notices his clenched fists, pale color, and diaphoretic forehead. She asks, "Are you all right? " Mr. J. responds, "Oh, I'm okay, just some minor discomfort."

Answer: Incongruence between verbal and nonverbal behaviors.

6.   A student nurse on community health rotation makes a home visit to teach a mother who has requested information on infant nutrition. During a teaching session, the client walks back and forth and gets ready to leave.

Answer: Hidden message, Why doesn't the mother value the information?

7.   A child sobs loudly. When asked what is wrong, he replies, "Nothing."

Answer: Incongruence between verbal and nonverbal behavior.

EXERCISE 5-C

Nonverbal Cues in Relationships

Purpose: To increase awareness of nonverbal cues that support or negate the meaning of the verbal content.

Teaching Tip

Write a physical behavioral cue word on the chalkboard or on an overhead transparency. Have each student write her or his interpretation of the meaning of the cue. Then compare student answers. Answers can be developed for the following common cue behaviors:

- Avoidance of eye contact
- Tapping fingers
- Slumped posture
- Frequent shifts in body weight
- Leaning forward toward speaker
- Frequent glances at watch

EXERCISE 5-D

Identifying Environmental Variables

Purpose: To sensitize the student to types of environmental factors that foster optimal nurse-client communication. To conserve time, assign the first part as an out-of-class activity.

Directions

1.   Ask students to recall their first day of college class or hospital clinical orientation.

2.   Have them list the factors that helped them obtain needed information.

3.   Have them list the factors that hindered obtaining needed information.

4. In group discussions, ask students to share identified factors with fellow students. Guide the discussion toward psychosocial characteristics such as anxiety level and presence or absence of supportive others. Next, focus on characteristics of the physical environment (noise level, temperature, lack of privacy, pain) that interfered with their ability to interact.

Answers: (An asterisk (*) indicates suggestions regarding the hospital.)

Facilitating Physical Factors: good acoustics, easy-to-see visual aids, moderate temperature (70°F), appropriate room size, door in rear of the room for late arrivals, privacy,* comfortable furniture

Hindering Physical Factors: temperature too hot or cold, nearby students who talk or rustle papers, noise from the next room,* hunger, poor lighting, pain,* visitors in the room,* semiprivate room*

Facilitating Psychological Factors: support from friends who are present, previous positive interaction with teacher or with medical caregiver,* success in a previous course, prepared for class, large class requiring minimal verbal participation, a small class that is easy to ask questions in, family nearby and helpful*

Hindering Psychological Factors: possible failure or poor grade, unremitting illness,* excessive demands by other life factors such as problems with boyfriend, high anxiety level, uncertainty about outcome,* worry about expenses*

Teaching Tip
If students are reluctant to participate initially, share your own perceptions about factors that hinder or help learning for students and for hospitalized clients.

EXERCISE 5-E
Validating Inferences about Nonverbal Messages

Purpose: To provide practice in validation skills in a nonthreatening environment, have students do some role-playing.

Directions: These may be written on a piece of paper, or the student may develop one directly from this list: pain, anger, sadness, confidence, anxiety, disapproval, relief, uncertainty, shock, disbelief, disgust, acceptance, disinterest, rejection, despair, uprightness. The other students must guess what behaviors the student is trying to enact.

Questions for Discussion
1. Which emotions were more difficult to guess from their nonverbal cues? Which ones were easier?
2. Was there more than one interpretation of the emotion?
3. How would you use the information you developed today in your future care of clients?

Chapter 6

Bridges and Barriers in the Therapeutic Relationship

INTRODUCTION

This chapter reviews the major conceptual components of effective relationships. The concepts of trust, caring, empathy, anxiety, mutuality, and stereotyping are defined, and contextual factors, such as personal space and confidentiality, are described. Nursing students should understand these concepts and be able to examine them in relation to their own behavior as well as that of their clients. Inability to master these concepts increases discomfort on the part of the student and the client.

Experiential exercises are provided to help students develop an understanding of each concept. It cannot be stressed too strongly that *active participation* in these learning exercises helps students work through the meaning of the chapter's content. Mastery of these skills will help the nurse provide better care.

There are eight exercises in this chapter of the text.

EXERCISE 6-1
Application of Caring

This exercise can be done for personal and for professional situations. Explore what is common in contrast to what is different.

EXERCISE 6-2
Techniques that Promote Trust

Purpose: To help students identify techniques that promote the establishment of trust. After providing practice time in using these skills, summarize examples on the chalkboard.

Teaching Tips
Use alternative strategies: If students have no clinical examples, try a few "trust" activities in class:

Have student A stand behind student B, who is instructed to fall backward (student A, of course, catches student B).

Have student A lead blindfolded student B around the room during break time. Discuss feelings. What makes one person trust another? What problems prevent trust?

EXERCISE 6-3
Identifying Empathetic Responses

Purpose: To help identify levels of empathy.

Directions: Read the client statement, then identify the nurse's response as to the correct empathy level, 1, 2, 3, 4, or 5, and place the number on the line to the left of the response.

Answers

Set 1

Level 1 a. Doctors like that ought to give up medicine.

Level 3 b. You feel that the doctor was confusing and didn't explain . . .

Level 1 c. What time is it now?

Level 5 d. You're angry that the doctor was unable to explain . . .

Level 5 e. You feel exasperated about not knowing . . .

Set 2

Level 3 a. You're fed up with needles and wish to be left alone.

Level 4 b. Getting needles is part of being in the hospital.

Level 5 c. You're angry about having intrusive procedures.

Level 1 d. Just remember to fill out your menu for tomorrow.

Level 5 e. With all these intrusive procedures, you feel vulnerable and defenseless, ready to go hide to get away from it all.

EXERCISE 6-4
Evaluating Mutuality

Purpose: To identify behaviors and feelings on the part of the nurse and the client that indicate mutuality.

Pitfalls: In small group situations, some students tend to dominate the discussion while others make no contribution. Group process techniques (see Chapter 12) may be used to foster participation. Teacher intervention or the use of sociograms can provide input to the members about the group process.

Teaching Tip

This exercise allows students time to share clinical experiences in a semistructured fashion. To ensure that this activity fosters group discussion and mutual goal sharing, it is recommended that the class be divided into small groups consisting of no more than eight in each. Suggest that one group member serve as recorder to take "minutes" of the discussion. The minutes can list examples of mutual goals established with clients. In a general discussion, these lists can be shared with the class.

EXERCISE 6-5
Confidentiality and Setting

Teaching Tip

Go around the room, and have one student quickly summarize each breach of confidentiality. The next student offers a suggestion to correct the breach.

EXERCISE 6-6
Identifying Verbal and Nonverbal Behaviors Associated with Anxiety

Purpose: To broaden the awareness of behavioral responses that indicate anxiety.

Directions: Assign this exercise as an out-of-class activity. Have students list as many anxious behaviors as they can think of. Each column contains a few examples to start. If desired, class time can be used to discuss the lists in a group and to add new behaviors to the list.

Teaching Tip

This exercise allows students to draw on past learning and experience to classify behaviors according to levels of anxiety. Corrective feedback may be given if the students tend to misclassify behaviors. Groups may be asked to share their lists if all the behaviors cannot be shown.

Some behaviors might be *verbal* (interrupting speech with "um," "ah," or "uh"; expressing anger to cover up anxiety; changing the subject frequently; not finishing sentences); or *nonverbal* (trembling; flushing; jerky body movements; darting eyes around;

drumming fingers on table; clearing the throat; cold, wet hands; or facial tic.)

Sample Answers

Verbal: Along with quavering voice, rapid speech, mumbling, defensive words, *add*—interrupting speech with "um," "ah," etc.; expressing anger to cover up anxiety; changing subject frequently; not finishing sentences.

Nonverbal: Along with nail biting, foot tapping, sweating, pacing, *add*—trembling, flushing, jerky body movements, darting eyes around, drumming fingers on table, clearing the throat, cold and wet hands, facial tic.

EXERCISE 6-7
Reducing Clinical Bias by Identifying Stereotypes

Purpose: To help identify general and personal stereotypes.

Teaching Tip

Break students up into small groups. Begining students may discuss any of the following stereotypes, which they should recognize as fairly blatant examples. More advanced students should focus on discussing responses based on a nurse's point of view for each of the clinical examples listed.

List of stereotypes, both positive and negative, might include:

- The Aryan race is a superior race.
- The only good Indian is a dead Indian.
- Latinos are family-oriented.
- Jews are money-hungry.
- Black is beautiful.
- The Irish are alcoholics.
- People on welfare are lazy.
- Italian men are great lovers.
- The blue-collar family is crude.
- Rich people are snobs.
- Men are strong, and women are tender.
- Taller children have higher intelligence scores (IQs).
- Little boys are troublesome; little girls are compliant.
- Women cannot make rational leadership decisions.
- Women who get raped asked for it.

EXERCISE 6-8
Personal Space Differences

Assign as an out-of-class activity, and use class time to write common themes on the blackboard, overhead transparency, or computer to stimulate general discussion.

ADDITIONAL EXERCISES

EXERCISE 6-A
Confidentiality and Problem Solving

Purpose: To offer a group opportunity to creatively solve difficult situations concerning the use of confidential information.

Directions: Study the example, then write the problem and list the steps you would take to solve it.

Example: Fifteen-year-old Susan, a client on the adolescent unit, tells you that she is on birth control pills but that her mother doesn't know. She asks you to promise not to tell anyone.

1. Write down the problem.
2. What steps would you take to resolve the problem?

Teaching Tip
You can use other clinical examples. Answers should include the nurse telling the client who and what she needs to tell but reassuring the client that her mother need not be told. Nurse might also work with the client on the mother-daughter relationship to enable the client to tell her mother.

EXERCISE 6-B
Identifying Behaviors of Intrusion into Personal Space

Purpose: To help students identify behaviors of another individual when a person enters his/her space.

Directions: Two volunteers role-play a situation. Student 1 (playing the client) is told that the other will be interviewing him for a history database. Student 2 is confidentially directed to slowly move items placed on the table closer to student 1 and, finally, to move his/her body closer.

Setting: A table and two chairs are facing each other. Items on the table include a soda can, ashtray, and pencils.

Questions for Discussion
1. How did the client respond when the nurse moved items toward him?
2. Did the client allow the items into his space or did he retreat?
3. What changes in the content of the conversation were observed? Clinical situations might also be discussed and examples cited.

Answers
In each case, students should be able to identify specific descriptions of the violation of the principles presented in the text. They are:

1. Failure to provide privacy for an intimate situation, an assumption of the client's feelings.

Action: Draw the curtain, shut the door, and drape the client.

2. The physician has shared difficult news with the client and has not allowed time for client to respond; or too many people are in the space with the client; or they intrude without warning the client.

Action: Remain with the client, and encourage him to talk while sitting by the bed without facing the client directly.

3. Intrusive equipment introduced into room without explanation to client; equipment closer than family; family treated as not important.

Action: Plan nursing activities so as not to interfere with family visit; explain all equipment and procedures; talk with family about the policy, and explain how they can help.

EXERCISE 6-C
Trust in Interpersonal Relationships

Purpose: To aid in differentiating behaviors that promote or abuse trust.

Directions: Mark T for true if the statement about nursing action would promote trust in a client.

T 1. Nurse introduces self and describes her role.
2. During diabetes teaching session, nurse confuses types of insulin.
3. Nurse tells the diabetic client not to clip his nails even though his physician told him that it was okay.
T 4. Nurse answers the call light promptly.
T 5. Nurse periodically stops in the client's room to determine whether he needs anything.

6. Nurse arranges to change a dressing at 1:30 but doesn't arrive to do so until 2:30.
7. Prior to surgery, the client knows that he may need to have several toes amputated; nurse reassures him, "Everything will be fine."
T 8. Nurse asks a visitor to step outside while she gives an injection; nurse then goes to find the visitor afterward to say that it's okay to return.

EXERCISE 6-D
Anxiety: Application to a Clinical Situation

Purpose: To increase self-awareness of anxiety.

Teaching Tip
This exercise may be conducted in small groups. Allow enough time for the class to hold a discussion and to compile a list of common causes of client anxiety.

Directions: Answer the following questions:

1. Describe the circumstances surrounding an anxiety-producing situation for a client.

Answers
- Uncertainty about the diagnosis or outcome
- Fear of pain
- Worry about financial hardship
- Concern about how illness will affect family, job, or other relationships or roles

2. Identify some common coping responses. Are they adaptive or maladaptive?

Answers
- Withdrawal = adaptive (if limited to short periods)
- Change in sleeping pattern = maladaptive
- Change in eating habits = maladaptive
- Tendency to develop narrow focus on single issue = maladaptive (if long term)
- Inability to attend to other activities = maladaptive
- Denial or blocking out of information = maladaptive
- Sarcasm = maladaptive
- Use of humor or laughter to relieve tension = adaptive
- Talking about anxiety and sharing with staff or other patients = adaptive

EXERCISE 6-E
More Clinical Bias

Purpose: To help students identify examples of nursing biases that need to be reduced.

Directions: Have students break into small groups. Have them identify their own personal stereotype relevant to alcoholics, spoiled children, large families, welfare recipients, senile elderly people, non-compliance. Have students identify appropriate ways to handle each situation to reduce bias.

Pitfalls: In any exercise in which the students are asked to reveal personal attitudes or beliefs that may not be acceptable to others in the group, some students feel vulnerable. Views may be interpreted negatively by others.

Teaching Tips
1. Have each group member review "rules for giving feedback" listed in the Prologue.
2. Focus discussion in an overall class summary on behaviors that are useful to nurses coping with biased behavior exhibited by a client.

Situation A
Mrs. Small, an emergency department nurse on night duty, reports to the day shift: "Oh, and a Mr. Johnson came in drunk last night around 3 a.m. He got into a fight and needs a few stitches in his forehead." The head nurse on the daytime shift learns from Mr. Johnson that he has been sitting and sleeping in the waiting room for the past 4 hours and has not yet seen a doctor, even though everyone else has been attended to.

Situation B
On break, Mrs. Smith complains about the 3-year-old boy to whom she is assigned. "He sure knows when to pour on the tears. There's nothing wrong with him until he sees you; then the tears start, but they stop as soon as you leave or his mother comes. He's just spoiled because they have a nanny at home who waits on him hand and foot."

Answers
Common coping strategies may include:
- Ignoring biased comments
- Accepting comments
- Offering neutral responses
- Conveying acceptance of the client but not of his or her beliefs

Chapter 7

Role Relationship Patterns

INTRODUCTION

This chapter focuses on role-acquisition concepts and reviews the role stress inherent in the assumption of multiple roles in a complex society. Teaching these concepts helps instructors formalize the role socialization process that must occur in basic nursing education.

General Guidelines and Teaching Tips

Professional role development is often taught in a leadership type of course late in the undergraduate curriculum, yet socialization into the nursing role occurs beginning with the first nursing course in the curriculum.

Reflect on the demands courses make on students.

1. How do demands differ in nursing courses compared with those made in other courses (e.g., attendance policy, penalties for lateness)?
2. What behaviors do you as a teacher reward? Are these congruent with those expected of the nurse giving client care?

Discussion of the content from this chapter is a justifiable use of class or seminar time because it promotes critical thinking, which is one of the characteristics the National League for Nursing uses in evaluating nursing educational programs.

There are seven exercises in this chapter of the text.

EXERCISE 7-1

Role Relations and Self-Concept

Teaching Tips

This exercise can be adapted for use on the day of the first client encounter. Student answers usually rate their degree of comfort with technical skills as a critical aspect of competence. Seniors might compare pregraduation competency self-perceptions with those of beginning students.

EXERCISE 7-2

Looking at My Development as a Professional Nurse

This exercise can be done as a journal across courses.

EXERCISE 7-3

Professional Nursing Roles

This exercise is usually enjoyable for students, although answers reported in seminar or class are often different from those expected by the instructor. Students seem to have little insight into the idea of the various kinds of credentials and need information to differentiate licensure, certification, advanced practice, and other terms.

Pitfalls: Interviews with nurses who express negative feelings about nursing can be disconcerting to students.

Teaching Tip

The class should discuss negative feedback from practicing nurses, and this feedback should be acknowledged as a valid response by some nurses to their conditions of practice, such as lack of autonomy. The focus should be placed on helping students identify ways in which a nurse in such a position might make changes for the better.

EXERCISE 7-4

Exploring a Vision of Professional Nursing

Students usually enjoy this exercise, especially toward the completion of the curriculum. They do tend to lean toward interviewing critical care nurses.

EXERCISE 7-5

Understanding Life Roles

Have a goal for the exercise; for example, one outcome might be to generate a list of roles implemented by each student. Compare roles of males and females.

EXERCISE 7-6
Giving Commendations

It may be easier to discuss strengths of someone else.

EXERCISE 7-7
Transferable Skills

Students might interview someone older, for example, a graduate of last year's nursing class.

ADDITIONAL EXERCISES

To Exercise 7-3, add questions to the interview about a potential legal issue confronted frequently by the nurse and about any ethical dilemma encountered. Because novice students seem to need help differentiating between legal and ethical issues, allow time for class or seminar or a postconference discussion.

EXERCISE 7-A
Acting as a Change Agent

Purpose: To identify a standard practice on the hospital unit that might need to be changed.

Directions: Have students participate in drafting a new standard of practice (e.g., new page for the procedure manual).

Answer
The process would begin with a review of existing practice literature. Perhaps other agencies might need to be surveyed to obtain information. Students would interview the practice and standards committee for the hospital and the unit representative to that committee. The student "committee" then drafts the proposed new standard or procedure and ideally presents this information to supervisors as well as staff, who have the power to change practice.

EXERCISE 7-B
Identifying Adaptive and Maladaptive Stress Coping Mechanisms for Persons Encountering Multiple Role Demands

Directions: Go quickly around the room, and ask students to name a coping strategy. Passing a soft foam ball across to the next person speeds up answers. Answers should list positive or adaptive coping strategies.

Suggested Answers
- Prioritizing essentials
- Giving oneself permission not to do nonessential tasks, such as cleaning house
- Taking time for oneself, such as pampering oneself with a bubble bath or going on shopping spree
- Exercise, such as working out at a gym

Multiple Role Relationships
Students often identify negative or nonadaptive coping strategies, such as drinking, overeating, and social isolation. These should be acknowledged, with more discussion focusing on ways to turn these around, substituting adaptive responses. Depersonalize any class discussions.

Nursing intervention implication would be to assess role overload in clients and use adaptive measures identified in the preceding answer in the learner's health teaching with clients.

Chapter 8

The Grief Experience: Life's Losses and Endings

INTRODUCTION

Loss involves the ending of a relationship by death or separation. Termination is one of the most difficult phases of the nurse–client relationship, yet successful resolution of this phase is of great importance. Discomfort about this aspect of the relationship sometimes results in a shortchanging or an avoidance of the grief process. Successful termination requires awareness of the feelings that emerge in all parties. Furthermore, many novice nurses during their working career have not yet dealt with concepts of death as a commonly encountered final termination.

The exercises in this chapter are designed to familiarize students with their own views of termination and to help them begin to think about their application to clinical practice. The focus of teaching initially needs to be placed on increasing students' awareness of their own reactions to loss. Instead of eliciting a series of personal revelations, draw out common themes and common reactions to any loss. Later exercises help to direct student attention to clinical situations.

Some of us have unresolved grief. These exercises may call forth some emotional responses. Be prepared by offering some office hours for a one-to-one discussion. If necessary, refer to a counselor.

There are six exercises in this chapter of the text.

EXERCISE 8-1

The Meaning of Loss

Purpose: To explore feelings related to loss.

Directions: Avoid allowing students to narrate personal experiences. Focus on common feelings.

Answers

Common feelings associated with loss: anger, sadness, apathy about other aspects of life, desire to regain what was lost, determination to overcome loss, and determination to be compensated

Adaptive coping: crying, verbalizing feelings about loss, and involvement in activities that give meaning to the loss

Maladaptive coping: extreme versions of the preceding behavior, profound depression, anhedonia (inability to feel pleasure), inability to form new attachments in order to avoid possible future loss, and avoidance behaviors

EXERCISE 8-2

A Personal Loss Inventory

This exercise maybe done as homework. In class, focus on which strategies were successful in facilitating coping.

EXERCISE 8-3

How Do I Grieve?

This exercise also may be done as homework.

EXERCISE 8-4

A Questionnaire About Death

Teaching Tip

Assign this exercise to be completed prior to class. In the class, discuss the usefulness of this activity in increasing the learner's recognition of his or her own personal values about death. Further discussion should focus on how these values will affect the student's ability to relate to clients who hold different views of death. Are their values acquired as part of the role socialization of caregivers that in the past emphasized "save the patient at all costs"?

EXERCISE 8-5

Blueprint for My Life Story

Purpose: To help students view life as an integrated process.

Directions: Assign as homework, then have the class discuss briefly whether the purpose of the exercise was achieved.

EXERCISE 8-6
Gift-Giving Role Play

Teaching Tip

This exercise deals with professional nurse–client termination issues. Because the purpose of this exercise is to help students develop therapeutic responses to clients who wish to give them gifts, focus on the ethics of accepting gifts for professional, reimbursed services. Use group discussion to examine the issues involved, such as the use of gifts to prolong a relationship and to postpone termination, to manipulate feelings, to induce guilt, or to restore equality in a relationship (e.g., "I owed you, but now we're even").

ADDITIONAL EXERCISES

EXERCISE 8-A
Describing Loss

Purpose: To increase sensitivity to an individual's coping strategies.

Directions: Interview someone who has suffered loss of a significant other. Have them describe what helped them cope successfully with the experience. Compare answers in a group of classmates. Are there common themes, such as a strong religious faith?

EXERCISE 8-B
Early Leave-Takings

Purpose: To help students get in touch with their own long-buried feelings and to apply them to current learning.

Directions: Consider the answers to these questions:

1. What is your earliest recollection of leaving your mother?
2. What did it feel like?
3. How did you deal with it?

Answer

If students are unable to recall feelings, items 2 and 3 could be related to the grieving process surrounding the breakup of a current relationship.

Chapter 9

Communication Styles

INTRODUCTION

This chapter can be enjoyable and useful for student experimentation. Let the students be creative. Ideas for students in group or out-of-class assignments might include videotaping, pantomime, role playing, imitating some of the facial expressions in Figure 9-1, cutting out of magazines pictures that display expression of a strong emotion.

There are three exercises in this chapter of the text.

EXERCISE 9-1
Gender Bias

Students seem to get deeply involved in expressing opinions about gender bias. Try to maintain a neutral affect. (It is easy to let our own bias enter the discussion even though we are the teachers). If the class is predominantly female, avoid "male bashing."

EXERCISE 9-2
Nurses' Clothing as Nonverbal Communication

Answers
1. Former symbols included a white cap specific to each nursing school, a white uniform (dress), white hose (no socks), and very white shoes; and no makeup or jewelry, except a nursing pin depicting the nursing school.
2. Without a cap, what symbolizes the nurse?
3. Today nurses with different functions dress quite differently. Pediatric nurses might wear pastels, often smocks with bright-colored animals or designs. Intensive care nurses, surgical nurses, and those in other specialty areas wear scrub gowns, sometimes with pants, often in a variety of bright colors. Flight nurses wear flight suits, and nurses making rounds for physicians often dress up in fashionable dresses or suits and may or may not wear a lab coat.

Perhaps the one common identifier is the large picture identity badge with the "RN" label, which is worn for security reasons these days rather than as a badge of the profession.

EXERCISE 9-3
Self-Analysis of Videotape

Expect beginning students to have a high level of anxiety about videotaping themselves. It is difficult to self-critique. Make sure the critique states some positive aspects. Avoid any type of evaluation or grade for this activity.

Additional Questions for Discussion
1. Are people blind to appearance?
2. Are people influenced by skin color, style of hair, dress, or jewelry?

ADDITIONAL EXERCISES

EXERCISE 9-A
Mime

Purpose: To increase awareness of facial cues in communication.

Time: 2 minutes; then 3 minutes for general class discussion.

Directions: Break the class into groups of three. Student 1 uses pantomime to act out one feeling. Student 2 attempts make a verbal guess about what feeling is being conveyed. Student 3 observes student 2's nonverbal responses. Report to class.

EXERCISE 9-B
Interpreting Nonverbal Cues

Purpose: To demonstrate the degree of error in attempting to interpret nonverbal cues without verifying the message by listening to vocal tone, pitch, and word pattern.

Directions: Watch television with the sound muted. Pay close attention to the nonverbal content of a series of commercials. If you haven't heard the commercial before, are you able to figure out what is being sold?

EXERCISE 9-C

Blinded to Appearance

Purpose: To increase awareness about how people respond to you.

Directions: Take two photographs of yourself, one in uniform with a very neat appearance and one in casual clothes with a very unusual hairstyle and mode of dress. Show the pictures to three strangers and ask them which one to put on your resume in seeking a job.

Chapter **10**

Developing Therapeutic Communication Skills in the Nurse–Client Relationship

INTRODUCTION

The content of this chapter is designed to help students develop communication skills required to successfully establish and manage professional relationships. The text describes specific techniques that help nurses explore, define, and clarify health needs with clients. In client interactions, the nurse must distinguish between congruent and incongruent messages and must validate nursing inferences with the client.

These experiential exercises provide opportunities to practice each communication skill described in the chapter. The learner can experiment with different communication strategies for dealing with typical blocks in communication.

There are 12 exercises in this chapter of the text.

EXERCISE 10-1

Active Listening

Teaching Tip

This exercise allows for practicing active listening using a familiar situation. If videotaping equipment is available, have students do this as an out-of-class activity and critique their own performances.

EXERCISE 10-2

Observing for Nonverbal Cues

Teaching Tip

This exercise works best as an out-of-class assignment. A television commercial may be substituted for a movie.

EXERCISE 10-3

Asking Open-Ended Questions

Focus on listing samples of open-ended questions. Sometimes this role-playing needs to be goal-directed, such as practicing asking health history questions.

EXERCISE 10-4

Differences in Active Listening Questions

Answers

Key: Open-ended questions are marked with an asterisk (*); focused questions are marked with a plus sign (+); closed-ended questions are marked with a minus sign (–).

- 1. Ms. Gai, did you have a productive therapy session?
+ 2. How do you feel about it now that you've learned that you will be staying at your daughter's house?
+ 3. What did the doctor say about your lower back pain?
- 4. Your tray will be here soon. Are you hungry?
* 5. And when you heard that, you felt . . . ?
- 6. When the doctor walked away, you felt rejected?
- 7. No one likes to be in pain; can I get you something for it?
+ 8. In the past, when your leg ached, what kinds of things helped it?
* 9. What do you think about being transferred to a nursing home?
+ 10. Tell me, what brought you to see the doctor today?
- 11. Are you having that problem with arthritis in your hand again?
* 12. What would you like to discuss today while we take a walk?
* 13. How are you?
+ 14. What happened to you after you fell down?
* 15. And then what did you think?
- 16. Do you feel like taking your medicine now or later?

EXERCISE 10-5

Listening for Themes

Purpose: To help students identify underlying themes in messages.

29

Questions for Discussion

1. Are the underlying themes recorded by the group consistent with the speaker's understanding of his or her communication?

2. Were the interpretations of pertinent information relatively similar or significantly different? If they were different, what implications do you think such differences have for nurse–client relationships in nursing practice?

Pitfalls: Supersensitivity to peer feedback is a potential problem. Review the rules for giving feedback listed in the Prologue to this *Instructors' Manual*. If feedback evokes negative feelings, this can be dealt with in a nonpersonal manner immediately in the classroom setting. One strategy is to depersonalize the verbal exchange (Cormier, 1984). Use a two-part statement that expresses an appreciation for sharing one's point of view while stating one's own position.

Model: "I understand the reason for . . . [your position] . . ., but I feel . . . is important.

Example: "I understand why you feel the client behaved inappropriately, but I feel that the important aspect of this situation was not the sexual content of the message but rather the staff's reaction to it."

Teaching Tip

Recording the students' presentations outside of class on videotape or audiocassette saves time. Have students critique their own presentations. When students denigrate another's comment in class, try using the model above or broaden the student's comment to illustrate one entire concept rather than a personal point of view. Supportive comments from other students also help the situation. Another technique is to verbally refocus discussion on the purpose or the objectives of the day's lesson.

Timely intervention by the instructor or other students can limit the use of damaging feedback from one or two class members.

EXERCISE 10-6
Minimal Cues and Leads

This exercise can also be assigned as homework. Have students watch 5 minutes of a talk show.

EXERCISE 10-7
Using Clarification

This exercise is self-explanatory.

EXERCISE 10-8
Practicing Paraphrasing

Purpose: To validate with the client the accuracy of perceptions of the objective content of the client's message and to convey to the client that you are interested and actually heard what was said.

Directions: For each statement, write one appropriately rephrased sentence.

1. "I'm on a diet, but I seem to be gaining a lot of weight even though I usually try to stick to it faithfully."

Appropriately Paraphrased Example: "You want to lose weight but your diet isn't working?"

Inappropriate: "You can't stick to your diet?"

2. "I need an operation but can't take the time to have it until my business is doing better."

Appropriately Paraphrased Example: "You need an operation but haven't got time?"

Inappropriate: "You won't take the time to have surgery?"

3. "The doctor just told me I have cancer but I'm not sure what he means."

Appropriately Paraphrased Example: "You understand you have cancer but don't know the details?"

Inappropriate: "You are not sure you have cancer?"

EXERCISE 10-9
Role-Play Practice in Differentiating Paraphrasing and Reflection

Questions for Discussion

1. What difficulties surfaced in trying to paraphrase the statements of clients?

Answer
The situation is often somewhat awkward for beginners.

2. Did the paraphrased statement encourage you to continue? Did you feel more understood as a result of hearing the listener's response? What did you learn personally from this exercise about paraphrasing as a listening response?

EXERCISE 10-10
Practicing the Use of Reflecting Responses

Teaching Tip

Assigning as an out-of-class homework assignment allows students time to practice the use of reflection.

EXERCISE 10-11
Practicing Summarization

Teaching Tip

Pick biomedical ethical issues of current concern or issues depicted in a currently popular movie. Have a volunteer summarize the issue so that everyone understands. Connect this activity to nursing skills by pointing out that summarization also can be used to identify progress in the therapeutic process and to explicitly identify the basis for further interactions or interventions.

EXERCISE 10-12
Therapeutic Use of Silence

Teaching Tip

After role-playing, have a general discussion to share feelings about the effective use of silence. Most people rush in to fill in a silent period unless they are trained to use silence therapeutically.

ADDITIONAL EXERCISES

EXERCISE 10-A
Identifying Underlying Feelings

Purpose: To provide practice in using nonverbal cues to expression of feelings.

Directions: Bring in pictures from home, or pick out several advertisements from magazines with two people talking to each other. Identify what kinds of feelings are being expressed.

Questions for Discussion
1. How did you reach your conclusions?
2. What kind of psychological enticement do you think the advertiser is trying to get across?

EXERCISE 10-B
The Value of Encouragers

Purpose: To practice and evaluate the efficacy of minimal cues and leads.

Directions
1. Think of a recent interpersonal problem you have encountered. Break up the group into groups of three. Student A is the protagonist, student B is the helping person, and student C is the observer. Student A relates the problem and indicates how he or she dealt with it and the outcome. Student B uses encouragers, minimal cues, and leads as outlined in the text. Student C observes the interaction and provides feedback.
2. Reverse roles, and this time the helping person should not use verbal cues and minimal leads as a listening response strategy. If time permits, each student can have an opportunity to practice each role.

Questions for Discussion
1. What were the differences when encouragers were not used? Was the communication as lively?
2. How did you feel to you while you were telling your story when the helping person used this strategy?

EXERCISE 10-C
Charades

Purpose: To experience the use of silence in a relationship.

Directions
1. This exercise takes place in small groups of four to six students.
2. Two individuals are selected. Student A plays the part of a boy; student B plays the part of a girl. The rest of the group sits in a circle around students A and B. The group's job is to act as observers, writing down what messages each person thinks are being conveyed and making notes about all nonverbal cues observed.
3. For 3 minutes, student A sits facing student B and nonverbally attempts to communicate with student B, asking her or him out on a date. Student B then has 3 minutes to reply, nonverbally telling student A where she or he lives, finding out how to dress for the date, and so forth.

Discussion

In a general discussion following this exercise, share the observations made by the observers, focusing on the nonverbal cues used to communicate. What strategies were used to overcome silence? How difficult is it to resist the urge to talk?

EXERCISE 10-D

The Discomfort of Silence

Purpose: To help students understand the diversity of silence.

Directions

1.   This role-playing exercise is to be done with a group.

2.   The class divides into two groups by counting off 1, 2, 1, 2, etc.

3.   All the 1s gather on one side of the room, all the 2s on the other.

4.   Instructions:

To the 1s: Select a client from the group of 2s and form a dyad. Pretend you are a new nurse meeting client 2 for the first time. Introduce yourself, and find out the client's name, reason for being in the hospital, current mood, and health status. You have 2 minutes.

To the 2s: Your role is that of an unhappy patient, unwilling to talk with another new nurse. Respond to 1's first question, but refuse to answer any other questions.

5.   The group leader will monitor the process and terminate interactions after 3 minutes or sooner if the group desires.

Discussion

In a general discussion, ask the 2s how they felt when they were asked questions they were forbidden to answer. Where were they uncomfortable? Ask them to estimate how long this exercise took.

Then ask the 1s how they felt when the client refused to talk. Were they frustrated? Angry? What did they do? Most people tend to try to fill the silence with social chatter. Did anyone try to do so?

In a therapeutic interaction, silence has several functions. Which of the following were noted during the class exercise?

1.   A period of silence can be used to assess our own level of anxiety.

2.   It can be used to assess the client's level of anxiety.

3.   It gives the nurse an opportunity to concentrate on making observations of the client's nonverbal behavior.

4.   Silence on the nurse's part encourages the client's verbal communication.

5.   A short period of silence allows the client time to formulate a thoughtful reply to the nurse's interaction.

If silence is utilized as a communication skill, several problems may arise. Which of the following were noted during the class exercise?

1.   Overuse leading to prolonged periods of silence can discourage further communication.

2.   Prolonged periods of silence can increase client or nurse anxiety.

EXERCISE 10-E

Identifying the Need for Validation

Purpose: To experience the process of validation

Directions

1.   When a client statement is unclear, the nurse may identify a need to seek validation from the client to confirm perception of the message.

Example: Client (sobbing): "That nurse had no business telling the doctor I wasn't taking my medicine. Now I can't go home."

Example: Nurse: "You're upset because you can't go home?"

Example: Client: "I'm a little under par today."

Example: Nurse: "You're feeling worse today than yesterday?"

2.   Write a sentence for each situation below that appropriately seeks validation.

   a.   Client: "You are late with my insulin; now my food won't be any good."

   b.   Client (grimacing): "This leg is playing up a bit."

   c.   Client (burping): "That medicine doesn't sit well."

   d.   Client: "Yeah, I know I'm supposed to take that pill before I eat."

EXERCISE 10-F

Integrating the Use of Communication Strategies

Purpose: To provide practice in using the major communications skills described in this chapter.

Directions

Study the following situations, and write a sentence illustrating the use of each skill listed.

Client: "I know you have to do your job, but it seems to me that you people have no consideration for patients. I get woken up at 5:00 a.m. to get the floor mopped, presented with a cold breakfast, and taken to physical therapy, and woken at night to get a sleeping pill. I find it exhausting. No wonder I'm not learning to regulate my insulin."

1. Listen actively
2. Open-ended question
3. Clarify
4. Paraphrase
5. Reflect
6. Summarize
7. Validate

EXERCISE 10-G

Attending Behaviors

Purpose: To help students experience the relevance of using attending behaviors in communicating.

Directions

1.   Students form groups of three, with one taking the role of the client, another taking the role of the nurse, and the third acting as observer. Students role-play a recent nursing situation or provide each triad with a clinical situation in which attending behaviors are not used. Replay the same situation with the use of the attending behaviors cited earlier.

2.   The observer shares impressions with the participants and compares them with the experience of the other students. The student who played the client in each situation describes the differences in feelings and communications in each of the role-playing situations.

3.   Reverse roles and repeat the exercise if desired.

EXERCISE 10-H

Observing Nonverbal Behavior

Purpose: To help identify nonverbal behaviors.

Directions

1.   The group leader makes up 3 x 5 inch cards prior to class. On each card is the name of a feeling (e.g., sad, happy, lonely, scared, afraid, confident, shy, proud, lovable, dejected, hopeless, helpless, hostile, annoyed, attractive, or pleased).

2.   Students draw a card and, in turn, act out the emotion nonverbally.

3.   The other students guess the emotion expressed nonverbally.

Questions for Discussion

1.   How difficult was it to express an emotion without words?

2.   Did some of the nonverbal expressions of the emotion have multiple meanings? If so, why do you think this occurred?

3.   Were some of the emotions that were expressed more or less universal in nature?

Answer: Anger, joy, despair, or grief

4.   What were some of the nonverbal cues that made it easier to guess certain nonverbal communications of feelings?

Answer: Facial expressions

Teaching Tip

To save time, as an alternate activity you can circulate five or six pictures cut from a magazine depicting happiness, anger, or other emotions. Have students write down their perceptions of the nonverbal messages. Do differences occur because of a different cultural context or social setting?

Chapter 11

Intercultural Communication

INTRODUCTION

It can be stated with certainty that every nurse will be required to deal with culturally diverse clients during her or his career. The content in this chapter is designed to increase nurses' awareness of their own cultural values. This content assists nurses to explore barriers and strategies useful in caring for clients from other cultures.

Teaching Tips

It is critical for the instructor to emphasize the to avoid making assumptions about clients because they seem to belong to a certain cultural or ethnic group. Within the limits of just one chapter, no author could discuss all the variations within a group or explore all of the many diverse cultures within society.

Nurses need to differentiate among subcultures. Not all non–English-speaking people are part of the same group. As with Asian Americans, Hispanics differ widely, depending on the family's country of origin. These differences are physiological as well as behavioral.

There are nine exercises in this chapter of the text.

EXERCISE 11-1
The Meaning of Culture

Teaching Tip

This exercise can be done very briefly in class. Use the chalkboard or an overhead transparency, and have students call out adjectives describing culture. Write a short list. Then poll students for positive or negative interpretations. Discuss differences in attitudes.

EXERCISE 11-2
Cultural Self-Assessment Exercise

Teaching Tip

Assign this exercise as a homework assignment.

EXERCISE 11-3
Recognizing Components of Group Culture

An alternative exercise is to have students watch a movie that deals with a different culture and submit a written or oral critique (e.g., *The Joy Luck Club, Norma Rae, A Family Thing, The Milagro Beanfield War, The Brother from Another Planet, Cry Freedom, La Familia*).

EXERCISE 11-4
Family Cultural Experiences

Teaching Tip

Focus on discussion of common themes.

Answers

1. Conceptually, customs, like other components of culture, begin with family experiences early in childhood.

2. Factors producing changes in generational family customs include changes in the dominant culture, "acculturation" in school, and the blending of customs occurring as offspring marry.

EXERCISE 11-5
Diversity in Nursing

This exercise is self-explanatory.

EXERCISE 11-6
Exploring Stereotypes

Younger students do not seem invested in the traditional stereotypes.

EXERCISE 11-7
Understanding Language Barriers

Teaching Tip

Focus on the importance of nonverbal communication and the use of pictures. Describe strategies used in large health care agencies (translators, multilingual teaching materials, and electronic aids, such as personal computer translators).

34

EXERCISE 11-8
Cultural Assessment

An alternative activity might be to take a current assessment tool and critique it for cultural specificity.

EXERCISE 11-9
Applying Cultural Sensitivity to Nursing Care

An alternative fun exercise is to have student groups do a brief presentation on cultural preferences, then provide foods of that culture as a class snack.

ADDITIONAL EXERCISES

EXERCISE 11-A
Cultural Stories

Purpose: To help the student develop an understanding of cultural differences.

Directions
1.   Interview someone from another culture using the categories listed in the text. The person can be a relative, a friend, or a client.
2.   Take turns sharing the information received with your classmates.
3.   List important points or summaries on a chalkboard or flip chart.

Questions for Discussion
1.   What did you find out about the culture that you didn't know before doing this exercise?
2.   Which cultural activities were most different from how you experience the same issues? Were some of them familiar to you?
3.   What did you learn about yourself in doing this exercise?

EXERCISE 11-B
Applications of Cultural Diversity Affecting Nursing Care

Purpose: To increase awareness of communication with clients.

Directions: Each student writes about a clinical situation in which he or she is a client from another culture who does not understand the nurse. This may require some time on the part of the students but will be of great interest and may have practical applications in clinical nursing situations.
1.   What strategies could the nurse use to communicate?
2.   How do cultural traditions become barriers to health care?

Teaching Tip
It may be best to divide the students into groups of two or three members. Students can share information they have gathered with the rest of the class or can make posters to display. They can use their existing database format and include items from the table in the text; if time allows, have students develop a nursing care plan.

Chapter 12

Communicating in Groups

INTRODUCTION

Students bring some skills to group situations. Over the years, they have learned to communicate socially in peer groups, family situations, and perhaps even in work groups. The content in this chapter is designed to help learners use existing group communications skills and develop additional skills that they will need to use on a daily basis to deliver care, establish policies, and act as change agents.

Group interactions can be both with formal groups (e.g., the employing agency, client families, and nursing associations) and with informal groups (e.g., colleagues, learning groups, and work groups). Increasingly, delivery of effective health care requires skills working with multiple groups of care providers.

Many students have only a beginning awareness of how groups function. In this chapter, exercises are designed to assist students in developing greater insight into basic concepts of group dynamics and group leadership styles. Participation in this exercise may enhance the learner's abilities to function as a group member or a group leader.

There are eight exercises in this chapter of the text.

EXERCISE 12-1
Role of Group Communication

Purpose: To increase the class members' appreciation for the role that group communication plays in their lives and to increase their awareness of existing skills.

Teaching Tip
To make this exercise more meaningful, focus on Question 6, guiding discussion toward how existing skills will be needed in future nursing practice.

EXERCISE 12-2
Member Commitment

Focus the discussion on identifying common themes.

EXERCISE 12-3
Identifying Norms

Purpose: To help identify norms operating in groups.

Directions: Have students divide a piece of paper into three columns. In the first column, students should list the norms that they think exist in their class or work group. In the second column, students should list the norms that they think exist in their family. The third column is for an analysis of commonalties or differences shared with the group, first related to the school or work group and then to the family.

Sample Answers

Class Norms	Family Norms	Common
Be on time	Don't yell	Respect adults
Pay attention	Tell Mom if	
Take notes	you won't be	
Don't talk	home for dinner	
Raise hand to		
ask a question		

EXERCISE 12-4
Headbands: Group Role Expectations

Purpose: To experience the pressures of role expectations, to demonstrate the effects of role expectations on individual behavior in a group, and to explore the effects of role pressures on total group performance.

Pitfall: Students find that this exercise, more than most, makes a lasting impression on them. Some students become quite angry or frustrated while participating, especially if they feel defeated in reaching their perceived goal; that is, an actual discussion of their opinion about nursing.

Teaching Tip
For this exercise, it is crucial to conduct a debriefing group discussion. Focus on how the students felt during the activity.

EXERCISE 12-5

Identifying Task and Maintenance Functions

Purpose: To compare task functions with maintenance functions.

Task functions: initiating, seeking information, clarifying, consensus-making, testing, and summarizing

Maintenance functions: encouraging, expressing, group feeling, harmonizing, compromising, gate-keeping, and setting standards

Teaching Tip

This exercise is usually more effective if participants sit in a circle. The topic should be one of interest to them; for example, how to help a friend who threatens suicide, whether new graduate nurses should work for a reduced salary while awaiting licensure, or whether nurses should be licensed at two entry levels.

EXERCISE 12-6

Clarifying Personal Leadership Role Preferences

Teaching Tips

Many students are reluctant to reveal feelings about leadership, especially if some leadership behaviors are required and evaluated in their clinical performance evaluations. Facilitate discussion by depersonalizing the discussion. You might ask students to recall a situation in high school when they had to organize a group activity or present a group project.

This exercise is best accomplished in small groups of no more than eight students, who may meet without the instructor, perhaps for the last 15 minutes of a scheduled class or in a clinical postconference.

EXERCISE 12-7

Group Closure and Expressing Affection

Teaching Tip

Instructors can model this process of closure by summarizing your lecture content at the end of each lecture. For the student experience, any type of summarization can be used.

EXERCISE 12-8

Learning about Support Groups

Pitfall: When we've done this activity with a large number of students without guiding their community contacts, some agencies have expressed a feeling of annoyance at being contacted by many students.

Teaching Tip

Have class members conduct their contact activity in groups instead of individually. Prevent multiple contacts by having each group select from a list you circulate so that no two groups contact the same agency.

ADDITIONAL EXERCISE

EXERCISE 12-A

Group Planning

Purpose: To help students experience the process of planning for a group relationship.

Directions

1. Break up into small groups of three to five students each.

2. Have each group select a different group experience to plan; for example, an adolescent group, a group for alcoholics, a group for preadolescent boys, a group for the elderly, or a support group for families of people with Alzheimer's disease.

3. Answer the following questions in relation to the group selected.

    a. What are the goals to be achieved? Are they realistic, stated concretely in behavioral terms, and relevant to meeting the identified self-care demands of the client?

    b. What types of interactions would be necessary to achieve them?

    c. What selection criteria would be necessary to ensure successful group participation?

    d. What norms should be established if group goals are to be met?

    e. What would be your role in the group?

    f. What communication techniques would be most appropriate to meet the needs of the group?

    g. How would you structure the first meeting in light of the group goals and specific needs of the target population?

    h. How will you go about meeting your objectives?

4. After the members of each group respond to the questions in relation to their specific group population, the responses can be shared with the larger group by each group in turn. The larger group can critique the responses of each group.

Questions for Discussion

1. How difficult was it to plan realistically for a specific client population?

2. As you developed your responses, were any of them interrelated?

3. What did you learn from doing this exercise?

Teaching Tip

If students have not yet had experience with varied client populations, they could become involved in planning some type of self-help group meeting on campus or in the community, such as a diet support group, a smoking cessation group, or another type of group.

Chapter 13

Communicating with Families

INTRODUCTION

There are a number of theories about family. The most useful theories treat families as systems interacting in a somewhat open way with the larger society. Communication is one component of family function, essential to all the other family functions.

Exercises in this chapter are designed to help the learner begin to appreciate and evaluate family communication processes.

There are 10 exercises in this chapter of the text.

EXERCISE 13-1
Constructing a Gendergram

Teaching Tips
Today's students have a difficult time gaining perspective about changes across time. As an alternative activity, have students critique a movie from the 1940s or a television family situation comedy (sitcom) from the 1950s in regard to how gender roles are portrayed. For example, in "Leave it to Beaver," June is a stay-at-home mom who wears dresses and pearls to vacuum the house.

EXERCISE 13-2
Family Structures and Processes

Teaching Tip
An easier version of this exercise is to have students evaluate a family with whom they have interacted with their clinical practice.

EXERCISE 13-3
Positive and Negative Family Interactions

Pitfall: When having students read aloud about an actual client's family, caution them to omit *all* identifying characteristics.

EXERCISE 13-4
Family Coping Strategies

Teaching Tip
You may want to use a videotaped family interaction so that all students evaluate the same family dynamics, such as roles and decision-making. The author has also used movie videos, assigned as homework, to teach family dynamics. Sample movie titles include *Ordinary People, Death of a Salesman, Eve's Bayou, This Boy's Life* (a true story), *Zhadou* (Chinese), *Ladybird, Ladybird* (British), *The 400 Blows* (French).

Pitfall: Young students or those with conservative values have been offended by some content, such as the graphic depiction of rape.

EXERCISE 13-5
Family Genogram

Because this exercise is intended to be used as a beginning effort to familiarize students with the concept of utilizing a genogram as a brief, graphic depiction of a family's health history, it adds interest if students diagram their own family of origin.

Pitfalls: Lack of familiarity with this format often results in diagrams that list an incomplete health history. Occasionally, students reveal some fairly sensitive information. The author has discontinued using this exercise as a graded activity because of its intrusiveness and the inability of adopted students to complete it. Instead, we have used the family depicted in the movie *Ordinary People* to diagram.

Teaching Tip
Differentiating between health history and family function may need to be explained carefully. Students are usually able to diagram three generations, including themselves. Adopted students who lack knowledge about their own history may interview another student. We use this exercise successfully even with

freshmen. It is helpful when the instructor can draw a genogram of his or her own family on the board or overhead transparency as a model while discussing the symbolic meaning of the diagram and what each line means for the family.

EXERCISE 13-6
Family Ecomap

Movies like those mentioned earlier can be substituted for a student's family of origin.

EXERCISE 13-7
Nursing Process Applied to Family Interactions

Answers (Case Study of the Monroe Family)
1.   Possible questions might include determining knowledge of risk factors, whether husband and wife have discussed his prognosis, what information the wife feels she has not received, whether they have discussed how his illness will change their roles in the family, usual patterns of (adaptive or maladaptive) coping with anxiety, and so forth.
2.   Possible diagnoses:

- Altered family processes
- Compromised family coping related to Mr. Monroe's denial
- Compromised family coping related to Mrs. Monroe's knowledge deficit
- Knowledge deficit
- Anxiety related to Mr. Monroe's heart condition, as evidenced by . . .

EXERCISE 13-8
Using Intervention Skill with Families

Students working with actual families require close supervision as well as knowledge of referral sources. Therefore, this exercise is best reserved for advanced students.

EXERCISE 13-9
Offering Commendations

This exercise is self-explanatory.

EXERCISE 13-10
Evaluating Nurse-Family Communication

You can simulate the family-nurse interaction by having several faculty members role-play a brief interaction (this is better when done for laughs, with the faculty in costume).

ADDITIONAL EXERCISE

Many variations on the above exercises can be done. Videos from the University of Calgary depicting family therapy can be used, students can role-play family vignettes, or commercial movies can be critiqued. In some schools, the students follow one family for several semesters.

EXERCISE 13-A
Communication Skills with Families

Discuss:

1.   How can a nurse best offer support to a family?
2.   What social service agencies are available to provide support?
3.   What barriers to communication exist across community agencies?

Teaching Tip
Students often perceive the positiveness of their nurse-family interaction based on feelings about their own competency. Perceptions about negative experiences often involve discomfort about handling anger or grief, which some students take personally. Discussion should be geared toward the role of the professional nurse and the importance of learning to deal with family emotions rather than focusing on the "rightness" or "wrongness" of accusations. Novice learners benefit from a structured assessment guide.

Chapter 14

Resolving Conflict Between Nurse and Client

INTRODUCTION

This chapter discusses the different ways in which conflict can be dealt with in relationships—by avoidance, false reassurance, aggression, bargaining, placating, collaboration, and problem-solving. Identifying the reasons for the conflict and attempting to resolve the underlying causes for problem behavior constitute the most effective approach. To utilize this strategy, the nurse must behave in an assertive manner rather than act aggressively or passively.

Teaching Tips

In discussing assertive versus nonassertive behavior, you might list several advantages and disadvantages on an overhead transparency (see Figure 14-1, *Instructor's Manual*).

Stay focused on the issue, the behavior. Avoid bringing up old situations, and ignore personal comments about your ability. Angel and Petronko (1987) cite some examples of ways to handle negative criticism occurring in the form of put-downs:

Put-down	*Response*
I don't know how your staff stands you!	They think I'm wonderful.
What's a pretty girl like you doing unmarried?	It's marvelous to have so much freedom.
Last night I had a real nurse; now I have to settle for a student.	Sounds like you got good care; I plan to give you good care today too!
Oh you're one of those nurses with a degree (from a coworker).	I plan to use my education to help us all work well together.

From Angel G, Petronko DK. *Developing the New Assertive Nurse*. New York: Springer, 1987.

Assertiveness is a skill that takes time to develop and one that must be practiced. Exercises provide opportunities to explore concepts related to assertiveness, aggressiveness, powerlessness, and problem-solving in simulated clinical situations.

There are six exercises in this chapter of the text.

EXERCISE 14-1
Personal Responses to Conflict

Purpose: To increase awareness of responses in conflict situations and which elements in the situations—the people involved, status, age, previous experience, lack of experience, place—contribute to one's sense of discomfort.

Directions: Divide students into smaller groups of two or three participants, and have them discuss a conflict situation for purposes of identifying feelings.

The following feelings are common correlates of interpersonal conflict situations that many people say they have experienced in conflict situations they haven't handled well:

Answer
Possible common feelings: annoyance, anger, antagonism, embarrassment, intimidation, hostility, exasperation, criticism, caught off guard, intrusion, competitiveness, superiority, inferiority, anxiousness, frustration, vengefulness, manipulation, outmaneuvering, obsequiousness, humiliation, deflation, disappointment, uneasiness, quarrelsomeness, emptiness, incompleteness, defensiveness, exclusion, devaluation, resentment, bitterness

Teaching Tips
Although these feelings generally are not ones we may be especially proud of, they are a part of the human experience. By acknowledging their existence within ourselves, we usually have more choice about how we will handle them.

Use the list of feelings generated by students to focus class discussion on common feelings identified by the group rather than responses by any one individual. Do not ask students to verbalize their conflict situation. Help students identify behaviors that lead to more positive outcomes. For example, if people are annoyed or angry, verbally acknowledging that this situation makes them angry may give them increased control over their response.

Variations: This exercise can be done as a homework assignment.

EXERCISE 14-2
Responding Assertively

Teaching Tip
Review the content in Figure 14-1 of the *Instructor's Manual*.

EXERCISE 14-3
Pitching the Assertive Message

This quick, fun exercise can be used to examine the effects of changes in vocal tone and pitch.

EXERCISE 14-4
Assertiveness Self-Assessment Quiz

Directions: Read and answer Yes, No, or Sometimes. A score of 10 or more items without a No answer suggests the need for assertiveness training. Do you:

1. Lack confidence in your nursing judgment?
2. Hesitate to express your feelings?
3. Feel self-conscious if someone watches you work?
4. Hesitate to call a physician about a client's problem?
5. Avoid questioning people in authority?
6. Use the phrase "I hate to bother you, but…"?
7. Avoid speaking up in class or in a clinic?
8. Show how upset you are when pressure builds up?
9. Feel that people take advantage of you?
10. Have trouble starting a conversation?
11. Find it difficult to compliment others?
12. Find it difficult to correct a coworker when she or he is wrong?
13. Make a negating comment when you receive a compliment?
14. Swear at others?
15. Hesitate to protest an unfair evaluation?
16. Hesitate to protest when asked to do someone else's work?
17. Tend to complain to others rather than to the person you have a problem with?
18. Avoid problems rather than try to solve them?

EXERCISE 14-5
Assertive Responses

Additional cases for further practice are listed in Exercise 14-A.

EXERCISE 14-6
Defining Conflict Issues

Purpose: To identify problem definitions in interpersonal conflict situations. Unless there is a concrete definition and consensual agreement about the nature of a conflict issue, effective problem-solving cannot occur. In every conflict situation, it is important to look for the following:

1. *Specific behaviors* (including words, tone, posture, facial expression)
2. *Feeling impressions* (including words, tone, intensity, facial expression)
3. *Need* (expressed verbally or through actions)

CASE 1

Mrs. Ali is an Indian client who doesn't speak much English. She just had her baby by cesarean section, and it is expected that she will remain in the hospital for at least 6 days. Her husband tells the nurse that she wants to breast-feed, but she has decided to wait until she goes home to begin because she will be more comfortable and she wants privacy. The nurse knows that breast-feeding will be more successful if it is initiated soon after birth.

Answers
Behaviors: The client's husband states that she wants to breast-feed but doesn't wish to start before going home. The wife is not initiating breast-feeding in the hospital.

Nursing Inference: Indirectly, the client is expressing physical discomfort, possible insecurity, and awkwardness about breast-feeding. She also may be acting in accordance with cultural norms of her country or family.

Underlying Needs: The need is for safety and security. Mrs. Ali probably will not be motivated to attempt breast-feeding until she feels safe and secure in her environment.

Figure 14-1

Disadvantages of behaving assertively:

- Self-directed anger
- Feelings of dissatisfaction
- Loss of self-respect
- Loss of autonomy
- Dependency
- Little likelihood of change occurring.

Advantages of behaving assertively:

- Feeling of satisfaction
- Increased self-respect
- More independence
- Able to stimulate change

The nurse receives criticism assertively by:

- Evaluating the source. Is this person's opinion valued? Have you heard this same criticism from others?
- Asking for clarification. Ask the person to give you specific examples of the behavior he or she is criticizing.
- Saying that you feel the criticism is unfair, if you really feel it is.
- Saying the criticism is justified, if you feel it really is.

CASE 2

Mrs. Strassner is returned to the unit from surgery following a radical mastectomy. The doctor's orders call for her to ambulate, cough, and deep-breathe and for nurses to encourage the client to use her arm as much as possible in self-care activities. Mrs. Strassner asks the nurse in a very annoyed tone, "Why do I have to do this? You can see that it is difficult for me. Why can't you help me?"

Answers

Behaviors: Noncompliance with the exercise order.

Nursing Inference: The client is expressing anger and perhaps some anxiety or fear.

Underlying Needs: Dependency needs, including a desire for the nurse to do for her rather than a willingness to assume responsibility for self-care, which health care providers view as important in order to maximize her recovery.

CASE 3

Mr. Cresa is a 31-year-old client with recently diagnosed terminal cancer of the pancreas. He answers the nurse's questions with monosyllables and turns his head away. When the nurse questions him, he says in a low voice: "There is no hope. They're going to keep me here until I die. Can't you give me my medication more often than every 3 hours—I'm going to die anyway."

Answers

Behaviors: Withdrawal from interaction with the nurse and a demand for more frequent medication.

Nursing Inference: The client is exhibiting apparent depression or hopelessness.

Underlying Needs: The expressed need is for medication, but the underlying need is to resolve the grief process and to discuss his prognosis and immediate future. The nurse can best help Mr. Cresa with problem-solving rather than engaging in a conflict about the timing of his medication.

ADDITIONAL EXERCISES

EXERCISE 14-A

Mrs. Stennett's Rights

Purpose: To gain the opportunity to experience different strategies in coping with conflict situations.

Directions: Have students role-play Mrs. Stennett's dilemma in groups of three, with one student as Mrs. Stennett, one in the role of the nurse, and one as observer.

Mrs. Stennett has been hospitalized for 3 weeks. She is in traction and cannot move around. Miss Mills, the nurse on duty, has an unusually heavy workload today because one of the aides called in sick. She has just given Mrs. Stennett a bed bath, straightened up her bed, and is getting ready to leave the room. Mrs. Stennett calls to her as she leaves the room, "Now you'll be back in a half hour to do my nails, won't you? They're so long, I'm afraid I will scratch myself. It's your professional duty to meet my needs."

The student in the nurse's role should respond to Mrs. Stennett's questions. After the role-play is completed, compare the effectiveness of different strategies.

Questions for Discussion

1.   Which strategies were most effective?

2.   Were the rights of both participants equally respected?

3.   How did you assess the client's problem and her level of readiness? What factors did you consider?

4.   As the observer, what did you notice about the interaction that diminished or escalated the sense of conflict?

5.   As the nurse, how did you feel in this situation? As the client?

6.   What similarities in approach were most useful across groups in resolving this conflict situation?

EXERCISE 14-B

Behavioral Responses to Interpersonal Conflict

Purpose: To experience the feelings associated with the three types of responses to conflict.

Directions: Choose a typical interpersonal conflict. Using the behaviors suggested in Box 14-3, have students role-play each of the different response positions. Pause in between each response position to reflect on the feelings generated by being in that position.

After each person has had a turn at each position, discuss the feelings and what your body felt like in each position. What other interpersonal conflict situations did this one remind you of? Which communication position felt most comfortable and why?

Pitfalls: Some students are reluctant to role-play in front of large groups. Asking for volunteers to role-play situations allows the less outgoing students to feel more comfortable.

Teaching Tip

Because this exercise is relatively easy to role-play and requires only brief responses, more students can become involved. The audience needs to be able to observe all the action because they will be asked to comment on body posture and other nonverbal cues seen during the role-play.

Example Answers

Student 1 says, "Do you mind if I smoke?" while already lighting up.

Student 2 (nonassertive response) waves smoke away but says, "Oh, go ahead."

Student 3 (aggressive response) says, "That's a filthy habit. Put out that cigarette immediately," in a harsh tone of voice.

Student 4 (assertive response) says with humor, "Give us a break and save that air pollution for later—p-p-please!"

Other conflict situations listed in the text can be used. Ask students to list several alternative behavioral or verbal responses. Assist the group in differentiating which of the hypothetical responses are nonassertive, appropriately assertive, or inappropriately aggressive.

Variation: This exercise can be done in pantomime.

ADDITIONAL CASE STUDIES

CASE 1: TIMING

The client just had abdominal surgery and refuses to deep-breathe, cough, or ambulate.

Answer: Suggested Interventions

The nurse could acknowledge the client's distress, offer to give pain medicine, and offer to return in an hour to help him ambulate. These actions show flexibility and an ability to modify actions in a way that recognizes the client's needs but at the same time challenges the client to collaborate in her own self-care.

An appropriately assertive statement might be, "Mr. Quinn, it's important for you to cough, deep-breathe, and move around in order to get your lungs clear and get your body systems moving again. However, I can see that you are in pain. Let's see if you can have something for it so that in an hour you are more comfortable and we can try again."

CASE 2: ANGER

Jane is a 15-year-old client with cancer. Following removal of her right leg, chemotherapy was begun. As a result, Jane lost most of her hair. Until now, the nurse has had a very good relationship with her. Today, however, Jane throws a book across the room as the nurse enters and says, "Get out of here; I don't want anyone to come in here; I hate my life."

Answer: Suggested Intervention

Any assertive statement at this time would probably go unheard. The nurse first needs to reflect on the anger expressed and to seek to have Jane put it into words.

CASE 3: ACTING OUT

Gerry, age 7, was admitted to the hospital after a car accident. In the weeks of hospitalization, he was initially tearful and then angry. By the second week, he exhibited hostility most of the time. He refuses to eat.

Answer: Suggested Intervention

In this invasive environment, the only control this child has is over interpersonal interactions, making them as aversive as possible, and over whether to eat. A care plan might be devised that would focus on lowering anxiety by providing predictability for some painful events, such as changing dressings at a specific time. The staff could avoid responding with anger but could provide reliable information about what is going to happen, when it will happen, and how it will feel.

Another strategy to reduce conflict is to allow Gerry to have some control (within limits set by the nurse), perhaps by allowing him to removing old dressings himself, decide whether to drink milk or eat a cheese sandwich, and the like.

Chapter 15

Health Promotion and Client Learning Needs

INTRODUCTION

Health teaching involves an integrated use of nurse-client communication concepts. The content in this chapter provides several theoretical models to help students conceptualize components of health promotion and education.

Exercises provide a structured opportunity for student practice of teaching skills in relatively nonthreatening situations. Many curricula provide course credit for clinical teaching projects done as a component of the intervention phase of the nursing process.

There are four exercises in this chapter of the text.

EXERCISE 15-1
Pender's Health Promotion Model

Teaching Tip
For novice learners, this exercise is best done with clients who have a single health problem rather than complex health care situations.

EXERCISE 15-2
Facilitating Readiness to Confront Medical Events

Answers
1. Pat would have to express some desire to change some aspect of this life situation. For example, he might talk about not wanting to end up like his uncle, who had a painful death from cirrhosis.

2. It would be important to assess the reasons for her anxiety. For example, she may have had some past experience involving an unfortunate chemotherapy outcome for a friend.

3. Examine some coping strategies he found useful in the past when threatened with loss of control or imperfection.

4. Information about social support systems and hospital policy. For example, can her family be with her? Can her friends visit? Can she use the bedside telephone? Then supply information about what she can expect to happen while hospitalized.

EXERCISE 15-3
Significant Learning Experiences

A possible focus for this evaluation activity might be to have students evaluate the advantages and disadvantages of the experiential approach to learning exemplified in the text (i.e., the use of learning exercises to promote active learning). An important component in determining the success of this teaching approach is whether time is allowed to complete the final discussion phase, in which students synthesize their learning (rather than just "doing" the exercises).

EXERCISE 15-4
Applying Maslow's Theory to Learning Readiness

Answers
There are an infinite variety of answers. Frequently, the most supportive nursing measures involve helping the client fulfill unmet needs at a lower level, for example, scheduling a teaching-learning session *after* a meal rather than trying to educate a hungry client.

ADDITIONAL EXERCISE

EXERCISE 15-A
Healthy People 2010 Goals

Directions: With students in small groups or as a class, have them brainstorm to make a list of goals similar to those in *Healthy People 2010*. These could be related to a specialty area of practice. For example, in pediatrics, a goal is "Reduce drug abuse (glue sniffing) by 50% in this community"; in obstetrics, a goal is "Reduce infant mortality in this state by 75%."

Another excellent reference for health promotion concepts is the U.S. Preventive Services Task Force (or the most recent edition).

U.S. Preventive Services Task Force. Report on Health Promotion. *Guide to Clinical Preventive Services*. Baltimore, Williams & Wilkins, 1998.

Chapter 16

Health Teaching in the Nurse–Client Relationship

INTRODUCTION

This chapter describes the nurse's role in health teaching. Three theoretical frameworks are presented to guide educational interactions with clients.

Exercises are provided to prepare students for implementing this role by allowing them to practice essential components for effective health teaching. Most curricula offer multiple opportunities for creative teaching experiences with classmates, with individual clients, and with groups of clients.

There are nine exercises in this chapter of the text.

EXERCISE 16-1
Guidelines for Reflective Journals

Purpose: Reflective journals are more than diaries of happenings; they also should reflect an attempt to analyze experiences critically. They may be especially useful during a psychiatric or mental health clinical rotation. Critical thinking is one of the criteria identified by the National League for Nursing, for which schools of nursing need to provide curriculum experience.

Teaching Tip
Student seminars or even some clinical postconferences are useful times to allow small group interactions among students for the purpose of critiquing teaching experiences. This synthesis activity is an essential component of the process that begins with presentation of didactic content, continues through application to practice, and culminates with reflection. When small group discussions are not possible, use this journal exercise to help promote synthesis.

EXERCISE 16-2
Using a Behavioral Approach

Teaching Tip
As an alternative, students would write behavioral objectives for an actual client teaching project. Students seem to need help writing goals that are mea-surable and realistic. Goals for teaching similar content to various age groups of clients might be compared across student groups using the box in Chapter 15 as a guide for gearing teaching to developmental age.

EXERCISE 16-3
Role-Play of an Assessment Interview

An alternative is to videotape and self-critique an interview.

EXERCISE 16-4
Developing Behavioral Goals

Teaching Tip
Have students review Chapter 2 on writing mutual goals for the nursing care plan. Apply these concepts to writing health education goals. Goals for all nursing care plans should be written in measurable, behavioral terms and should include long-term as well as short-term goals.

Alternative Exercise: The same outcomes can be obtained if students are asked to include at least one health education goal on each care plan.

EXERCISE 16-5
Developing Teaching Plans

Use guidelines presented in Chapters 15 and 16.

EXERCISE 16-6
Using Advanced Organizers as a Teaching Strategy

This exercise is self-explanatory.

EXERCISE 16-7
Giving Teaching Feedback

Pitfalls: The pitfalls inherent in providing feedback are described in the Prologue.

Teaching Tip

Review the rules for giving feedback (see Prologue) with your students. Remind students to avoid giving or interpreting feedback in a destructive, negative manner.

EXERCISE 16-8

Coaching Exercise

Teaching Tip

Use Figure 16-1 to guide discussion.

EXERCISE 16-9

Group Health Teaching

Teaching Tip

Our undergraduate students plan and present similar health promotion teaching projects as part of clinical experiences in the community. Teaching projects with obstetrical clients are conducted in conjunction with hospital clinical rotations, and projects during pediatric and community health rotations consist of arranged presentations given to schoolchildren. This reflects a trend toward incorporating more ambulatory community-based experiences and expands on the role of the nurse in health promotion, as described in Chapter 15.

Outcome evaluation should be a part of this experience. Suggested methods are examination of videotapes or audiotapes, evaluation of teaching materials, content outline and narrative records of the experience, and measurements of learning, such as noted in pretest/post-tests, return demonstrations, changes in behavior, or even learner participation.

ADDITIONAL EXERCISE

EXERCISE 16-A

Teaching Plan Critique

Directions

1.   Obtain a copy of one of the health education curriculum units designed by the state education office (e.g., Department of Public Instruction). For example, most states have the DARE drug awareness curriculum, which is offered to sixth graders. Many states have developed model awareness curriculum models for acquired immunodeficiency syndrome (AIDS). You might ask health education and physical education teachers to share one of their own lesson plans.

2.   Critique the model lesson plan. Most programs designed for young people involve more than just information exchange. They focus on how to solve problems or make decisions (critical thinking approach) as well as use of value-clarification strategies and development of communications skills for use in difficult situations in interacting with peers (the social learning model). Newer models also may incorporate some techniques for personalizing probability of risk (health belief model).

3.   Have students discuss which aspects of these model lessons might be applicable to student-client teaching situations.

Chapter 17

Communicating with Clients Experiencing Communication Deficits

INTRODUCTION

This chapter provides a framework for consideration of the nurse who deals with some of the potential problems that arise in relationships between nurses and clients with specialized communication difficulties.

Exercises are designed to sensitize novice nurses to the special problems encountered by clients with sensory problems.

There are four exercises in this chapter of the text.

EXERCISE 17-1
Loss of Sensory Function in Geriatric Clients*

Purpose: To sensitize participants to the feelings often experienced by older adults as they lose sensory function by having the younger individual "walk in the older person's shoes."

Teaching Tip
Have all the equipment ready—a large bag of cotton balls and plastic wrap, or use old, donated eyeglasses with transparent tape applied over lenses. Stress safety.

_____

* Exercise developed by B. J. Glen, RN, EdD, former member of National Standards Committee for the Association for Gerontology in Higher Education.

EXERCISE 17-2
Hearing Loss

As an alternative, students might use swimmer's earplugs and attend class.

EXERCISE 17-3
Blindness

Teaching Tip
Students really enjoy this exercise. Have them do it on their lunch hour so that they have to use dollars, count change, step off curbs, pour into cups that might overflow, or eat food with utensils. Emphasize to the

"sighted" students that they are entrusted with the safety of the blindfolded students.

Variation: Collect old eyeglasses, and have students apply transparent tape over the lenses. This step distorts their straight-ahead vision but leaves some peripheral vision, simulating cataracts or retinal degeneration.

EXERCISE 17-4
Schizophrenia Communication Simulation*

This exercise is self-explanatory. It is best used with students during their psychiatric/mental health nursing clinical experience.

_____

* Idea suggested by Dr. Ann Newman, University of North Carolina at Charlotte.

ADDITIONAL EXERCISE

EXERCISE 17-A
Developing Trust

Directions: Have students pair up with a partner, preferably someone who is not their friend, with one person standing in front of the other. The person in front closes his or her eyes and falls backward into the arms of the person standing behind. Either partner may use words to guide the experience. Following this experience, the seeing partner helps the people with their eyes closed to their seats.

Questions for Discussion
1. How did it feel to risk harm by putting faith in another?
2. Do clients with sensory impairment hesitate to trust strangers even if they are health professionals?
3. What did you learn about yourself from doing this exercise that might be useful in your practice?

Pitfall: Students quickly become frustrated with this exercise.

Teaching Tip

Keep the exercise brief. Focus discussion on feelings of frustration, miscommunication, and so on.

Chapter 18

Communicating with Children

INTRODUCTION

The days are long past when we communicated with children as if they were small adults. Communication with children involves its own unique set of skills. Consideration must be given to a child's level of developmental needs, including the child's:

- Physiological capability to process the information given
- Level of cognitive maturity in thinking processes
- Rate of acquiring vocabulary and language skills
- Sense of self
- Dependency needs and willingness to interact with adults

The exercises in this chapter and the information in the boxes have been developed to supply guidelines to nurses caring for children of all ages, with an emphasis on caring for ill children.

There are seven exercises in this chapter of the text.

EXERCISE 18-1
Using a Mutual Storytelling Technique

Teaching Tip
To give practical experience with this technique, have students do this exercise outside class with well children. If a child reveals significant problems, ethically you may need to provide referrals.

EXERCISE 18-2
Age-Appropriate Medical Terminology

Answers

Medical Term	Suggested Age-Appropriate Terminology
Cardiac catheterization	Heart picture
NPO *(nil per os)*	No food; cannot eat or drink
Urine specimen	Wee-wee, pee-pee, tinkle . . ., in a cup
Anesthesia	Sleep medicine, mask with sweet air, medicine so you won't feel anything
Infection	Germs inside your body, something that makes you sick
Inflammation	Sore, ow-ie, the sick, red part of your body
Isolation	Your own special place, pretend space capsule, a rule to keep germs in this room
Intake and output	Counting drinks, measuring in a cup everything you eat or tinkle
Operating room	Special room where the doctor works, the doctor's fix-it room
Sedation	Calm-down medicine, quiet medicine
Nausea	Sick tummy, funny feeling in your tummy that makes you throw up
Vital signs	Counting your heartbeats, checking your temperature
Enema	Tube to put fluid in your bottom to help you go to the bathroom
Injection	Shot, poke with a needle
Dressings	Bandage
Disease	Sickness
IV	Fluid in your arm, needle under the skin

(continued next page)

Medical Term	Suggested Age-Appropriate Terminology
Abdomen	Tummy, gut
Defecation	Poop, No. 2, poo-poo
Catheter	Tube for pee
Discharge	Go home, leave, go bye-bye with Mommy
Phagocytosis	Soldier cells that kill germs
Irritable	Grouchy, grumpy
Dehydration	Dry
Micturition	Pee, wee-wee, No. 1
Fatigue	Sleepy, tired
Headache	Head that hurts
Penis	Weenie, thing, boy-part

Discussion

What words are more appropriate for a 4-year-old than for an 8-year-old? Think of any experiences you might have had as a child client or you may have observed. What were some of the troublesome words you found in these experiences?

Teaching Tips

This is a marvelous exercise we have used in pediatric nursing classes and in courses teaching growth and development. Photocopy the list of adult vocabulary words. Cut out each set of words into separate slips of paper. Put these into a container that can be passed quickly around the room. (If possible, use a seasonal theme container, a plastic pumpkin in the fall for Halloween, an Easter basket in the spring, and so on, to give the idea that we are doing this exercise for fun!) Each student to whom the container is passed reaches in, selects a slip of paper, reads it to the class, and then quickly supplies an age-appropriate word conveying the same meaning to a 4-year-old child.

EXERCISE 18-3

Pediatric Nursing Procedures

Questions for Discussion: Put yourself in the place of the nurse who is preparing a 4-year-old boy for a painful procedure:

1. What essential information does he need?
2. If this is a frequently repeated procedure, how can you make him feel safe before and after the procedure?
3. How soon ahead of time do you prepare him?

Answers

1. Values to communicate regarding painful procedures include:
   - Purpose of the procedure
   - Necessity in terms of projected value to the child
   - A role the parents can perform in strengthening the child's ability to tolerate pain by lending their support
   - Be honest about whether it will hurt!
2. Strategies frequently used on pediatric units include:
   - Performing painful procedures in a place outside the child's bed or room
   - Signaling nonpainful care by wearing one color of smock and using another color when discomfort will be involved
   - Allowing the child some choices
   - Avoiding combining painful procedures with daily care
   - Communicating truthfully about whether a procedure will hurt
3. With a child of a young age, it may be more effective to get the painful procedure over with as quickly as possible and then to comfort the child or to use therapeutic measures, such as play therapy afterward, to allow the child to master the experience. Do not prepare the child too far ahead of time (more than 1 hour), because it will increase his or her anxiety.

EXERCISE 18-4
Preparing Children for Treatment Procedures

Answer

Common themes relate to:

1. The need to assess current level of knowledge about the procedure
2. Assessing the child's developmental and cognitive limits on the child's ability to understand your information
3. Assessing whether the child is ready to listen to new information
4. The need to adapt your teaching style and vocabulary level to the child's cognitive level of understanding

EXERCISE 18-5
Strategies for Conducting an Assessment on the Toddler or the Preschooler

Answer

One helpful strategy is to have the child sit in the mother's or father's lap, facing away from the nurse; then casually put the stethoscope around to the child's chest. For preschoolers, it is helpful to let them listen, play with the equipment, or have a fuzzy toy attached to the stethoscope. For both groups, using distraction is great!

EXERCISE 18-6
Working with the Newly Diagnosed HIV-Positive Teenager

Use the questions provided to stimulate discussion. Emphasize that there are no wrong answers for coping with the situation.

EXERCISE 18-7
Conflicts Experienced by Care Providers of HIV-Positive Children

Use the questions provided to stimulate discussion. Emphasize that there are no wrong answers for coping with the situation.

Chapter 19

Communicating with Older Adults

INTRODUCTION

As the population ages, most nurses will need to master ways to communicate therapeutically with older adults in varying stages of health and illness. Problems in communication arise when the elderly person has cognitive or sensory deficits.

Helping confused elderly clients continue to use functional areas and strong points while compensating for those aspects of care the client can no longer manage are two aspects of communicative skills. Family members familiar with the verbal communication of the dysarthric client can be used as a go-between when necessary.

This chapter describes barriers to communication with older people. Further strategies to enhance nurse-client communication are outlined in the last additional exercise activity.

Possible **barriers** to communication with older people include:

- Diminished cognitive power and memory
- Attitudinal differences (youth-oriented culture, shifting values)
- Limitations in mobility
- Physical isolation and decrease size of social network
- Sensory losses
- Limited verbal ability (dysphasia, aphasia)
- Limited concentration span

There are three exercises in this chapter of the text.

EXERCISE 19-1

Psychosocial Strengths and Resiliency

It helps to have a few structured questions before doing the interview. Some students really enjoy doing this interview with an elderly relative. Use the discussion questions to focus class discussion.

EXERCISE 19-2

What Is It Like to Experience Sensory Decline?

This is a fun exercise students can approach in a light-hearted manner. Have students do this exercise at home or across campus during a class break. If they take a walk, make sure that they are able to function safely.

EXERCISE 19-3

Hearing the Stories of Older Adults

This exercise is designed to raise the sensitivity level of novice nurses to the views of older adults.

Directions: In interviewing an older adult, have students apply Erikson's framework, Maslow's model, or another framework as they write up two to three paragraphs analyzing the developmental status of the adult they interviewed:

- What experiences did the adult have growing up, dating, working, or founding a family?
- How did the elderly person adjust to retirement and growing older?
- What are the person's happiest moments?
- What was the hardest thing the person ever had to do?
- What does the person regard as his or her most significant contribution?
- How does the adult view aging, illness, and death?

Teaching Tip

Students might go to a nursing home or extended-care facility, an adult day care center, or a religious group to do this interview, but the most beneficial experiences students have had with this exercise have come from interviewing one of their own older relatives. Many students have been amazed at what their relative has done and have found it a very enriching experience. Even when the experience is negative and the relative is found to be bitter and despairing, the students seem to benefit from their analysis. Use a few minutes of class discussion to pool ideas about what factors shaped the outcomes differences.

Undergraduate students have successfully used **Internet discussion rooms** created on the class Web site to post interview summaries. To increase cognitive processing, have students meet in small workgroups, read interview results to each other, and identify common themes. Use an **Internet discussion room** to post these themes.

ADDITIONAL EXERCISES

EXERCISE 19-A
Into Aging

We highly recommend the simulation game, *Into Aging*. Although extensive preplanning and a number of equipment items (signs, poker chips) are required, once these items are assembled, they can be reused. It takes about 1 hour of class time, including the debriefing, but students have been vocal in saying that it is well worth their time.

From Hoffman TL, Reif SD. *Into Aging: A Simulation Game*. Thorofare, NJ: Charles B. Slack, Inc., 1978.

EXERCISE 19-B
Age-Appropriate Interventions

Purpose: To stimulate discussion of appropriate interventions.

Directions: Discuss the following cases.

CLIENT PROBLEM 1

Problem: Client exhibits disturbed attention

Nursing Diagnosis: Inadequate coping related to organic memory loss

Nursing Goal: Minimize factors that contribute to inattention

Nursing System: Supportive, educative

Method of Assistance: Guiding, supporting, providing an understanding environment

Nursing Interventions

1. Look directly at the client when communicating.

2. Call the client's name several times.
3. Position yourself in the client's line of vision when communicating.
4. Rest your hand on the client's hands.
5. Give clear, distinct, simple directions in a step-by-step fashion.
6. Direct conversation toward concrete, familiar objects.
7. If lapses in attention occur, let the client rest a few minutes before re-engaging his or her attention.
8. Provide simple activities that will encourage purposeful action.
9. Repeat messages slowly, calmly, and patiently until the client shows signs of comprehension.
10. Vary media and words to fit the client's ability to comprehend the message.
11. Modify environmental stimuli that affect attention.
12. Help the client's family understand that inattention and failure to respond are due to the client's inability to process the information cognitively.

CLIENT PROBLEM 2

Problem: Disorientation, increasing demands on coping mechanisms

Nursing Diagnosis: Knowledge deficit related to organic memory loss

Nursing Goal: Decrease disorientation and help client to master immediate environment

Nursing System: Partly compensatory

Method of Assistance: Guiding, supporting, acting, or doing for, providing a developmental environment

Nursing Interventions

1. Frequently orient the client to time, place, and person using clocks, calendars, and visual aids. Label drawers, and provide written reminders.
2. Establish a set, well-known routine for the client to follow.
3. Address the client by name and title ("Good morning, Mr. Tate") to reinforce a sense of identity.
4. Repeat basic information frequently during the day.

5. Do not allow the client to ramble incoherently. Fill in words on the basis of what you can understand.
6. Use visual cues such as pictures and gestures to supplement auditory senses.
7. Create a calm, quiet, and unhurried atmosphere.
8. Speak slowly and distinctly. Use simple words.

9. Give the client enough time to answer.
10. Moderate or avoid stressful situations to decrease stimuli that would destroy perceptions or cause sensory overload.

Adapted from Burnside I. *Psychosocial Nursing Care of the Aged,* 2nd ed. New York: McGraw-Hill, 1980; Arnold E: Tips for caregivers. *ADRA Newsletter,* 1985; and Niewenhuis R: Breaking the speech barrier. *Nursing Times* 85(15):34-36, 1989.

Chapter 20

Communicating with Clients in Stressful Situations

INTRODUCTION

This chapter examines the origin and manifestation of stress. Focus is placed on assessment of client stress and on intervention strategies with clients. The need for nurses to care for themselves is described in a detailed discussion of burnout. Useful burnout-prevention tactics are discussed in terms of application to professional role functions.

Exercises provided in this chapter may contribute insight into client stress management. They also may be applied pragmatically to the learners' own professional and personal lives.

There are six exercises in this chapter of the text.

EXERCISE 20-1
The Relationship Between Anger and Anxiety

Teaching Tip
Focus class discussion on item 5, identifying categories of behaviors or situations that make many people angry. In item 6, knowing that anxiety may underlie a client's anger allows nurses to depersonalize their responses and concentrate on treating the cause of the client's anxiety.

EXERCISE 20-2
Coping Exercise

Students generally have already identified their best coping mechanisms. What is new is listening to those used by others. Avoid judgments. Once one student volunteers a behavioral strategy, ask the class members whether they or others they know use this behavior. This technique can defuse some of the judgmental nature of evaluating the listed behaviors as adaptive or as maladaptive.

EXERCISE 20-3
Role-Play: Handling Stressful Situations

Teaching Tip
Use the discussion questions to focus the class.

EXERCISE 20-4
Community Resources for Stress Management

Many communities now offer written pamphlets or books listing agencies and their services. Another resource can be the telephone book, which may include a special section listing social service agencies.

Pitfall: Agency personnel tend to become annoyed if many students indiscriminately try to access them with the same request for information.

Directions: Divide the class into workgroups, and have one representative contact each agency to avoid multiple contacts. Then share this information among all students in the class, perhaps developing a referral list of community services that can be given to primary care providers.

EXERCISE 20-5
Progressive Relaxation Exercise

This exercise is self-explanatory and can be done in the classroom. In fact, some instructors use a similar exercise at the beginning of every class.

EXERCISE 20-6
Burnout Assessment

If you use this exercise, remember that you are ethically obligated to refer those with high scores to a helping resource.

ADDITIONAL EXERCISES

EXERCISE 20-A
Assessing Stress as a Stimulus

Directions: Apply the Holmes and Rahe scale to the case study about Marge as caregiver to her husband with Alzheimer's disease or to any case study.

Answers: Application of the Holmes and Rahe scale to the given case situation suggests that Marge's level of stress places her in the 51% probability of illness category.

EXERCISE 20-B
Meditation

At the end of a busy clinical day, use a brief silent meditation period in conjunction with the relaxation exercise as a way to begin a postconference.

EXERCISE 20-C
Conflicts Experienced by AIDS Caregivers

Directions: Divide students into small groups. Have them read the following case study and answer questions. Answers can be compared in the larger classroom group.

CASE STUDY

Janet is a 24-year-old nurse working at St. Mary's Hospital, a large acute care facility in the Midwest. She graduated with a BSN 2 years ago and, after working 1 year on a medical unit, transferred to a new unit exclusively for clients with acquired immunodeficiency syndrome (AIDS). She enjoys her work, finding the clients' physical and social conditions challenging, and she welcomes the opportunity to practice holistic nursing. She also enjoys the learning environment of the unit and likes her coworkers and colleagues.

However, there has always been an area of stress in Janet's life. She still lives with her parents, and they have never liked the fact that she works with AIDS clients. Recently she has developed a serious relationship with a young man and is considering marriage. This young man shares her parents' concerns about her work, and they are all now putting pressure on her to change jobs. She doesn't want to give up the job she loves and feels that to do so would be deserting the clients who need her, with whom she has established therapeutic relationships. At the same time, she doesn't want to live in conflict with the people she loves.

Questions for Discussion
1.   Because this stress is of long standing, how has Janet previously successfully coped with it?
2.   What factors are operating to increase her stress?
3.   What options would you suggest for Janet?

Teaching Tip
Emphasize that there are no wrong answers for coping with this situation. Many nurses do cope by withdrawing from similar stressful situations. A more adaptive response, however, might be to use the situation as a growth experience, an opportunity to educate others about transmission of human immunodeficiency virus (HIV). You might encourage the students to add information to this case study to reflect their own families' feelings about caring for AIDS clients.

Answers
Emphasize in the discussion that there are no wrong answers for coping with this situation. Many nurses do resolve this type of stress by withdrawing from the situation. A more adaptive response, however, might be to use this situation as a growth experience, as an opportunity to educate her significant others about AIDS transmission, disease progression, and care needs. Beyond merely providing her family with information, Janet might create a more humanistic understanding by inviting them to meet a few of her clients. She might even offer them the opportunity to contribute something to the lives of her clients, perhaps by serving as volunteers.

Contributed by Gail Tumulty, PhD, RN, former Director of Nursing, King Faisal Hospital, Saudi Arabia.

Chapter 21

Communicating with Clients in Crisis

INTRODUCTION

Crisis theory is one of several middle-level theories of great pragmatic use to nurses in practice. Although this theory is not broad enough to provide a framework for all nursing practice, it provides a basis for handling the crises that sometimes arise in every nurse's career. Strategies for crisis intervention are based on concepts pioneered by Lindemann, Caplan, and, more recently, Aquilera.

The exercises provided are designed to give the learner greater insight and time to practice techniques while still in a nonthreatening learning environment.

There are three exercises in this chapter of the text.

EXERCISE 21-1
Understanding the Nature of Crisis

Teaching Tip

Because of the sensitive nature of some information new students reveal, it may be better to handle this as a written assignment, read in confidence only by the instructor. For example, in one of our recent classes, 24% of the students revealed themselves as victims of sexual abuse, while others detailed unplanned pregnancies and other crises.

EXERCISE 21-2
Interacting in Crisis Situations

This exercise provides experience in using the three-stage model of crisis intervention via role play about the following situation.

CASE STUDY

Julie is a 23-year-old woman who has been married for 3 years. Her husband, Jack, is 25 and a law student. They were married when she was a senior in college; she graduated with a degree in social sciences but has been unable to find work in her chosen field. As a result, she has been working full time as a secretary. Her husband worked part time as a security guard and attended school full time. During their second year of marriage, Julie unexpectedly became pregnant. Jack had to quit school to support her during her last trimester. He continued to do so 2 months after the baby was born.

Eventually, Jack was able to return to school and Julie to work. While the baby was a burden, they loved her and were managing. When Julie went back to work, they found a reliable babysitter who lived two doors away. Four days ago, she received a call from the hospital to meet with a staff doctor with her husband. When they arrived at the hospital, they were informed by the doctor that their daughter had died of sudden infant death syndrome at the babysitter's home.

Both Jack's and Julie's parents came to stay with them until the baby's burial. They buried her yesterday morning, and the relatives left in the afternoon. This morning, after Jack left for work and the baby's feeding time came, Julie found herself preparing the baby's formula. She became overcome with feelings and began to cry. She also began feeling angry with her husband and family. She also felt guilty for feeling that way. She says she feels as if she is going crazy. She can't stop thinking about the baby and has constant vivid images of her whenever she is alone. Julie is flooded with a host of emotions she is unable to identify or control.

Rating Scale: A student group member rates the "counselor's" performance with a number from 1 (least effective) to 5 (most effective) for these items:

1. Did the nurse/counselor engage the client?
2. Did the nurse/counselor accurately reflect the client's feelings?
3. Did the client appear to share sensitive emotional information with the nurse/counselor?
4. Did the nurse/counselor communicate openness and a nonjudgmental attitude toward the client?
5. Did the nurse/counselor use brief, concise sentences?

6. Did the counselor utilize the compound sentence when connecting emotional reactions to stresses?

7. Did the client and nurse/counselor establish a mutually understood definition of the problem?

8. Did the nurse/counselor allow the client to do most of the talking and explaining?

9. Was the client able to arrive at useful alternatives as a result of the interview?

10. Did the nurse/counselor and client plan actions that the client could begin using right away?

Questions for Discussion

1. What did you learn from doing this exercise?

2. What would you want to do differently as a result of this exercise when communicating with the client in crisis?

3. What was the effect of using the three-stage model of crisis intervention as a way of organizing your approach to the crisis situation?

Rating scale developed by T. Perfetti, 1982.

Teaching Tips

An alternative is to play a videotape and have the entire class analyze the same interaction and then compare and discuss findings.

Another interesting alternative, if equipment is available, is to have the students break into groups and make a short home videotape to be shown and analyzed by the class. Some additional guidelines for evaluating videotaped interactions are provided in the beginning of this *Instructor's Manual*.

For more advanced students, substitute an actual clinical situation they have encountered for the role-play example they have provided in the book.

EXERCISE 21-3

Personal Support Systems

This exercise should be used as a homework assignment.

ADDITIONAL EXERCISE

EXERCISE 21-A

Communication with the Newly Diagnosed HIV-Positive Adolescent

Directions: Read the case situation and answer the following questions.

CASE STUDY

Bill, age 17 years, seeks treatment for gonorrhea. He is hospitalized for further diagnostic testing and treatment after his initial work-up reveals a compromised immune system and that he is seropositive for the human immunosuppressive virus 1. For 2 days on the unit, he has cried and cursed and been uncooperative. The staff tends to avoid Bill when possible.

A team of physicians begins a bone marrow aspiration procedure in the treatment room after obtaining his absent parents' consent by phone. (They have expressed condemnation and have not yet been in to visit.) The technician comes in and out of the room, getting equipment, while the physicians concentrate on completing the procedure. No one is speaking to Bill, who alternately screams and cries and becomes very quiet.

1. What crisis interventions and communication techniques could a student nurse make as she squeezes into this small room to observe the procedure?

2. What assessment would you make about Bill's feelings about his diagnosis?

3. What can be inferred about Bill's behavior during this procedure?

4. What interventions could an experienced nurse make this week with all groups of professional caregivers?

5. What interventions might be made with his family?

6. What additional data are needed before beginning any HIV/AIDS teaching with Bill?

Answers

Nonverbal touch and verbal reassurance about what is happening next and time to completion would be appropriate communication efforts.

Efforts by an experienced clinician could be directed to:

- The client, to help him verbalize the anxiety underlying his anger.
- The nurses and physicians on the staff, to help them recognize the cause of their avoidance behaviors.
- The family, to support them enough to allow them to mobilize some support for their son.

For longer-term intervention and therapy, a referral may be needed. When Bill's anxiety is decreased enough to allow him to learn about his condition, assessment should focus on what he knows about the course of the disease, any personal experiences he has associated with HIV/AIDS, and his feelings about his situation.

Chapter 22

Communicating with Other Health Professionals

INTRODUCTION

This chapter examines professional relationships and discusses how to apply communication concepts to collegial conflict situations. Additional material describes the nature of professional workgroups. Because failed change efforts occur as a result of a lack of understanding of group process principles, the application of these principles to work groups is discussed.

Exercises are designed to increase awareness of related concepts and to offer learners some limited experience with professional conflict situations.

There are 10 exercises in this chapter of the text.

EXERCISE 22-1
Client Advocate Role-Play

Teaching Tip
The case example is useful with learners who do not have clinical experiences.

EXERCISE 22-2
Community Resources

When this exercise was provided in an earlier chapter, it was noted that the instructor needed to structure contacts with community agencies to avoid becoming an unnecessary annoyance.

EXERCISE 22-3
Applying Principles of Delegation

This exercise is for advanced students.

EXERCISE 22-4
Feelings about Authority

Purpose: To become conscious about feelings toward authority figures.

Teaching Tip
Make sure that the activity is graded on the basis of participation, not on content. It may help to have students do this exercise as a homework assignment

and discuss it in class. When some students respond by being intimidated and some respond with anger, are these differences due to personality or the situation?

EXERCISE 22-5
Applying Principles of Confrontation

Divide the class into two groups, and have them role-play the case presented in the text. Use the guidelines provided in the text in confronting each problem. Remind the class that the night shift must take vital signs, give complete bed baths, and get clients ready for morning procedures between 5 and 7 a.m.

- Identify the real concerns
- Clarify each groups assumptions
- What is the real issue?

EXERCISE 22-6
Barriers to Interprofessional Communication

Discussions based on this exercise offer practice in understanding of the basic concepts of client advocacy, communication barriers, and peer negotiation in simulated nursing situations.

CASE STUDY A

Dr. Tanlow interrupts Ms. Serf as she is preparing pain medication for 68-year-old Mrs. Gould. It is already 15 minutes late. Dr. Tanlow says he needs Ms. Serf immediately in room 20C to assist with a drainage and dressing change. Knowing that Mrs. Gould, a diabetic, will respond to prolonged pain with vomiting, Ms. Serf replies that she will be available to help Dr. Tanlow in 10 minutes (during which time she will have administered Mrs. Gould's pain medication).

Dr. Tanlow, already on his way to room 20C, whirls around, stating loudly, "When I say I need assistance, I mean now. I am a busy man, in case you hadn't noticed." If you were Ms. Serf, what would be an appropriate response?

Answer

An empathetic statement recognizing how busy the doctor is, a restatement of own immediate responsibility to protect client (client advocate), a statement of expectation that doctor will put client need as priority, a request that the doctor have some flexibility, and a description of alternative possibilities, such as seeking supervisor's assistance.

CASE STUDY B

A newly hired nurse is helping a resident draw femoral blood. The nurse states that although she has never assisted with this procedure, she is thoroughly familiar with the technique through the hospital manual. The nurse requests that if the resident should require anything different from the manual, he should tell her so.

The resident responds, "You should have practiced this with someone else. I shouldn't be stuck with a neophyte. Ha Ha! Get it? Neophyte, instead of needle." How should the nurse respond?

Answer

Clarify the issue, state own feelings.

CASE STUDY C

Mrs. Warfield, the nursing supervisor, remains on Unit C most of the evening with Mr. Whelan, who is working his first evening shift as charge nurse. Toward the end of the evening, Mr. Whelan asked Mrs. Warfield if there was a special reason she was spending so much time on the unit. Mrs. Warfield replied vaguely that she always does that with first-time charge nurses.

Two days later, Mr. Whelan received a written report about his evening as charge nurse that was negative in nature and particularly critical of the fact that the supervisor had to spend so much time on Unit C. A copy of the report went to the head nurse on Unit C and to Mr. Whelan's personnel file. How would you respond if you were Mr. Whelan?

Answer

Use steps in Box 22-6, and make appointment with supervisor and head nurse for confrontation. Have a clear goal in mind (to get report modified or removed from record).

CASE STUDY D

Mrs. Swick had been working the evening shift for 8 months. When she was hired, she was promised

in writing that she would be moved to a permanent day-shift assignment as soon as a replacement could be found for the evening shift. Recently, two new nurses have been hired and assigned to permanent days.

After writing a note to the supervisor brought no response, Mrs. Swick scheduled an appointment to discuss her schedule with her supervisor. After the appointment, her supervisor began scheduling her on days, but her new assignment requires once a month a 2-day rotation to nights, a day off (which she used to sleep following her night shift), consistently followed by 5 straight days. How would you approach this situation if you were Mrs. Swick?

Answer

Same as answer to Case Study C above.

EXERCISE 22-7
Goals and Objectives in Workgroups

This exercise helps students identify professional goals in workgroups.

Teaching Tip

Have students answer the questions in the text based on their experience in some other setting. When discussing situations in class, avoid instructor/school-student conflict discussions. Objectives should reflect what student personally hoped to achieve as a group participant as well as what she or he contributed to the overall group task.

EXERCISE 22-8
Problem Diagnoses

Use this exercise with advanced students.

EXERCISE 22-9
Brainstorming: A Family Dilemma

Teaching Tip

Use a **discussion room** on the **Internet Web site** you create for this class. Have students post their answers and require them to read peer postings and to reply to at least one.

EXERCISE 22-10
Staff-Focused Consultation

This exercise can be done with students role-playing the case from this chapter in the text.

ADDITIONAL EXERCISES

EXERCISE 22-A

Differentiating Responses in Collegial Relations

Directions: Refer to the case example of the crying child in the text. Think of different types of responses to this communication. Write down your first reactions.

Questions for Discussion

1. How emotional is your first reaction?
2. Formulate your own assertive response, and discuss with classmates how it differs from the ones offered.
3. What does your response tell you about your style?
4. Next, look at the put-down response, and discuss with your classmates what is unprofessional about it.

EXERCISE 22-B

The Car: Feedback of Group Membership Styles

This exercise has been useful to some instructors trying to dramatize content on group process.

Teaching Tips

1. Strategies for managing conflict situations:
   a. Prepare carefully by organizing information and monitoring and managing own anxiety.
   b. A sense of timing. Address one issue at a time.
   c. Focus on the issue in the present, not in the past.
   d. Make a request for behavior change, if necessary, not for a change in feelings or attitude.
   e. Provide feedback and evaluate conflict resolution.
2. Strategies effective in conflict resolution with other health professionals.
   a. Describe specific examples and avoid judgmental generalizations.
   b. Focus on future, things that can be changed.
   c. Clearly state why the change is needed.
   d. Acknowledge at the outset that any evaluation is inherently subjective.
   e. Encourage mutual problem solving—a solution that meets both parties' needs.
   f. Don't focus on the problem as much as on the solution, and express respect and confidence that the person can improve.
   g. Develop a plan and state expectations and time limit/time frame.

Adapted from Booth R. Conflict and conflict management. In DJ Mason, SW Talbot (eds): *Political Action Handbook for Nurses*. Menlo Park, CA, Addison-Wesley, 1985; and Harmon S: Giving constructive criticism and aplomb. *Medical Laboratory Observor*, March, pp 24-27, 1991.

Chapter 23

Documentation in the Age of Computers

INTRODUCTION

Novice learners need a structured format to communicate the meaning of gathered data to others. In this chapter, the learner is introduced to methods for gathering and documenting data for agency files about clients and their families. The instructor should help students identify differences between what constitutes legally sufficient documentation and the more comprehensive nature of the clinically sufficient entry. Employing agencies stress the importance of correct and comprehensive documentation as a defense against malpractice law suits, especially when injury has occurred. The nursing profession more rigorously focuses on documenting meeting standards of care and making entries that record progression in client status toward stated health goals.

Exercises in this chapter are designed to offer practice in organizing assessment data. Use of such information in formulating nursing diagnoses is highlighted as a mechanism for communicating information about the client to other health care professionals.

There are three exercises in this chapter of the text.

EXERCISE 23-1
Charting Nursing Diagnoses

Teaching Tip

Focus discussion on how changing the wording of a diagnosis empowers nurses by presenting them with a problem for which they have many nursing interventions, thus allowing them to take independent "nursing" actions.

Answers

Example 1. Inability to communicate was not an accurate appraisal of the situation. By reframing the diagnosis, the nurse can implement many steps to decrease social isolation.

Example 2. The nurse cannot treat all, but by reframing these diagnoses to pain, the nurse can in-

dependently employ many nonpharmacologic interventions to eliminate the pain

EXERCISE 23-2
The Process Record

Purpose: To provide the student with practice in writing process recordings.

Teaching Tips

Students may photocopy the sample form for the Interpersonal Process Record (IPR) provided in this manual as many times as needed. Instructors may develop alternative formats as desired. Extensive directions for using the IPR sheet are given in the book.

This exercise is designed for beginning students. It is designed to teach beginning skills in recording and analyzing a typical nurse-client interaction. The process record is an excellent tool for assisting beginning students to identify the level of their communication skills while providing an opportunity for postinteraction analysis.

The first two columns record the conversation of the client and of the nurse verbatim. The last of the three columns should be used to identify or categorize specific communication skills used and to critically evaluate their effectiveness. When nurse comments have been effective or ineffective, students should cite concepts from communications theory that might explain what happened. Suggestions for alternative nurse communications should be made to recommend more effective ways in which to interact with the client.

Following the student's self-critique, many instructors choose to collect and read the IPRs, adding their own comments and suggestions as needed to give the student further insight into the communication process. We have found that requiring a series of weekly process records helps students acquire needed communication skills. As students gain experience in doing process records, it becomes easier. Their written comments generally indicate development of skill and refinement of analytical abilities.

It is *critical* to establish a milieu of trust and a climate of learning. Even the most experienced nurses can find areas that need improving in their use of communication techniques. The student comes to this exercise with a mindset expecting grading deductions for errors. Instructors need to emphasize that this is different. The expectations are that in the last column the student will demonstrate insight in her or his analysis for the interaction. "Credit" is given for this part of the learning activity. It would be a useless learning process if all the material in column 2 were "perfect."

Pitfalls: Some students initially have some difficulty developing complete process records. Often they express concern that they will forget parts of their conversation with the client. In their first attempt at a process recording, few students are able to comment accurately on the types of communication skills they used.

EXERCISE 23-3
The Interpersonal Process: Related Concepts

Teaching Tip

Assign this exercise before class, then discuss it just during class, preferably in dyads. It may be a more interesting learning experience if each student is instructed to write down two or three goals prior to initiating a nurse-client interaction. Analysis then can include whether these goals were achieved and why or why not. This may help beginning students develop more realistic goals.

Example

A student intending to interview a newly admitted 18-year-old client established these goals:

1. Orient K.M. to the unit by providing a tour and a pamphlet on hospital policies.
2. Use communication skills to explore feelings about diagnosis and impending surgery.
3. Begin preoperative teaching.

CASE STUDY

When the student approached K.M., she was talking on the telephone with her boyfriend and was totally unresponsive to the student's request for 15 minutes of her time. The same thing happened when the student returned an hour later and asked K.M. to terminate her phone conversation. The student left without speaking to the client again.

Later, when the student reflected on these interactions, she was able to recognize how angry she felt when this adolescent client disregarded her professional requests. After writing the incidents up on a process recording, the student was able to make some suggestions for alternative goals that might have been mutually acceptable to K.M. and to the nursing staff, including scheduling a meeting for a specific time later in the afternoon.

ADDITIONAL EXERCISES

EXERCISE 23-A
Practice Using a Process Recording

Directions: Take the sample process record. Have students cover the last column and write in their own comments. Compare with those given in the sample.

EXERCISE 23-B
Developing Nursing Diagnoses

Purpose: To increase familiarity with psychosocial nursing diagnoses.

Directions

Take each one of a standard list of diagnoses, and write a second component to tailor it to a specific client you have worked with. Some examples are listed as follows.

Example 1. Impairment of communication . . . (associated with Japanese spoken as a first language).

Example 2. Moderate anxiety . . . (associated with separation from kin).

Example 3. Impaired self-concept . . . (related to profound sensory impairment).

Answers

Beginning learners tell us that the most difficult aspect involved in writing diagnoses is understanding the language. It takes a while to develop actual understanding instead of a "cookbook" use of a list of diagnoses.

Test Bank

COMMUNICATION TEST BANK INTRODUCTION

The communication test bank accompanies the Arnold and Boggs *Interpersonal Relationships* textbook and is a section of the Instructor's Manual. **It may be copied for use with students in conjunction with the textbook.** The following information accompanies each question:

- The correct answer
- Identification of the topic
- The step of the nursing process to which the question relates
- The cognitive level of the question:
  Knowledge
  Comprehension
  Application
  Analysis
- Difficulty level of the question
  Easy
  Moderate
  Hard
- Rationale

EXAMPLE

1. Nurse Jones demonstrates the application of modern nursing theory when she:
   1) Administers insulin to a client with diabetes
   2) Assists a physician with a pelvic examination
   3) Teaches a client techniques of breast self-examination
   4) Makes up a client's bed

Correct Answer: 3
Topic: Theoretical Perspectives
Step of the Nursing Process: Implementation
Cognitive Level: Application
Difficulty: Easy
Rationale: Modern nursing theory has broadened the definition of health with a strong emphasis on disease prevention and health promotion.

CHAPTER 1

Theoretical Perspectives and Contemporary Issues

1. Which of the following best describes the role of theory in the nurse–client relationship?
   1) Theory provides a common language
   2) Theory is the essence of the nurse–client relationship
   3) Theory varies with changes in health care delivery
   4) Theory guides nursing practice

Correct Answer: 4
Topic: Theory as a Guide to Practice
Step of the Nursing Process: All Phases of the Nursing Process
Cognitive Level: Comprehension
Difficulty: Moderate
Rationale: Theory provides nurses with a systematic way to view client situations and a logical way to organize and interpret data.

2. Nurse Jones demonstrates the application of modern nursing theory when she:
   1) Administers insulin to a client with diabetes
   2) Assists a physician with a pelvic examination
   3) Teaches a client techniques of breast self-examination
   4) Makes up a client's bed

Correct Answer: 3
Topic: Theoretical Perspectives
Step of the Nursing Process: Implementation
Cognitive Level: Application
Difficulty: Easy
Rationale: Modern nursing theory has broadened the definition of health with a strong emphasis on disease prevention and health promotion.

3. Nursing theory originated with which of the following nursing leaders?
   1) Virginia Henderson
   2) Martha Rogers
   3) Dorothea Orem
   4) Florence Nightingale

Correct Answer: 4
Topic: Nursing Theory Development
Step of the Nursing Process: All Phases of the Nursing Process

Cognitive Level: Knowledge
Difficulty: Easy
Rationale: Theory development began when Florence Nightingale published her notes on nursing in 1859.

4. Virginia Henderson, Sister Callista Roy, Jean Watson, Dorothea Orem, and Rosemary Parse are best known for:
   1) Developing nursing theories
   2) Linking theory to practice
   3) Validating existing theory
   4) Measuring clinical outcomes

Correct Answer: 1
Topic: Theoretical Perspectives
Step of the Nursing Process: All Phases of the Nursing Process
Cognitive Level: Comprehension
Difficulty: Easy
Rationale: These are some of the nursing leaders who developed the original theories of nursing.

5. Nursing's metaparadigm:
   1) Helps bind nursing to other professions
   2) Consists of three elements: person, health, and nursing
   3) Makes nursing's functions unique
   4) Is a view of the immediate environment

Correct Answer: 3
Topic: Nursing Knowledge
Steps of the Nursing Process: All Phases of the Nursing Process
Cognitive Level: Knowledge
Difficulty: Easy
Rationale: Nursing's metaparadigm is a worldwide view that makes its functions unique.

6. Nurse Green, when admitting Mr. Brown to the medical-surgical unit, asks him about cultural issues. By doing this, Nurse Green is demonstrating use of the concept of:
   1) Person
   2) Environment
   3) Health
   4) Nursing

Correct Answer: 2
Topic: Nursing Knowledge
Step of the Nursing Process: Assessment
Cognitive Level: Application
Difficulty: Moderate
Rationale: The concept of environment includes cultural and religious beliefs.

7. Mary, a young mother, tells you, "I'm worried because my son needs a blood transfusion. I don't know what to do, because blood transfusions cause AIDS." Which central nursing concept is represented in this situation?
   1) Environment
   2) Caring
   3) Health
   4) Person

Correct Answer: 4
Topic: Nursing Knowledge
Step of the Nursing Process: Implementation
Cognitive Level: Application
Difficulty: Moderate
Rationale: With the concept of person, nurses provide educational and emotional support to families.

8. Performing a dressing change using sterile technique is an example of which pattern of knowledge?
   1) Empirical
   2) Personal
   3) Aesthetic
   4) Ethical

Correct Answer: 1
Topic: Patterns of Knowing
Step of the Nursing Process: Implementation
Cognitive Level: Comprehension
Difficulty: Moderate
Rationale: Empirical knowledge is the scientific rationale for skilled nursing interventions.

9. The nurse–client relationship, as described by Peplau:
   1) Would not be useful in a short-stay unit
   2) Allows personal and social growth to occur only for the client
   3) Leaves the client with a greater sense of well-being

4) Describes phases of the relationship that are mutually exclusive

Correct Answer: 3
Topic: Nursing Theory in the Nurse–Client Relationship
Step of the Nursing Process: All Phases of the Nursing Process
Cognitive Level: Knowledge
Difficulty: Moderate
Rationale: An important aspect of the nurse–client relationship is to leave the client with a greater sense of well-being than before the encounter.

10. Which of the following is the purpose of the nurse–client relationship? To foster:
    1) spiritual well-being of the client
    2) understanding of the client's health problem
    3) physical health of the client
    4) a partnership with the client

Correct Answer: 4
Topic: Nursing Theory in the Nurse–Client Relationship
Step of the Nursing Process: All Phases of the Nursing Process
Cognitive Level: Knowledge
Difficulty: Moderate
Rationale: The purpose of the nurse–client relationship is to have a meaningful, shared experience in which personal-social growth occur for both nurse and client.

11. Which of the following represents *exploitation*, the third phase of the nurse–client relationship, according to Peplau?
    1) John Adams, RN, meets with the client, Mr. Jones, to obtain data
    2) John Adams, RN, develops the nursing diagnosis, Anxiety about upcoming surgery
    3) John Adams, RN, develops the goal to decrease Mr. Jones' anxiety within two sessions
    4) John Adams, RN, teaches Mr. Jones to perform relaxation techniques

Correct Answer: 4
Topic: Nursing Theory in the Nurse–Client Relationship
Step of the Nursing Process: Implementation
Cognitive Level: Application
Difficulty: Moderate

Rationale: The exploitation phase uses resources to help the client resolve issues.

12. The identification phase of the nurse–client relationship:
    1) Sets the stage for the rest of the relationship
    2) Correlates with the assessment phase of the nursing process
    3) Focuses on mutual clarification of ideas and expectations
    4) Uses community resources to help resolve health care issues

Correct Answer: 3
Topic: Nursing Theory in the Nurse–Client Relationship
Step of the Nursing Process: Planning
Cognitive Level: Knowledge
Difficulty: Moderate
Rationale: The identification component focuses on mutual clarification.

13. Anger directed at the nurse by the family of a client newly diagnosed with cancer can best be understood in the context of:
    1) Martin Buber's I-Thou relationship
    2) Abraham Maslow's hierarchy of needs
    3) Carl Jung's concepts of adult development
    4) Sigmund Freud's ego defense mechanisms

Correct Answer: 4
Topic: Contributions from Other Disciplines
Step of the Nursing Process: Implementation
Cognitive Level: Application
Difficulty: Moderate
Rationale: Freud identified ego defense mechanisms that a person uses to protect the self from anxiety. One of these is the projection of anger.

14. Which of the following theorists viewed the professional's relationship with the client as a means to helping the client grow and change?
    1) Maslow
    2) Rogers
    3) Erikson
    4) Buber

Correct Answer: 2
Topic: Contributions from Other Disciplines
Step of the Nursing Process: All Phases of the Nursing Process

Cognitive Level: Knowledge
Difficulty: Moderate
Rationale: According to Carl Rogers, if the professional could provide a certain type of relationship, the client would find the capacity to grow and change.

15. Nurse Smith wants to provide medication education to a group of clients with a diagnosis of schizophrenia. It would be most helpful for nurse Smith to keep in mind the concepts of:
    1) Freud's transference and countertransference
    2) Roger's person-centered relationship
    3) Maslow's self-actualization
    4) Erikson's principles of personality development

Correct Answer: 2
Topic: Contributions from Other Disciplines
Step of the Nursing Process: Planning
Cognitive Level: Analysis
Difficulty: Moderate
Rationale: Rogers' concepts are applicable for nurse–client teaching formats.

16. Which of the following statements about communication theory is true?
    1) Primates are able to learn new languages to share ideas and feelings
    2) Concepts include only verbal communication
    3) Perceptions are clarified through feedback
    4) Past experience does not influence communication

Correct Answer: 3
Topic: Communication Theory
Step of the Nursing Process: All Phases of the Nursing Process
Cognitive Level: Knowledge
Difficulty: Moderate
Rationale: Feedback is necessary to confirm that participants have the same understanding of the message.

17. In the circular transactional model of communication:
    1) Systems theory concepts are included
    2) People take only complementary roles in the communication

3) The context of the communication is unimportant
4) The purpose of communication is to influence the receiver

Correct Answer: 1
Topic: Communication Theory
Step of the Nursing Process: All Phases of the Nursing Process
Cognitive Level: Comprehension
Difficulty: Moderate
Rationale: Systems theory concepts of feedback and validation are included.

18. Feedback:
    1) Occurs in some interactions
    2) Involves only verbal responses
    3) Does not include validation
    4) Can focus on the feelings generated

Correct Answer: 4
Topic: Communication Theory
Step of the Nursing Process: All Phases of the Nursing Process
Cognitive Level: Knowledge
Difficulty: Moderate
Rationale: Feedback can focus on content, relationship, feelings, or events.

19. As a nursing student, you are expected to engage in therapeutic communication with clients. Which of the following statements represents therapeutic communication when a student discovers a client crying in bed?

1) "Hi, Joe, I'm the nurse who will be doing your treatments today."
2) "Hi, Joe, will you listen to me so that I can help you get better?"
3) "Hi, Joe, this is what is going to happen during surgery."
4) "Hi, Joe, can we talk about what seems to be bothering you?"

Correct Answer: 4
Topic: Therapeutic Communication
Step of the Nursing Process: Assessment
Cognitive Level: Application
Difficulty: Moderate
Rationale: This statement is goal-directed. Its purpose is to promote client well-being.

20. _____ could be used to describe the current focus of the health care delivery system:
    1) Tele-health
    2) The medical model
    3) Nursing's metaparadigm
    4) Capitated health care

Correct Answer: 3
Topic: Contemporary Issues
Step of the Nursing Process: All Phases of the Nursing Process
Cognitive Level: Comprehension
Difficulty: Moderate
Rationale: The focus of health care delivery today is on use of a public health framework rather than on a traditional model. Nursing's metaparadigm, with the emphasis on the interrelationship between person and environment, emphasizes health promotion and prevention.

CHAPTER 2

Professional Guides to Action in Interpersonal Relationships

1. Legal documents developed at the state level that govern the provision of professional nursing care are known as:
    1) NCLEX
    2) Nurse Practice Acts
    3) Professional standards of care
    4) Tort laws

Correct Answer: 2
Topic: Nurse Practice Acts
Step of the Nursing Process: All Phases of the Nursing Process

Cognitive Level: Knowledge
Difficulty: Moderate
Rationale: Nurse Practice Acts define nursing's scope of practice and outline nurse's rights, responsibilities, and licensing requirements.

2. A preoperative assessment shows that a client's hemoglobin is dropping. The anesthetist orders 3 units of blood to be administered. The nurse

administers the first unit before discovering that the client is a Jehovah's Witness, as documented in the record. This is an example of:

1) Professional conduct
2) A negligent act
3) Physical abuse
4) Breaching client confidentiality

Correct Answer: 2
Topic: Legal Standards
Step of the Nursing Process: All Phases of the Nursing Process
Cognitive Level: Application
Difficulty: Easy
Rationale: The nurse was negligent by not checking the record and by failure to inform and obtain verbal consent of the client for the procedure.

3. Which of the following is a violation of client confidentiality? Reporting:

1) a communicable disease
2) child abuse
3) gunshot wounds
4) client data to a colleague in nonprofessional setting

Correct Answer: 4
Topic: Legal Standards-Confidentiality
Step of the Nursing Process: All Phases of the Nursing Process
Cognitive Level: Knowledge
Difficulty: Easy
Rationale: Releasing information to people not directly involved in the client's care is a breach of confidentiality.

4. A 16-year-old female trauma victim arrives in the emergency department and requires emergency surgery. The nurse knows that:

1) A parent or guardian must give consent
2) The client can give consent if she provides proof of emancipation
3) The client must first be evaluated for competence before consent is obtained
4) Surgery can be performed without consent

Correct Answer: 4
Topic: Informed Consent
Step of the Nursing Process: All Phases of the Nursing Process
Cognitive Level: Application
Difficulty: Hard

Rationale: Surgery can be performed without consent as it is a life-threatening emergency.

5. In regard to informed consent, which of the following statements is true?

1) Only legally incompetent adults can give consent
2) Only parents can give consent for minor children
3) It is not required that the client be told about the cost and alternatives to treatment
4) Consent must be voluntary

Correct Answer: 4
Topic: Informed Consent
Step of the Nursing Process: All Phases of the Nursing Process
Cognitive Level: Knowledge
Difficulty: Moderate
Rationale: For legal consent to be valid, it must be voluntary.

6. Which of the following provide the health care team with information regarding the client's wishes regarding life-prolonging treatment protocols?

1) Advance directives
2) Informed consent
3) Statement of client's rights
4) Professional code of ethics

Correct Answer: 1
Topic: Advance Directives
Step of the Nursing Process: All Phases of the Nursing Process
Cognitive Level: Knowledge
Difficulty: Moderate
Rationale: Clients can put individual preferences in writing that are recognized by law.

7. The client has a living will in which he states he does not want to be kept alive by artificial means. The client's family wants to disregard the client's wishes and have him maintained on artificial life support. The most appropriate initial course of action for the nurse would be:

1) To tell the family that they have no legal rights

2) To tell the family that they have the right to override the living will because the patient cannot speak
3) Report the situation to the hospital's ethics committee
4) Allow the family to ventilate their feelings and concerns while maintaining the role of client advocate

Correct Answer: 4
Topic: Advance Directives
Step of the Nursing Process: Implementation
Cognitive Level: Analysis
Difficulty: Moderate
Rationale: This is the most appropriate action at the time to assist the family to deal with their loss and come to terms with their family member's wishes.

8. The nurse collects both objective and subjective data. An example of subjective data is:
1) Blood pressure: 140/80 mm Hg
2) Skin color jaundiced
3) "I have a headache"
4) History of seizures

Correct Answer: 3
Topic: Nursing Process
Step of the Nursing Process: Assessment
Cognitive Level: Knowledge
Difficulty: Easy
Rationale: Subjective refers to the client's perception.

9. One evening as you are on duty as a registered nurse, you observe a client pacing the floor. You approach the client and make the following statement to validate an inference:
1) "You are anxious so let's talk about it."
2) "Let's try some deep breathing to help you relax."
3) "You seem anxious. Will you tell me what is going on?"
4) "Clients who pace usually need to talk to a physician. Should I call yours?"

Correct Answer: 3
Topic: Nursing Process
Step of the Nursing Process: Assessment
Cognitive Level: Application
Difficulty: Moderate
Rationale: The nurse has inferred that the client is anxious but needs to ask further questions to validate the information.

10. Developing a nursing diagnosis is the second phase of the nursing process. Mr. Brown, scheduled for a bilateral inguinal hernia repair the next day, is observed pacing on the unit. After it has been validated that Mr. Brown is anxious about his upcoming surgery because he is afraid of pain, a relevant nursing diagnosis would be:
1) Anxiety related to surgery
2) Pain related to anxiety about surgery, as evidenced by pacing
3) Anxiety related to fear of postoperative pain, as evidenced by pacing
4) Pacing related to fear of postoperative pain

Correct Answer: 3
Topic: Nursing Process
Step of the Nursing Process: Nursing Diagnosis
Cognitive Level: Application
Difficulty: Hard
Rationale: Anxiety is the problem to be addressed. Related to connects the problem to the etiology (fear of pain). The third part of the statement identifies the clinical evidence (pacing) that supports the diagnosis.

11. Which of the following is an outcome for a client with a broken leg?
1) The client will develop an ambulation program within one month
2) Encourage the client to ambulate with cast using crutches
3) The client asks, ""When will I walk again?"
4) Alteration in mobility caused by a broken leg

Correct Answer: 1
Topic: Nursing Process
Step of the Nursing Process: Outcome Identification
Cognitive Level: Application
Difficulty: Hard
Rationale: Outcomes are goals that are measurable, achievable, and client-centered.

12. Which of the following is an independent intervention for a client, Mary Ann, who has been admitted to the hospital for a surgical procedure? She states to you "I am very anxious about my surgery, which is scheduled for tomorrow."

1) "Let me give you some medication to make you more comfortable"
2) "Let's talk about your feelings regarding the surgery"
3) "Let me check your vital signs now"
4) "Let me help you with this breathing machine in preparation for the surgery"

Correct Answer: 2
Topic: Nursing Process
Step of the Nursing Process: Implementation
Cognitive Level: Application
Difficulty: Moderate
Rationale: Independent nursing interventions can be provided by nurses without direction from other health care professionals.

13. Setting goals with the client occurs during which step of the nursing process?
    1) Assessment
    2) Planning
    3) Implementation
    4) Evaluation

Correct Answer: 2
Topic: Nursing Process
Step of the Nursing Process: Outcome Identification and Planning
Cognitive Level: Knowledge
Difficulty: Easy
Rationale: Outcome identification occurs during the planning phase.

14. Defining the problem occurs during which step of the nursing process?
    1) Diagnosis
    2) Planning
    3) Intervention
    4) Evaluation

Correct Answer: 1
Topic: Nursing Process
Step of the Nursing Process: Diagnosis
Cognitive Level: Knowledge
Difficulty: Moderate
Rationale: Alterations in health status that require nursing interventions are defined in the diagnosis step of the nursing process.

15. When evaluating the client's progress toward goal achievement, the nurse should ask the following question:
    1) Did the client tell the truth?
    2) Were the goals realistic?
    3) Did the physician diagnose the client's condition correctly?
    4) Was the length of stay too short?

Correct Answer: 2
Topic: Nursing Process
Step of the Nursing Process: Evaluation
Cognitive Level: Comprehension
Difficulty: Moderate
Rationale: The goals must be realistic and achievable for the interventions to be effective.

16. The nursing process helps the nurse:
    1) Maintain confidentiality
    2) Attain self-actualization
    3) Maintain therapeutic communication
    4) Organize observations and perform care

Correct Answer: 4
Topic: Nursing Process
Step of the Nursing Process: All Phases of the Nursing Process
Cognitive Level: Comprehension
Difficulty: Moderate
Rationale: The nursing process helps the nurse organize data, develop diagnoses, and perform interventions.

17. Which of the following describes a critical pathway?
    1) It is documentation in measurable terms
    2) It is based on nursing diagnosis
    3) It directs collaborative practice
    4) It is developed collaboratively with the client

Correct Answer: 3
Topic: Critical Pathways
Step of the Nursing Process: All Phases of the Nursing Process
Cognitive Level: Knowledge
Difficulty: Moderate
Rationale: Critical pathways are interdisciplinary clinical management frameworks.

CHAPTER 3

Clinical Judgment: Applying Critical Thinking and Ethical Decision Making

1. Which of the following types of thinking reflects the nursing process?
    1) Habits
    2) Inquiry
    3) Mnemonics
    4) Practice

    Correct Answer: 2
    Topic: Types of Thinking
    Step of the Nursing Process: All Phases of the Nursing Process
    Cognitive Level: Knowledge
    Difficulty: Moderate
    Rationale: A structured method of thinking is used in all steps of the nursing process.

2. Which of the following personality characteristics is a barrier to critical thinking?
    1) Accepting change
    2) Being open-minded
    3) Stereotyping
    4) Going with the flow

    Correct Answer: 3
    Topic: Critical Thinking
    Step of the Nursing Process: All Phases of the Nursing Process
    Cognitive Level: Comprehension
    Difficulty: Moderate
    Rationale: Stereotyping is a cognitive barrier to critical thinking.

3. The ethical decision-making model in which good is defined as maximum welfare or happiness is known as:
    1) The utilitarian model
    2) The human rights–based model
    3) The duty-based model
    4) Kant's model

    Correct Answer: 1
    Topic: Ethical Reasoning
    Step of the Nursing Process: All Phases of the Nursing Process
    Cognitive Level: Knowledge
    Difficulty: Moderate

Rationale: The utilitarian model is also known as the goal-based model, in which the duties of the nurse are determined by what will achieve maximum welfare.

4. Which of the following case examples represents the ethical concept of distributive justice?
    1) A famous baseball player receives a heart transplant
    2) An elderly client who has government insurance is denied standard cancer treatment
    3) During a visit to his physician's office, a client demands antibiotics for his cold and is given a prescription
    4) A client suffering from cirrhosis of the liver is placed on a transplant list

    Correct Answer: 2
    Topic: Ethical Theories
    Step of the Nursing Process: All Phases of the Nursing Process
    Cognitive Level: Analysis
    Difficulty: Hard
    Rationale: The decision to deny expensive treatments or to deny acute care to everyone over a certain age owing to scarce treatment resources is an example of the concept of distributive justice.

5. Conceived values are defined as:
    1) Values taught by one's culture
    2) Values an individual uses daily
    3) Two values that are in conflict
    4) Values determined by commitment

    Correct Answer: 1
    Topic: Values
    Step of the Nursing Process: All Phases of the Nursing Process
    Cognitive Level: Knowledge
    Difficulty: Moderate
    Rationale: These are conceptions of the ideal that have been taught by one's culture.

6. Carol Green, RN, values autonomy or self-determination as well as the preservation of life. This is an example of:

1) Conceptions of the ideal
2) Cognitive dissonance
3) Operative values
4) Commitment

Correct Answer: 2
Topic: Values
Step of the Nursing Process: All Phases of the Nursing Process
Cognitive Level: Application
Difficulty: Moderate
Rationale: Cognitive dissonance refers to two conflicting values.

7. Which of the following statements is true about the critical thinking process?
    1) It is a linear process
    2) The skills are inborn
    3) It involves self-reflection
    4) It assists nurses in criticizing the health care system

Correct Answer: 3
Topic: Critical Thinking
Step of the Nursing Process: All Phases of the Nursing Process
Cognitive Level: Comprehension
Difficulty: Moderate
Rationale: Critical thinking involves "thinking about thinking."

8. Differences between the critical thinking skills of a novice nurse and an expert nurse include:
    1) The expert nurse is able to diagnose faster than the novice
    2) Unlike the novice nurse, the expert nurse does not need to question and reassess
    3) The novice nurse utilizes past knowledge; the expert stays in the here and now
    4) The expert nurse organizes data more efficiently than the novice nurse

Correct Answer: 4
Topic: Critical Thinking
Step of the Nursing Process: All Phases of the Nursing Process
Cognitive Level: Comprehension
Difficulty: Moderate
Rationale: The novice nurse does not organize facts as efficiently.

9. John Smith, a client suffering from schizophrenia, has been stabilized with long-acting

haloperidol, an antipsychotic medication that he receives by injection every 3 weeks. The physician switches his medication to Seroquel, a new antipsychotic oral medication that John must take twice a day. He complains that he cannot afford the new medication and will not be able to remember to take it. The physician replies, "I can't help that, I have to treat you the way I think is best." John's nurse may experience:
    1) Paternalism
    2) Cognitive dissonance
    3) Nonmaleficence
    4) Moral distress

Correct Answer: 4
Topic: Ethical or Moral Dilemmas
Step of the Nursing Process: All Phases of the Nursing Process
Cognitive Level: Application
Difficulty: Moderate
Rationale: Moral distress results when the nurse knows what is right but is bound to do otherwise.

10. Which of the following steps in applying critical thinking to clinical decision-making corresponds with identification of personal values?
    1) First
    2) Second
    3) Third
    4) Fourth

Correct Answer: 2
Topic: Critical Thinking
Step of the Nursing Process: All Phases of the Nursing Process
Cognitive Level: Knowledge
Difficulty: Easy
Rationale: In step 2, personal values are identified.

11. The best method by which nurse educators can teach professional values is:
    1) Reading the ANA code
    2) Laissez-faire
    3) Role-modeling
    4) Values clarification

Correct Answer: 3
Topic: Professional Values
Cognitive Level: Knowledge
Difficulty: Moderate

Rationale: Professional values are transmitted by tradition and are modeled by expert nurses.

12. Which of the following describes the highest functional level of the values clarification process?
    1) Prizes a value
    2) Acts upon value system
    3) Chooses a value
    4) Understands value system

Correct Answer: 2
Topic: Professional Values
Step of the Nursing Process: All Phases of the Nursing Process
Cognitive Level: Knowledge
Difficulty: Moderate
Rationale: Acting on a value is the strongest evidence in the values clarification process.

13. The client's values:
    1) Must coincide with those of the nurse
    2) Are considered only during assessment
    3) Influence the nurse's interventions
    4) Are not influenced by culture

Correct Answer: 3
Topic: Values
Step of the Nursing Process: All Phases of the Nursing Process
Cognitive Level: Comprehension
Difficulty: Moderate
Rationale: Understanding the client's value system is important for developing the most appropriate interventions.

14. Values clarification can be incorporated within the intervention phase of the nursing process by identifying:
    1) conflict areas
    2) care guidelines
    3) client's values
    4) specific nursing diagnoses

Correct Answer: 2
Topic: Values
Step of the Nursing Process: Implementation
Cognitive Level: Comprehension
Difficulty: Hard
Rationale: The intervention used identifies values as guidelines for care.

15. During the third step in the critical thinking process:
    1) New data are obtained
    2) Values are clarified
    3) Existing information is compared with past knowledge
    4) The problem is identified

Correct Answer: 3
Topic: Critical Thinking Process
Step of the Nursing Process: All Phases of the Nursing Process
Cognitive Level: Comprehension
Difficulty: Moderate
Rationale: During step 3, existing information is compared with the past knowledge.

16. Betsy Green, student nurse, can best learn the steps in critical thinking by:
    1) Reading journals
    2) Classroom instruction
    3) Repeated practice
    4) Developing a mnemonic

Correct Answer: 3
Topic: Critical Thinking
Step of the Nursing Process: All Phases of the Nursing Process
Cognitive Level: Application
Difficulty: Moderate
Rationale: The most effective method of learning the steps in critical thinking is by repeatedly applying them to clinical situations.

CHAPTER 4

Self-Concept in the Nurse–Client Relationship

1. Pelau described the third stage of self-develop-
    ment as:
    1) Matching of behavior with appraisals
    2) Repeated appraisals
    3) Appraisals being made by significant
       others
    4) Reappraisal of self
    Correct Answer: 1
    Topic: Self-Concept
    Step of the Nursing Process: All Phases of the
    Nursing Process
    Cognitive Level: Knowledge
    Difficulty: Moderate
    Rationale: In the third stage, behavior emerges to
    match the appraisals.

2. An integral part of a birthing class for prospec-
    tive parents is a tour of the delivery room.
    Which of the following concepts does this
    represent?
    1) Holistic construct
    2) Psychological centrality
    3) Social norm
    4) Body image
    Correct Answer: 2
    Topic: Psychological Centrality
    Step of the Nursing Process: Implementation
    Cognitive Level: Application
    Difficulty: Moderate
    Rationale: Being in the hospital assumes psycho-
    logical centrality. By orienting the parents to the
    delivery room, the impact of being in a new and
    unfamiliar setting is reduced.

3. Janet Brown, RN, admits Mr. Albert, chief
    executive officer of the hospital, for diagnostic
    tests. Mr. Albert has never been a patient in the
    hospital before. Janet knows that Mr. Albert:
    1) Will feel secure
    2) Will likely have limited coping skills
    3) Will need to be given instructions only once
    4) Can find his way around the unit
    Correct Answer: 2
    Topic: Self-Concept
    Step of the Nursing Process: All Phases of the
    Nursing Process

Cognitive Level: Application
Difficulty: Moderate
Rationale: The client who has never been hospitalized has more limited coping skills than one who
has had experience.

4. Which of the following represents the role of
    the nurse–client relationship in the develop-
    ment of self?
    1) It acts as an interpreter of the client's
       behavior
    2) It is part of the self-system
    3) It helps the client develop patterns of
       behavior
    4) It helps the client reprise a situation
    Correct Answer: 4
    Topic: Self-Concept
    Step of the Nursing Process: All Phases of the
    Nursing Process
    Cognitive Level: Comprehension
    Difficulty: Moderate
    Rationale: The nurse offers the client an interper-
    sonal bridge between external events and internal
    perceptions.

5. A 50-year-old businessperson is admitted to the
    hospital for an appendectomy. Complications
    develop, and the client requires specialized
    breathing equipment. Which of Erikson's
    stages of psychosocial development is repre-
    sented in this situation?
    1) Integrity versus Despair
    2) Autonomy versus Shame and Doubt
    3) Intimacy versus Isolation
    4) Identity versus Identity Diffusion
    Correct Answer: 1
    Topic: Erikson's Model of Psychosocial Develop-
    ment
    Step of the Nursing Process: All Phases of the
    Nursing Process
    Cognitive Level: Application
    Difficulty: Moderate
    Rationale: In the Integrity versus Despair stage,
    the focus is on the meaning of life and worth. The

focus is not always age-related, and anyone facing death has the need to assess his or her life.

6. You are caring for a client who is complaining about pain in his right leg. However, this client has lost his right leg. Which of the following concepts is represented in this situation?
   1) Role performance
   2) Body image
   3) Self-esteem
   4) Personal identity

Correct Answer: 2
Topic: Self-Concept
Step of the Nursing Process: Diagnosis
Cognitive Level: Application
Difficulty: Hard
Rationale: This concept refers to an individual's perception of the body.

7. According to Driever, the self that arises out of how the individual perceives the expectations of others is:
   1) The moral-ethical self
   2) Self-consistency
   3) Self-ideal/self-expectancy
   4) The perceptual self

Correct Answer: 3
Topic: Self-Concept
Cognitive Level: Knowledge
Difficulty: Moderate
Rationale: This ideal self arises out of the perception of others' expectations.

8. Which of the following statements about perception is true?
   1) Perception is a function of the senses
   2) Perception is an interpersonal process
   3) Positive images are retained longer than negative ones
   4) Perception contributes greatly to self-concept

Correct Answer: 4
Topic: Perception
Step of the Nursing Process: All Phases of the Nursing Process
Cognitive Level: Comprehension
Difficulty: Hard
Rationale: Perceptual processes contribute significantly to the self-concept in the way individuals think about themselves and others.

9. Jim, a 12-year-old, states, "I am different from others in my physical education class because I am the class dunce." Identify the type of perceptual alteration represented in this example:
   1) Distorted reality
   2) Selective attention
   3) Self-fulfilling prophecy
   4) Cognitive distortion

Correct Answer: 3
Topic: Perceptual Alterations in Self-Concept
Step of the Nursing Process: All Phases of the Nursing Process
Cognitive Level: Application
Difficulty: Moderate
Rationale: A self-fulfilling prophecy occurs when a person's perception actually predicts his or her behavior.

10. Consider the three-step process for perceptual checks. What would your response be to Mary, who states, "I am an obese, compulsive person."
   1) "Can you tell me more about this?"
   2) "Is it difficult for you to be this way?"
   3) "I wouldn't worry about being very neat."
   4) "It is OK to be this way; you are not hurting anyone."

Correct Answer: 1
Topic: Three-Step Process for Perceptual Checks
Step of the Nursing Process: All Phases of the Nursing Process
Cognitive Level: Analysis
Difficulty: Moderate
Rationale: The first step describes precisely the behavior of concern.

11. Six-year-old Sarah has been admitted for a tonsillectomy. Allowing her time to examine and handle equipment is an intervention used to address which element of her personal identity?
   1) Perception
   2) Cognition
   3) Emotion
   4) Spirituality

Correct Answer: 2
Topic: Personal Identity
Step of the Nursing Process: Implementation
Cognitive Level: Application

Difficulty: Moderate
Rationale: Imaging is important for children. Handling the equipment would assist in Sarah's learning process.

12. When caring for a client with a diagnosis of paranoid schizophrenia, the nurse should remember that:
    1) Disordered behaviors lead to faulty perceptions
    2) Disordered behaviors lead to cognitive distortions
    3) Cognitive distortions lead to faulty perceptions
    4) Faulty perceptions lead to cognitive distortions

Correct Answer: 4
Topic: Cognitive
Step of the Nursing Process: All Phases of the Nursing Process
Cognitive Level: Application
Difficulty: Moderate
Rationale: Cognitive distortions occur in response to a faulty perception.

13. In the middle of her class presentation on self-concept, Beverly Jones, student nurse, notices that a classmate has fallen asleep. Beverly immediately decides that her presentation must be boring and that she will fail this assignment and subsequently obtain a poor grade in the course. This is an example of:
    1) Selective attention
    2) Negative self-talk
    3) Self-fulfilling prophecy
    4) Negative feedback

Correct Answer: 2
Topic: Cognitive
Step of the Nursing Process: All Phases of the Nursing Process
Cognitive Level: Application
Difficulty: Moderate
Rationale: Self-talk produces a thought that can lead to a value attachment characterizing a person as good or bad.

14. In late adolescence, the individual makes a commitment to a set of beliefs. This stage of faith development is known as:
    1) Paradoxical-consolidative
    2) Mythical-literal
    3) Individuating-reflective
    4) Intuitive-projective

Correct Answer: 3
Topic: How Faith Develops
Step of the Nursing Process: All Phases of the Nursing Process
Cognitive Level: Knowledge
Difficulty: Moderate
Rationale: The individuating-reflective stage occurs in adolescence.

15. Which of the following statements is true of self-esteem?
    1) It is an objective emotional process
    2) Achievements lead to high self-esteem
    3) It is an emotional process of self-judgment
    4) It is a concept that becomes fixed

Correct Answer: 3
Topic: Self-Esteem
Step of the Nursing Process: All Phases of the Nursing Process
Cognitive Level: Comprehension
Difficulty: Moderate
Rationale: Self-esteem develops from a person's perceptions of worth.

16. To become a skilled interviewer, one needs to first:
    1) Know something about one's own perceptions
    2) Become involved with one's client
    3) Learn to control one's feelings
    4) Practice objectivity

Correct Answer: 1
Topic: Self-Awareness
Step of the Nursing Process: All Phases of the Nursing Process
Cognitive Level: Knowledge
Difficulty: Easy
Rationale: The nurse's self-concept in the nurse–client relationship is as important as that of the client.

CHAPTER 5
Structuring the Relationship

1. Which of the following is not a violation of confidentiality?
   1) Talking about the client's symptoms in front of family members
   2) Using a client's name in a social conversation
   3) Describing a difficulty with a client in a care conference
   4) Reading a friend's chart on another hospital unit

Correct Answer: 3
Topic: Confidentiality
Step of the Nursing Process: All Phases of the Nursing Process
Cognitive Level: Comprehension
Difficulty: Moderate
Rationale: Sharing information with the health care team is not a breach of confidentiality.

2. When administering medications for human immunodeficiency virus to Mr. George, he tells you, "I should just stop taking them and get it over with." A therapeutic response would be:
   1) "You have to take these! If you stop, you will get very sick."
   2) "You're just feeling depressed right now. You'll feel better later."
   3) "Let's talk about what seems to be making you feel so hopeless."
   4) "You have the right to refuse treatment."

Correct Answer: 3
Topic: Therapeutic Relationship
Step of the Nursing Process: All Phases of the Nursing Process
Cognitive Level: Application
Difficulty: Hard
Rationale: The therapeutic relationship involves listening closely to the client and focusing on the client's concerns.

3. Her physician has informed Mrs. Harridan, an actress, that she requires surgery for a serious abdominal problem. Mrs. Harridan states to you, "I will have the surgery after I attend the annual Academy Awards." Select the most appropriate mutual goal for Mrs. Harridan:

   1) Mrs. Harridan will accept the recommended medical regimen
   2) Mrs. Harridan will alternate activity with rest throughout the day
   3) Mrs. Harridan will take a leave of absence from her work schedule
   4) Mrs. Harridan will check her blood pressure four times a day

Correct Answer: 2
Topic: Client-Centered Approach
Step of the Nursing Process: Planning phase
Cognitive Level: Application
Difficulty: Hard
Rationale: The goal should empower the client to achieve maximum health and well-being. Having her balance rest with work is a mutual goal.

4. Nurse Jones' father was an abusive man who died of alcoholism. After coming on duty, she finds that she has been assigned to a 45-year-old man who is in alcohol withdrawal. Her best therapeutic action would be to:
   1) request another assignment
   2) deliver care in short contacts to avoid projecting negativity
   3) examine her personal biases
   4) monitor the client's physical status closely

Correct Answer: 3
Topic: Self-Awareness
Step of the Nursing Process: All Phases of the Nursing Process
Cognitive Level: Application
Difficulty: Moderate
Rationale: Self-awareness is important so that biases are not projected onto the client.

5. Beth Clark, RN, returns to work after her two days off to find that a substitute nurse has changed the treatment plan of her favorite client. Beth becomes angry and critical of the other nurse in front of the client. This is an example of:

   1) Overinvolvement
   2) A client-centered approach
   3) Professional focus
   4) Disengagement

Correct Answer: 1
Topic: Boundaries
Step of the Nursing Process: All Phases of the Nursing Process
Cognitive Level: Application
Difficulty: Moderate
Rationale: Feeling resentment toward and discounting the actions of other professionals are signs of overinvolvement.

6. Being able to fully understand the experience of another without loss of self is known as:
   1) Therapeutic use of self
   2) Sympathy
   3) Empathy
   4) Authenticity

Correct Answer: 3
Topic: Therapeutic
Step of the Nursing Process: All Phases of the Nursing Process
Cognitive Level: Knowledge
Difficulty: Easy
Rationale: Empathy is the capacity to feel with the client without pity.

7. The three phases of interviewing, when the client is present, are:
   1) Confidentiality, trust, empathy
   2) Listening, hearing, feeling
   3) Orientation, working through problems, termination
   4) Getting details, thoughts, answers

Correct Answer: 3
Topic: Phases of the Nurse–Client Relationship
Step of the Nursing Process: All Phases of the Nursing Process
Cognitive Level: Comprehension
Difficulty: Easy
Rationale: The client is not present during pre-interaction.

8. Which of the following personality characteristics may affect a nurse's ability to function in a therapeutic manner, if they were to be disclosed?
   1) I am shy
   2) I get angry when I am criticized
   3) I find it hard to handle conflict
   4) I have difficulty getting up in the morning

Correct Answer: 2
Topic: Therapeutic Relationships
Step of the Nursing Process: All Phases of the Nursing Process
Cognitive Level: Application
Difficulty: Moderate
Rationale: The nurse needs to remain emotionally objective in a relationship with a client.

9. In the pre-interaction phase of the nurse–client relationship:
   1) Professional goals are communicated directly to the client
   2) The content of the interaction is vital, and the environment has little importance
   3) The client is not part of this phase of the interaction
   4) It is the nurse's knowledge of principles and responsibilities that guarantees a successful relationship

Correct Answer: 3
Topic: Pre-interaction Phase
Step of the Nursing Process: Assessment
Cognitive Level: Comprehension
Difficulty: Moderate
Rationale: During the pre-interaction phase, the nurse develops the physical and psychological environment for the interaction.

10. Which of the following is a nontherapeutic statement during the orientation phase of a relationship?
    1) "I am the nurse who will be caring for you today."
    2) "My job is to make you better."
    3) "I will be talking with you while I provide care."
    4) "You will be receiving care from an assistant and myself."

Correct Answer: 2
Topic: Orientation Phase
Step of the Nursing Process: Assessment
Cognitive Level: Application
Difficulty: Moderate
Rationale: This is a nontherapeutic statement. The nurse's role is to assist the client to achieve mutually defined goals.

11. The nurse practices nondirective listening during which of the following phases of the nurse–client relationship?
    1) Orientation
    2) Pre-interaction
    3) Termination
    4) Working

Correct Answer: 1
Topic: Phases of the Nurse–Client Relationship
Step of the Nursing Process: Assessment
Cognitive Level: Knowledge
Difficulty: Easy
Rationale: The nurse listens attentively to incorporate sensory data with verbal information.

12. According to Peplau, which of the following is the engagement phase of the relationship?
    1) The client explores thoughts, feelings, and ideas
    2) The nurse meets the client
    3) The client's problems are identified
    4) The nurse evaluates what the client has said

Correct Answer: 1
Topic: Nurse–Client Relationship
Step of the Nursing Process: Implementation
Cognitive Level: Application
Difficulty: Moderate
Rationale: Exploration occurs during the identification component of the working phase after trust has been established.

13. During which of the following phases of the nurse–client relationship does the client become more self-directing?
    1) Orientation
    2) Pre-interaction
    3) Identification
    4) Exploitation

Correct Answer: 4
Topic: Phases of the Nurse–Client Relationship
Step of the Nursing Process: Implementation
Cognitive Level: Application
Difficulty: Easy
Rationale: The nurse assists the client in using resources to resolve issues.

14. Which stage of the nursing process corresponds with the exploitation part of the working phase of the therapeutic relationship?

    1) Diagnosis
    2) Assessment
    3) Implementation
    4) Planning

Correct Answer: 3
Topic: Therapeutic Relationship
Step of the Nursing Process: Implementation
Cognitive Level: Comprehension
Difficulty: Moderate
Rationale: The exploitation phase corresponds to the implementation phase of the nursing process in which nurses assist clients in using resources to resolve issues.

15. When does the nurse first start planning for termination of the nurse–client relationship?
    1) From the initial encounter
    2) After goals have been achieved
    3) When the client so desires
    4) During the working phase of the relationship

Correct Answer: 1
Topic: Termination Phase of the Nurse–Client Relationship
Step of the Nursing Process: Evaluation
Cognitive Level: Knowledge
Difficulty: Easy
Rationale: Preparation for termination begins during the orientation phase, when the nurse explains the time, duration, and focus of the relationship.

16. The difference between therapeutic communication and social communication is:
    1) Enjoyment
    2) Amount of listening
    3) Worth to participants
    4) Focus

Correct Answer: 4
Topic: Therapeutic Communication
Step of the Nursing Process: All Phases of the Nursing Process
Cognitive Level: Comprehension
Difficulty: Easy
Rationale: Therapeutic communication has a specific purpose and a health-related goal.

17. Which of the following is true about the helping relationship?

1) Understanding should always be put into words
2) Both parties have equal responsibility for the relationship
3) Self-disclosure for both parties is expected
4) Understanding does not always have to be put into words

Correct Answer: 1

Topic: Helping Relationship
Step of the Nursing Process: All Phases of the Nursing Process
Cognitive Level: Knowledge
Difficulty: Moderate
Rationale: Understanding should be put into words to avoid misinterpretation.

CHAPTER 6

Bridges and Barriers in the Therapeutic Relationship

1. Which of the following describes caring?
   1) It is difficult to demonstrate professionally
   2) It is an ethical responsibility
   3) It is an intuitive process
   4) It is not influenced by past experience

Correct Answer: 2
Topic: Caring
Step of the Nursing Process: All Phases of the Nursing Process
Cognitive Level: Comprehension
Difficulty: Moderate
Rationale: Caring is a part of nursing ethics.

2. Which of the following should be achieved first in establishing the nurse–client relationship?
   1) Trust
   2) Empathy
   3) Mutuality
   4) Empowerment

Correct Answer: 1
Topic: Nurse–Client Relationship
Step of the Nursing Process: All Phases of the Nursing Process
Cognitive Level: Comprehension
Difficulty: Easy
Rationale: Trust must be established before a therapeutic relationship can develop.

3. Acknowledgment of the message and obvious feelings occur during which level of empathy?
   1) Level 1
   2) Level 2
   3) Level 3
   4) Level 4

Correct Answer: 4

Topic: Empathy
Step of the Nursing Process: All Phases of the Nursing Process
Cognitive Level: Knowledge
Difficulty: Easy
Rationale: Acknowledgment of the message and obvious feelings demonstrates the nurse's willingness to care about client's concerns.

4. Which of the following describes mutual goals? Mutuality is based on:
   1) client goals
   2) interdisciplinary health team goals
   3) the nurse's goals
   4) the physician's goals

Correct Answer: 1
Topic: Mutuality
Step of the Nursing Process: Planning
Cognitive Level: Comprehension
Difficulty: Moderate
Rationale: Mutuality means that both client and nurse are committed to enhancing the client's well-being based on client goals, not on goals of the health team, nurse, or physician.

5. Which of the following is a violation of client confidentiality?
   1) Sharing of information about communicable disease
   2) Reporting a client's problem during a change of shift
   3) Photographing a client wound to monitor the healing process
   4) Recording another client's behavior in the client's health record

Correct Answer: 4
Topic: Confidentiality
Step of the Nursing Process: All Phases of the Nursing Process
Cognitive Level: Analysis
Difficulty: Moderate
Rationale: Having a co-client named in another client's chart is a violation of confidentiality.

6. Bias begins with which of the following?
    1) Stereotyping during early education
    2) Family and early childhood experiences
    3) Limited contact with other cultures
    4) Uncomfortable experiences with culturally diverse clients

Correct Answer: 2
Topic: Bias
Step of the Nursing Process: All Phases of the Nursing Process
Cognitive Level: Knowledge
Difficulty: Moderate
Rationale: Biases are learned during childhood and are reinforced by life experiences.

7. Which of the following describes proxemics? Study of:
    1) the relationship between the message and the topic at hand
    2) implied meanings within individuals
    3) the use of space by humans
    4) the emotional personal space boundary

Correct Answer: 3
Topic: Proxemics
Step of the Nursing Process: All Phases of the Nursing Process
Cognitive Level: Knowledge
Difficulty: Easy
Rationale: Proxemics is the study of an individual's use of space.

8. Which of the following is a barrier to communication?
    1) Past experiences
    2) Unconditional acceptance
    3) Self-awareness
    4) Gender differences

Correct Answer: 1
Topic: Barriers to Communication

Step of the Nursing Process: All Phases of the Nursing Process
Cognitive Level: Comprehension
Difficulty: Moderate
Rationale: The ability to become a caring professional is influenced by past experience.

9. Which of the following is true about trust?
    1) The sender feels it
    2) It is difficult to demonstrate professionally
    3) It is an intuitive process
    4) The receiver feels it

Correct Answer: 4
Topic: Trust
Step of the Nursing Process: All Phases of the Nursing Process
Cognitive Level: Comprehension
Difficulty: Easy
Rationale: With development of interpersonal trust, the client feels safe.

10. Which of the following is an appropriate "I" statement?
    1) "Mr. Jones, I think you should go to bed now."
    2) "Mr. Jones, I would like you to go to bed now."
    3) "Mr. Jones, I don't think you should sit in the chair."
    4) "Mr. Jones, I thought we agreed that you would return to bed at this time."

Correct Answer: 4
Topic: "I" Statements
Step of the Nursing Process: Interventions
Cognitive Level: Application
Difficulty: Moderate
Rationale: This statement demonstrates mutuality; the nurse and client have collaborated to set a goal.

11. Upon entering the room, Rachel Singh, RN, finds her client, Mabel Brown, standing in the middle of the room wringing her hands. Nurse Singh notices that Mabel has put her street clothes on over her pajamas. On further examination, it is noted that Mabel is pale and hyperventilating with elevated vital signs. Which level of anxiety is Mabel experiencing?
    1) Mild
    2) Moderate

3)   Severe
4)   Panic
Correct Answer: 3
Topic: Anxiety
Step of the Nursing Process: Assessment
Cognitive Level: Analysis
Difficulty: Moderate
Rationale: Signs of severe anxiety include elevated vital signs, impaired problem-solving, and confused mental state.

12. Which of the following situations is an example of the nurse's use of empathy?
    1)   Setting up a rehabilitation placement for a client addicted to heroin
    2)   Sitting quietly holding a client's hand while she cries following the news that she has inoperable cancer
    3)   Giving a bed bath to a client who suffers from a right-sided cerebrovascular accident (CVA)
    4)   Telling a client all about the fun you had last night at one of the local clubs
Correct Answer: 2
Topic: Empathy
Step of the Nursing Process: Implementation
Cognitive Level: Application
Difficulty: Hard
Rationale: The nurse is offering the client time and attention as well as validation and touch.

13. John Adams, RN, knocks on the client's door and waits for her to answer before entering the room. He is demonstrating:
    1)   Nonverbal communication skills
    2)   Respect for the client's personal space
    3)   Respect for the client's confidentiality
    4)   Respect for the client's gender difference
Correct Answer: 2
Topic: Personal Space

Step of the Nursing Process: All Phases of the Nursing Process
Cognitive Level: Application
Difficulty: Moderate
Rationale: Giving warning before entering a client's room demonstrates respect for personal space.

14. Which of the following is true regarding personal space?
    1)   Individuals living in a Western culture need 40 square feet of personal space
    2)   Women need more space than men do
    3)   People need less space when they are anxious
    4)   The elderly need more control over their space
Correct Answer: 4
Topic: Personal Space
Step of the Nursing Process: All Phases of the Nursing Process
Cognitive Level: Knowledge
Difficulty: Easy
Rationale: The elderly need control over personal space, specifically over human touch.

15. Which of the following is not a step in the caring process?
    1)   Acknowledging the client's point of view
    2)   Assisting the client to problem-solve
    3)   Showing an intent to care
    4)   Assisting the client to understand the expectations of the health care team
Correct Answer: 4
Topic: Caring Process
Step of the Nursing Process: All Phases of the Nursing Process
Cognitive Level: Application
Difficulty: Easy
Rationale: The nurse needs to respond to the client's expectations for health care.

CHAPTER 7
Role Relationship Patterns

1. Which of the following case examples represents role relationship?
   1) Janice is the supervisor for a group of 50 people
   2) Melissa is a 20-year-old college student
   3) Andy is a 15-year-old who lives with his mother, grandmother, and two brothers
   4) John is a 20-year-old who lives alone

Correct Answer: 3
Topic: Role Relationship
Step of the Nursing Process: All Phases of the Nursing Process
Cognitive Level: Comprehension
Difficulty: Moderate
Rationale: Role relationship refers to human connections with others.

2. Which aspect of role reflects self-worth?
   1) Role transition
   2) Role performance
   3) Role relationship
   4) Role socialization

Correct Answer: 2
Topic: Role
Step of the Nursing Process: All Phases of the Nursing Process
Cognitive Level: Knowledge
Difficulty: Easy
Rationale: Role performance is important in defining identity and self-worth.

3. Anne Jones, age 45, is admitted to the psychiatric unit with a diagnosis of major depression. During the nursing assessment, it is discovered that Anne's symptoms started soon after her youngest child left for college. This situation is an example of:
   1) Role performance
   2) Role transition
   3) Role relationship
   4) Role stress

Correct Answer: 2
Topic: Role Relationship Patterns
Step of the Nursing Process: All Phases of the Nursing Process

Cognitive Level: Application
Difficulty: Moderate
Rationale: Role transition occurs when developmental life crises alter role function.

4. Tom Green, RN, has been practicing as a nurse for 4 years on a psychogeriatric unit. While assessing an elderly client admitted for psychosis, he discovers that the client has a history of breast cancer and no prior psychiatric history. He immediately notifies the medical physician and orders copies of recent test results that were performed at another facility. According to Benner, Tom is practicing at which developmental stage of proficiency?
   1) Advanced beginner
   2) Competency
   3) Proficiency
   4) Expert

Correct Answer: 3
Topic: Professional Role Development
Step of the Nursing Process: Assessment
Cognitive Level: Application
Difficulty: Hard
Rationale: The proficiency stage marks the transition from novice to expert and occurs approximately 3 to 5 years into practice.

5. Burnout is another name for:
   1) Role pressure
   2) Role ambiguity
   3) Role transition
   4) Role stress

Correct Answer: 4
Topic: Role Stress
Step of the Nursing Process: All Phases of the Nursing Process
Cognitive Level: Knowledge
Difficulty: Easy
Rationale: Overtime role stress leads to burnout.

6. Jane White, RN, has been up all night with her sick daughter. She leaves the child with the babysitter and goes into work because she

knows that the unit is already short-staffed. Jane suffers from:

1) Role ambiguity
2) Role conflict
3) Role pressures
4) Burnout

Correct Answer: 2
Topic: Role Stress
Step of the Nursing Process: All Phases of the Nursing Process
Cognitive Level: Application
Difficulty: Moderate
Rationale: Role conflict can occur when the nurse feels torn between multiple life roles.

7. Greg Chin, RN, decides that he will sign up to attend a diabetes workshop after a client was admitted to the unit with an insulin pump that was unfamiliar to Greg. This is an example of:

1) Role performance
2) Client advocacy
3) Role responsibility
4) Professional self-awareness

Correct Answer: 4
Topic: Professional Nursing Roles
Step of the Nursing Process: All Phases of the Nursing Process
Cognitive Level: Application
Difficulty: Moderate
Rationale: Self-awareness allows the nurse to recognize continuing education needs.

8. George, age 45, sustained a back injury in an auto accident, resulting in disability status regarding his job as a truck driver. As his nurse, what would you say to help George identify skills transferable to a future position?

1) "I am sorry to learn about your job loss."
2) "Your wife stated that you were a reliable, trustworthy worker."
3) "Think of your strengths associated with your previous job position."
4) "The career office really considers you employable."

Correct Answer: 3
Topic: Implementation
Step of the Nursing Process: Implementation
Cognitive Level: Analysis
Difficulty: Hard

Rationale: Personal strengths are unique traits that can be transferred to other positions.

9. Nurse Beam offers the George family a list of community resources and support groups and encourages them to become involved in the local lupus chapter. This is an example of which professional nursing role responsibility?

1) Client advocate role
2) Teaching role
3) Caregiver role
4) Consultant role

Correct Answer: 1
Topic: Professional Role Responsibility
Step of the Nursing Process: Implementation
Cognitive Level: Application
Difficulty: Moderate
Rationale: Nurses use the client advocate role by motivating clients to become informed, active participants in their health care.

10. Mrs. Edmunds, age 80, has a fractured hip. During your first meeting, she asks you about the nature of her condition? Your response:

1) "You have a fractured femur," stated in a loud voice
2) "You will have to speak to your physician about your diagnosis."
3) "Do you wish to call your son to discuss it with him, since he talked with the doctor?"
4) "When you fell at home, you broke your hip."

Correct Answer: 4
Topic: Client's Rights
Step of the Nursing Process: Implementation
Cognitive Level: Application
Difficulty: Hard
Rationale: The patient has the right to obtain understandable information concerning diagnosis from direct caregivers.

11. Nurse Green, RN, is conducting an interview with the Albert family. Mr. Albert has just been diagnosed with Alzheimer's disease. Nurse Green wants to assess family role relationships. What would be an appropriate question?

1) "What are your likes and dislikes?"
2) "Who assumes responsibility for decision-making?"
3) "How would you describe your job?"

4) "How do you like to be treated?"
Correct Answer: 2
Topic: Role Relationships
Step of the Nursing Process: Assessment
Cognitive Level: Analysis
Difficulty: Moderate
Rationale: It is important to assess the impact on the family of the illness. It is necessary to find out who is the decision-maker in the family. If it is the client, that will have more of an impact on the family.

12. Caring, generosity, and compassion represent essential values associated with:
    1) Aesthetics
    2) Altruism
    3) Justice
    4) Truth
Correct Answer: 2
Topic: Professionalism
Step of the Nursing Process: All Phases of the Nursing Process
Cognitive Level: Knowledge
Difficulty: Easy
Rationale: Altruism represents concern for the welfare of others.

13. Nancy Jones, RN, observes the unit housekeeper giving her name and phone number to a client. Nancy reports this incidence to her clinical manager. This is an example of which essential value of truth?
    1) Maintaining confidentiality
    2) Allocating resources fairly
    3) Obtaining sufficient data before reporting infractions of policies
    4) Safeguarding the individual's right to privacy
Correct Answer: 3
Topic: Professional Behaviors
Step of the Nursing Process: Intervention
Cognitive Level: Application
Difficulty: Moderate
Rationale: This is a behavior reflecting the essential value of truth. The nurse in this situation is protecting the client from possible exploitation by the employee.

14. Which of the following is a nursing diagnosis associated with alteration in self-concept/role performance?
    1) Sleep pattern disturbance
    2) Anticipatory grieving
    3) Altered thought processes
    4) Impaired communication
Correct Answer: 2
Topic: Self-Concept
Step of the Nursing Process: Diagnosis
Cognitive Level: Comprehension
Difficulty: Moderate
Rationale: Anticipatory and dysfunctional grieving are associated with self-concept/role performance.

15. Mr. Sterling's wife, Beth, died 18 months ago. The Sterlings had been married for 40 years. Since her death, Mr. Sterling has stopped all social contacts, isolates himself in his apartment, and says he would like to go to sleep and not wake up. A nursing diagnosis for Mr. Sterling related to self-concept might be:
    1) Hopelessness related to death of spouse
    2) Ineffective coping related to loss of spouse, as evidenced by isolation, hopelessness
    3) Loss of spouse resulting in dysfunctional grieving and suicidal ideation
    4) Isolation and hopelessness related to death of spouse
Correct Answer: 2
Topic: Alteration in Self-Concept/Role Performance
Step of the Nursing Process: Diagnosis
Cognitive Level: Analysis
Difficulty: Hard
Rationale: The problem in Mr. Sterling's case is his inability to cope since his wife's death.

CHAPTER 8

The Grief Experience: Life's Losses and Endings

1. Which of the following statements is true about grief and loss?
    1) Not all losses produce grief
    2) Feelings associated with various losses differ
    3) Grief is a normal response to loss
    4) Grief follows a predictable pattern in stages

    Correct Answer: 3
    Topic: Grief and Loss
    Step of the Nursing Process: All Phases of the Nursing Process
    Cognitive Level: Comprehension
    Difficulty: Moderate
    Rationale: Grief is a normal human response to the stress of losing something.

2. Anticipatory grief:
    1) Has the same characteristics as actual grief
    2) Is more stable than actual grief
    3) Can be completed as a process
    4) Includes hope that loss will not occur

    Correct Answer: 4
    Topic: Anticipatory Grief
    Step of the Nursing Process: All Phases of the Nursing Process
    Cognitive Level: Comprehension
    Difficulty: Easy
    Rationale: With anticipatory grief, there is always the hope that the anticipated loss will not occur.

3. You are caring for Mr. Ramos, who is expected to die within a month. He states, "I can't go on anymore, help me!" You know Mr. Ramos is in the _____ stage of dying.
    1) Anger
    2) Denial
    3) Acceptance
    4) Depression

    Correct Answer: 4
    Topic: Stages of Death and Dying
    Step of the Nursing Process: Assessment
    Cognitive Level: Analysis
    Difficulty: Easy
    Rationale: Clients in this stage recognize and grieve their losses.

4. Which of the following does not fall under the category of complicated grief?
    1) Somatization disorder
    2) Chronic sorrow
    3) Chronic grief
    4) Absent grief

    Correct Answer: 2
    Topic: Complicated Grief
    Step of the Nursing Process: All Phases of the Nursing Process
    Cognitive Level: Comprehension
    Difficulty: Easy
    Rationale: Chronic sorrow is a normal response to an ongoing loss such as chronic illness. It differs from chronic grief, which results in dysfunctional behavior such as attempts to keep the dead person alive.

5. Mr. Hamilton has been given 6 months to live after being told he has stage 4 cancer of the lung. Evidence that he is in the bargaining stage of death and dying is expressed by:
    1) "Not me"
    2) "Why me?"
    3) "Yes, me"
    4) "Let me"

    Correct Answer: 4
    Topic: Stages of Grieving and Death and Dying
    Step of the Nursing Process: All Phases of the Nursing Process
    Cognitive Level: Application
    Difficulty: Moderate
    Rationale: This option represents the bargaining stage, in which the client bargains with God ("If you'll just *let me* live longer, I'll...").

6. Joy Chow has just received the biopsy reports that indicate recurrence of breast cancer. The response indicating the acceptance stage of death and dying would be:
    1) "The test results are incredible."
    2) "The test results are positive."
    3) "The test results are negative."
    4) "The test results will be repeated next week."

Correct Answer: 2
Topic: Stages of Death and Dying
Step of the Nursing Process: All Phases of the Nursing Process
Cognitive Level: Application
Difficulty: Moderate
Rationale: This response indicates that the client has accepted the inevitable.

7. Stoicism and denial of grief are examples of how _____ can affect family coping with death:
    1) Kübler-Ross
    2) Culture
    3) Developmental level
    4) Prior experience

Correct Answer: 2
Topic: Culture
Step of the Nursing Process: All Phases of the Nursing Process
Cognitive Level: Knowledge
Difficulty: Moderate
Rationale: The American culture does not value "falling apart" during times of grief, but values stoicism and a general denial of grief. Stoicism and denial of grief are examples of cultural influences.

8. Bruce Green has just been transferred to your facility from another hospital at his insistence. He is demanding a second opinion because he feels that "they must have made a mistake." As his nurse, you know that the best communication technique to use with Mr. Green is to:
    1) Clarify the client's response
    2) Reflect the client's behavior
    3) Summarize the client's behavior
    4) Acknowledge the client's feelings

Correct Answer: 2
Topic: Denial
Step of the Nursing Process: All Phases of the Nursing Process
Cognitive Level: Application
Difficulty: Moderate
Rationale: An important skill for the nurse is to be able to take the client's position. This is not the time to promote change. Denial is a coping mechanism being used by this client.

9. You are seeing 8-year-old Billy in the nurse's office at school because he received a bloody nose in a scuffle with another child while playing at recess. You discover that Billy's parents have recently divorced. You know that:
    1) Billy still has both parents and should not be experiencing a sense of loss
    2) Billy has gotten over his grief because he is able to play outside
    3) Billy needs to be referred for grief counseling
    4) Billy's behavior is expected

Correct Answer: 4
Topic: Bereavement and the Family System
Step of the Nursing Process: Assessment
Cognitive Level: Analysis
Difficulty: Moderate
Rationale: Children often show anger and acting-out behavior in response to a significant loss.

10. In evaluating care of dying clients, the nurse knows that her interventions have been unsuccessful if the:
    1) client does not get past the stage of denial
    2) client dies in peace surrounded by loved ones
    3) client died in pain
    4) nurse refused to allow the client to be sad

Correct Answer: 4
Topic: Role of Nurses Working with Dying Clients
Step of the Nursing Process: Evaluation
Cognitive Level: Comprehension
Difficulty: Moderate
Rationale: The client needs to be sad and cry. If the nurse assumes that it is bad for the client to be sad, the client may smile to keep the nurse happy and thus be blocked from expressing true feelings.

11. You have been caring for 15-year-old Tara, who is dying. She states to you, "I know I am not going home again. I think it is harder for my parents than me. Will you talk to them for me?" Which of the following is the best response?
    1) "It is true that you will be dying soon, but you must be honest with your parents."
    2) "That's not true, but I will talk to your parents."

3) "You are having a bad day, so I will be back later to see if you need anything else."

4) "Yes, I will talk to your parents, but you need to talk to them also. I will help you with that."

Correct Answer: 4
Topic: Roles of Nurses Working with Dying Clients
Step of the Nursing Process: Intervention
Cognitive Level: Analysis
Difficulty: Moderate
Rationale: The nurse may need to help families talk about the child's terminal illness.

12. Which of the following is an inappropriate intervention for termination of the nurse–client relationship?

1) Allow client to express their feelings

2) To avoid upsetting the client, the nurse keeps her feelings to herself

3) Examine negative components of the relationship

4) Identifying client's support system

Correct Answer: 2
Topic: Termination of the Nurse–Client Relationship
Step of the Nursing Process: Implementation
Cognitive Level: Comprehension
Difficulty: Moderate
Rationale: It is important for the nurse to share constructive feelings with the client.

13. An appreciative client offers Jane Green, a professional nurse, a beautiful bracelet. Jane knows she must handle gift-giving by:

1) Adhering to the policy of the facility

2) Refusing to accept the bracelet in a gentle, tactful manner

3) Accept or refuse based on the uniqueness of the relationship

4) Accept the gift, but also remind the client of intangible gifts

Correct Answer: 3
Topic: Termination
Step of the Nursing Process: Evaluation
Cognitive Level: Application
Difficulty: Moderate
Rationale: Accepting or refusing a gift involves judgment and being true to what you know or feel about a client.

14. Brian Smith, RN, has been working in a long-term care facility for several years. He and his wife are moving to another state. He knows that his role in dealing with the termination of his relationship with his clients is to:

1) Prepare clients for termination

2) Inform clients that he will "keep in touch"

3) Instruct clients that they have benefited from the relationship

4) Discuss feelings with clients during the last encounter

Correct Answer: 1
Topic: Termination
Step of the Nursing Process: Implementation
Cognitive Level: Application
Difficulty: Moderate
Rationale: Clients need to be adequately prepared for termination well in advance.

15. How does use of the nursing process differ during the termination phase of the nurse–client relationship from other health care situations?

1) Assessment

2) Diagnosis

3) Planning

4) Intervention

Correct Answer: 3
Topic: Termination of the Nurse–Client Relationship
Step of the Nursing Process: Planning
Cognitive Level: Comprehension
Difficulty: Moderate
Rationale: Some of the objectives and plans for termination are decided independently by the nurse, not mutually with the client.

16. Joyce Li is suffering from anxiety related to the impending termination of the relationship with her nurse, Betsy. An effective nursing intervention used by Betsy would be to:

1) Analyze the accuracy in assessing the client's feelings about impending termination

2) Allow the client to express fears related to impending termination

3) Request that the client report when there is a decrease in anxiety

4) Determine client's self-care deficit related to termination

Correct Answer: 2

Topic: Losses and Endings
Step of the Nursing Process: Implementation
Cognitive Level: Analysis
Difficulty: Hard
Rationale: An important intervention is to allow clients to express their feelings.

17. Anne Jones, student nurse, has finished her rotation on the outpatient psychiatric unit. Her client, Betty Burk, diagnosed with borderline personality disorder, comes into the clinic displaying superficial scratches to both forearms. Which of the following is a nursing diagnosis for Betty related to losses and endings in the nurse–client relationship?
    1) Noncompliance about impending termination of nurse–client relationship
    2) Knowledge deficit about impending termination of nurse–client relationship
    3) Self-care deficit related to impending termination of nurse–client relationship
    4) Anxiety related to the impending termination of nurse–client relationship
Correct Answer: 4
Topic: Losses and Endings
Step of the Nursing Process: Diagnosis
Cognitive Level: Analysis
Difficulty: Hard
Rationale: The client's anxiety has led to the regression in her behavior.

CHAPTER 9
Communication Styles

1. Which of the following is a description of meta-communication?
    1) Communication style
    2) Nonverbal communication
    3) Verbal communication
    4) Nonverbal and verbal communication
Correct Answer: 4
Topic: Communication Styles
Step of the Nursing Process: All Phases of the Nursing Process
Cognitive Level: Comprehension
Difficulty: Moderate
Rationale: Meta-communication refers to all the factors that influence how the message is perceived. It includes both verbal and nonverbal behaviors.

2. Greg Smith, RN, puts his arm around his elderly client when he assists her to transfer into the chair. The client may interpret this as:
    1) A positive gesture only
    2) A method of control
    3) Denotation
    4) Paralanguage
Correct Answer: 2
Topic: Nonverbal communication
Step of the Nursing Process: Implementation
Cognitive Level: Application
Difficulty: Moderate

Rationale: Touching a client can be interpreted as a means of control.

3. A description of denotative meaning is a:
    1) personalized meaning of a word or phrase
    2) meaning generally shared by individuals
    3) meaning shared by families
    4) meaning generally shared within a specific culture
Correct Answer: 2
Topic: Communication Styles
Step of the Nursing Process: All Phases of the Nursing Process
Cognitive Level: Knowledge
Difficulty: Easy
Rationale: Denotation reflects a generalized meaning assigned to a word.

4. When describing your client's symptoms of relapse to Dr. Singh, you say, "Bill stopped taking his medications last week, then hit the booze." Dr. Singh looks at you blankly. This is an example of:
    1) Connotation
    2) Information processing
    3) Time span between messages
    4) Nonverbal cultural variations

Correct Answer: 1
Topic: Communication Styles
Step of the Nursing Process: All Phases of the Nursing Process
Cognitive Level: Application
Difficulty: Moderate
Rationale: Connotation refers to the use of words in a personalized way that is culturally specific.

5. You are assigned to care for Mr. Green, a 45-year-old teacher with multiple sclerosis. Which communication behavior will have the most impact on Mr. Green?
   1) What you say
   2) Tone of voice
   3) Sense of confidence
   4) Eye contact
Correct Answer: 2
Topic: Communication Styles
Step of the Nursing Process: All Phases of the Nursing Process
Cognitive Level: Application
Difficulty: Moderate
Rationale: Tone of voice is important because it affects how the verbal message is interpreted. When tone of voice does not fit the words, the message is likely to be discounted.

6. The communication components are:
   1) Language, vocalization, and nonverbal messages
   2) Pitch, tone, and paralanguage
   3) Proxemics, touch, and kinesics
   4) Eye contact, facial expressions, and nonverbal messages
Correct Answer: 1
Topic: Communication Styles
Step of the Nursing Process: All Phases of the Nursing Process
Cognitive Level: Knowledge
Difficulty: Moderate
Rationale: Components of communication include verbal, nonverbal, and oral delivery of the message.

7. Most person-to-person communication is:
   1) Verbal
   2) Process
   3) Nonverbal
   4) Content

Correct Answer: 3
Topic: Communication Styles
Step of the Nursing Process: All Phases of the Nursing Process
Cognitive Level: Knowledge
Difficulty: Easy
Rationale: Most person-to-person communications are nonverbal. Actions speak louder than words.

8. In response to your question, "How are you?", Mary states, ""I am fine." As she turns away, you note that she is crying. This is an example of:
   1) Nonverbal communication
   2) Incongruence
   3) Proxemics
   4) Congruence
Correct Answer: 2
Topic: Communication Styles
Step of the Nursing Process: All Phases of the Nursing Process
Cognitive Level: Application
Difficulty: Easy
Rationale: When nonverbal and verbal cues do not match, this is known as incongruence.

9. Mr. Lombardi, age 55, responds to questions inappropriately. The nurse should do which of the following?
   1) Assume that Mr. Lombardi is depressed and seek further information
   2) Ask other staff members whether Mr. Lombardi is sick
   3) Leave Mr. Lombardi alone for now and return to reassess
   4) Observe Mr. Lombardi's nonverbal behavior
Correct Answer: 4
Topic: Nonverbal Communication
Step of the Nursing Process: Assessment
Cognitive Level: Application
Difficulty: Moderate
Rationale: Nonverbal communication can be used to make accurate inferences about a person.

10. You are assigned to care for Mrs. Wilson, an 84-year-old woman who has suffered a right-sided stroke. Which of the following nonverbal behaviors should you consider using?

1) Facial expression
2) Tone of voice
3) Touch
4) Sense of confidence

Correct Answer: 3
Topic: Communication Styles
Step of the Nursing Process: Implementation
Cognitive Level: Application
Difficulty: Moderate
Rationale: Touch is one of the most powerful ways to communicate nonverbally. It is particularly useful with elderly clients, who may have decreased visual and auditory acuity or other sensory deprivations.

11. When performing an assessment on your newly admitted client, you as the nurse want to determine the client's response to touch. You would:
    1) Touch the client
    2) Use timing with touch
    3) Ask the client
    4) Shake the client's hand

Correct Answer: 3
Topic: Communication Styles
Step of the Nursing Process: Assessment
Cognitive Level: Application
Difficulty: Moderate
Rationale: It is important to obtain the client's permission to be touched because the interpretation of touch varies across culture and gender.

12. Which of the following is an example of expressive touch?
    1) Giving a client a bath
    2) Holding a client's hand
    3) Taking a client's temperature
    4) Giving a client a back rub

Correct Answer: 2
Topic: Nonverbal Communication
Step of the Nursing Process: Implementation
Cognitive Level: Application
Difficulty: Easy
Rationale: Holding a client's hand is a form of therapeutic nonverbal communication.

13. Your client, Jim, states that he is feeling fine, yet you observe that he has a tense body posture and a frown on his face. You infer that

he is experiencing pain, you are able to make this inference by knowledge of:
1) Confirming responses
2) Denotation
3) Proxemics
4) Kinesics

Correct Answer: 4
Topic: Nonverbal Communication
Step of the Nursing Process: Assessment
Cognitive Level: Application
Difficulty: Moderate
Rationale: The nurse was able to observe the patient's body language to infer pain.

14. In relation to gender differences in communication, which of the following are true?
    1) Men use more verbal communication in interpersonal relationships
    2) Women smile more often
    3) Men require less personal space than women
    4) Men have a greater range of vocal pitch

Correct Answer: 2
Topic: Gender Differences
Step of the Nursing Process: All Phases of the Nursing Process
Cognitive Level: Comprehension
Difficulty: Moderate
Rationale: Women smile more often and generally use more facial expressions than men when communicating.

15. Social cognitive competency refers to:
    1) The ability to use verbal and nonverbal interventions
    2) Understanding the relationships between the roles of the sender and receiver
    3) Being able to embrace the client's perspective
    4) Interpreting the emotional content by observing body language

Correct Answer: 3
Topic: Interpersonal Competence
Step of the Nursing Process: All Phases of the Nursing Process
Cognitive Level: Knowledge
Difficulty: Moderate
Rationale: Social; cognitive competence is the ability to interpret from the point of view of each of the participants.

16. Which of the following messages would validate the worth of the individual?
    1) The nurse says, "Take that tray to 6 bed 2"
    2) "I want to know about your physical symptoms following the chemotherapy"
    3) "Now dear, we are going to have a nice bath"
    4) "I would like to meet your family, and we could talk to them about your after care"

Correct Answer: 4
Topic: Validation of Individual Worth
Step of the Nursing Process: All Phases of the Nursing Process
Cognitive Level: Application
Difficulty: Moderate
Rationale: Getting to know the client's family is a confirming message to the client.

CHAPTER 10

Developing Therapeutic Communication Skills in the Nurse–Client Relationship

1. You organize your assignment so that you can spend time with your client who has just found out about his positive HIV status. You know that the interaction should focus on:
    1) Professional needs
    2) The client's progress towards wellness
    3) Your progress in carrying out the treatment plan
    4) The client's needs

Correct Answer: 4
Topic: Therapeutic Communication
Step of the Nursing Process: All Phases of the Nursing Process
Cognitive Level: Application
Difficulty: Easy
Rationale: All therapeutic communication must focus on client needs.

2. The nurse demonstrates that she understands the concept of *attending behaviors* by being aware of:
    1) the impact of your communication on others
    2) the client's verbal and nonverbal communication
    3) barriers to effective communication
    4) the use of medical terminology and cultural meanings

Correct Answer: 2
Topic: Attending Behaviors
Step of the Nursing Process: All Phases of the Nursing Process
Cognitive Level: Application

Difficulty: Moderate
Rationale: Attending behaviors refer to the nurse's focus on the client with the purpose of understanding their situation, the nurse uses meta-communication and minimal verbal cues. The nurse "listens" to the client.

3. You are caring for Melissa, a 15-year-old client suffering from acute leukemia. You want to actively listen to her concerns and understand her meanings. You know that a barrier to active listening is:
    1) Nonjudgmental behavior
    2) Treatment-centered behavior
    3) Dependent behavior
    4) Individualized behavior

Correct Answer: 2
Topic: Barrier to Active Listening
Step of the Nursing Process: Implementation
Cognitive Level: Application
Difficulty: Moderate
Rationale: The nurse can become preoccupied with physical care, and this acts as a barrier to active listening.

4. What is the most common cause of communication breakdown in a nurse–client relationship?
    1) Timing
    2) Changing the subject
    3) Interrupting
    4) Listening skills

Correct Answer: 4
Topic: Attending Behavior
Step of the Nursing Process: All Phases of the Nursing Process
Cognitive Level: Comprehension
Difficulty: Moderate
Rationale: Barriers to active listening skills can result from the nurse or client factors. Examples of this are preoccupation, personal insecurity, and discomfort.

5. You enter the client's room with the intent of allowing the client to express her feelings in relating to her cancer diagnosis. You notice that she is crying and clutching her incision line. After validating physical discomfort, you:
    1) Administer an analgesic and postpone the interaction
    2) Sit with her and hold her hand
    3) Explain that pain is expected following surgery but that it is important to move around to avoid complications
    4) Acknowledge the pain, but state that you are there to address her emotional pain

Correct Answer: 1
Topic: Barriers to Active Listening
Step of the Nursing Process: All Phases of the Nursing Process
Cognitive Level: Analysis
Difficulty: Moderate
Rationale: Physical discomfort can halt communication. The nurse needs to address the client's pain before attempting other interventions.

6. Shirley Hunt, RN, is conducting a medication education group for mentally ill clients. One of the clients states, "I don't think everyone needs medications. What about psychotherapy? Can you tell me about that?" What is an appropriate response by the nurse?
    1) Talk to the group about the benefits of psychotherapy
    2) Tell the group that psychotherapy is ineffective and that they need medication
    3) Acknowledge the question, but explain the time limitations and that the focus of this particular group is medication education
    4) Explain that it is the physician's decision as to the type of treatment modality for each client

Correct Answer: 3
Topic: Active Listening
Step of the Nursing Process: Implementation
Cognitive Level: Application
Difficulty: Hard
Rationale: Using this response, the nurse is able to return to the focus of the topic under discussion.

7. Nurse Jones, RN, wants to teach her client, Mr. George, how to administer insulin and wants to find out his concerns about his newly diagnosed diabetes. She knows that the best method of communicating therapeutically with Mr. George is to:
    1) Talk to him in the visitors' lounge
    2) Talk to him within his personal space
    3) Communicate with him using touch
    4) Talk to him face to face at his bedside

Correct Answer: 4
Topic: Conditions that Influence Communication
Step of the Nursing Process: Implementation
Cognitive Level: Application
Difficulty: Moderate
Rationale: Facing the client while making direct eye contact fosters trust. The physical environment influences effective communication (too many distractions or not enough privacy).

8. Which of the following is the best sequence of communication techniques during an assessment interview? Begin with:
    1) Asking focused questions and closed-ended questions
    2) Giving information and proceeding to stating observations
    3) Broad leads and moving to listening techniques
    4) Giving information and moving to focused questions

Correct Answer: 3
Topic: Building Rapport
Step of the Nursing Process: Assessment
Cognitive Level: Application
Difficulty: Moderate
Rationale: A broad opening allows the client to tell his story without imposing the nurse's ideas. The nurse needs to concentrate on what is being said and to listen for key words and issues.

9. You ask your newly admitted client, "What can we do to help you?" You know that this open-ended question will:
   1) Put the client at ease
   2) Allow the client to answer the question
   3) Achieve unrestricted description by the client
   4) Result in specific information from the client

Correct Answer: 3
Topic: Open-Ended Questions
Step of the Nursing Process: All Phases of the Nursing Process
Cognitive Level: Application
Difficulty: Moderate
Rationale: Open-ended questions cannot be answered with a "yes" or "no." They allow the client to elaborate his issues.

10. Which of the following is the best questioning sequence during a client interview in which the client is communicative and not in an emergency situation? Start with:
    1) focused questions and proceed to open-ended questions
    2) open-ended questions and proceed to focused questions
    3) closed questions and proceed to open-ended questions
    4) open-ended questions and proceed to closed questions

Correct Answer: 2
Topic: Asking Questions
Step of the Nursing Process: Assessment
Cognitive Level: Application
Difficulty: Moderate
Rationale: Start with open-ended questions to allow the client to tell his story in his own way. Use focused questions to obtain more specific information.

11. Mabel Brown has been admitted for investigation of frequent falls. Which of the following is a circular question that you would ask Mabel?
    1) "Tell me more about your falls at home."
    2) "How will this hospitalization affect your family?"
    3) "Have you experienced dizziness and imbalance before?"
    4) "Can you tell me what brought you in?"

Correct Answer: 2
Topic: Circular Questions
Step of the Nursing Process: Assessment
Cognitive Level: Application
Difficulty: Moderate
Rationale: Circular questions focus on the context in which an illness occurs in relation to the impact on family members.

12. A client states, "I can't sleep all night because the nurses are noisy." Choose the response that represents the nurse's recognition of the client's theme.
    1) "I will speak to the supervisor about your complaint."
    2) "You cannot sleep because of the noise level at night."
    3) "You need to understand that nurses communicate with other clients during the night."
    4) "I will tell the night nurses that you complained."

Correct Answer: 2
Topic: Themes
Step of the Nursing Process: All Phases of the Nursing Process
Cognitive Level: Application
Difficulty: Moderate
Rationale: A theme is the underlying feeling associated with concrete facts. It refers to seeing the experience as the client sees it, not what causes it, why it exists, or what purpose it serves.

13. Your client tells you, "I have had surgery before but never this major. What if I cannot return to work and support my family?" Your response is, "You are wondering if the operation will affect your ability to assume your normal roles." This is an example of which therapeutic listening response?
    1) Clarification
    2) Paraphrasing
    3) Restatement
    4) Validation

Correct Answer: 2
Topic: Listening Responses
Step of the Nursing Process: All Phases of the Nursing Process
Cognitive Level: Application
Difficulty: Moderate

Rationale: Paraphrasing is a response whereby the nurse transforms the message into his or her own words without losing the meaning.

14. You are engaged in an assignment in which you must interview a fellow student for 30 minutes. This student talks about her career plans, possible jobs after graduation, and her part-time work. After 10 minutes, she has stopped and you both sit in silence. Which of the following would be the best response?
    1) "Tell me more about how you selected your career goals?"
    2) "Who is the most significant person in your life?"
    3) "What impact will these plans have on your life?"
    4) Remain silent until she breaks the silence

Correct Answer: 3
Topic: Communication Skills
Step of the Nursing Process: All Phases of the Nursing Process
Cognitive Level: Application
Difficulty: Hard
Rationale: A silent pause can be helpful, but long silences become uncomfortable. Asking a focused question allows the interviewer to obtain more specific information.

15. As you listen to a client, you need to provide feedback that is:
    1) Descriptive, general, and content-focused
    2) Client-focused, evaluative, and content-focused
    3) Well-timed, general, and descriptive
    4) Process-focused and descriptive

Correct Answer: 4
Topic: Feedback
Step of the Nursing Process: All Phases of the Nursing Process
Cognitive Level: Knowledge
Difficulty: Moderate
Rationale: Effective feedback is specific rather than general and descriptive rather than evaluative or judging.

16. Mary states to her nurse, Betty, "I am having a tough time, and I am scared about the future." Which of the following responses represents the best feedback by Betty?
    1) "I know what you mean."
    2) "You should do something about it."
    3) "I really don't think you are having a tough time."
    4) "You are having a tough time, and you are scared."

Correct Answer: 4
Topic: Feedback
Step of the Nursing Process: All Phases of the Nursing Process
Cognitive Level: Application
Difficulty: Moderate
Rationale: This feedback focuses on specific behaviors and is descriptive.

17. A client has just arrived in the emergency department following a motor vehicle accident. She is unconscious. You have to contact the family by telephone. You know that:
    1) You should refuse and have the physician make the call
    2) Keep the explanation simple and give plenty of details to reduce anxiety
    3) Tell them it is an emergency and to rush to the hospital
    4) Remain calm, give a brief, simple explanation of what has happened

Correct Answer: 4
Topic: Telephone Communication
Step of the Nursing Process: All Phases of the Nursing Process
Cognitive Level: Application
Difficulty: Moderate
Rationale: Details should not be given at this time. Communication is kept simple with clear directions as to the next step.

CHAPTER 11

Intercultural Communication

1. Cultural competence:
   1) Involves knowledge of standardized clinical nursing skills
   2) Requires careful reflection of one's own values
   3) Involves multilingualism
   4) Understanding that there are few individual differences within the same culture

   Correct Answer: 2
   Topic: Cultural Competence
   Step of the Nursing Process: All Phases of the Nursing Process
   Cognitive Level: Knowledge
   Difficulty: Moderate
   Rationale: Cultural competence starts with self-awareness.

2. Which of the following defines cultural diversity?
   1) Differences among cultural groups
   2) Cultures viewed as neither inferior nor superior to one another
   3) Distinguishing characteristics that differentiate a group from the predominant culture or society
   4) A heterogeneous society in which several diverse cultural world views can coexist

   Correct Answer: 1
   Topic: Cultural Diversity
   Step of the Nursing Process: All Phases of the Nursing Process
   Cognitive Level: Knowledge
   Difficulty: Easy
   Rationale: The nurse needs to recognize that there are significant variations within cultural groups.

3. Which of the following groups carries value-laden stereotypes?
   1) American Indians, African Americans, Sicilian Italians
   2) Teenaged mothers, the homeless, the elderly
   3) American Indians, African Americans, AIDS clients
   4) Hispanics, the homeless, African Americans

   Correct Answer: 2
   Topic: Stereotyping
   Step of the Nursing Process: All Phases of the Nursing Process
   Cognitive Level: Comprehension
   Difficulty: Easy
   Rationale: The belief that certain individuals or groups of people are inferior is a value-laden stereotype. Stereotypes can be applied to the disabled, to people of various races, and to the elderly.

4. When communicating with a client from Thailand, you know that it is best to:
   1) Use technical language appropriately
   2) Use client nodding as an indicator of understanding
   3) Ask the client several questions
   4) Allow time for the client to respond

   Correct Answer: 4
   Topic: Intercultural Communication
   Step of the Nursing Process: All Phases of the Nursing Process
   Cognitive Level: Application
   Difficulty: Moderate
   Rationale: Allowing time gives the client the opportunity to translate the message. It also helps to convey interest and respect and helps decrease anxiety.

5. Mrs. Lee is an Asian client who communicates with the nursing staff indirectly with a family member present. Which nursing diagnosis applies to this situation?
   1) Altered perception related to altered abstraction
   2) Noncompliance related to client's cultural influences
   3) Impaired verbal communication related to sociocultural dissonance
   4) Altered role performance related to illness

   Correct Answer: 3
   Topic: Language Barriers
   Step of the Nursing Process: Diagnosis
   Cognitive Level: Analysis
   Difficulty: Moderate

Rationale: The problem is that the client is unable to communicate directly with the nursing staff because of a language barrier.

6. You are doing an admission assessment on an Asian client. The intake includes a cultural assessment. You would ask the client:
    1) "Does a minister, priest, or rabbi visit you?"
    2) "Do you feel understood and loved?"
    3) "What language do you prefer to speak?"
    4) "Does life have meaning and value for you?"

Correct Answer: 3
Topic: Language Barriers
Step of the Nursing Process: Assessment
Cognitive Level: Application
Difficulty: Moderate
Rationale: It is important to assess the client's need for an interpreter and the need for communication strategies, such as pictures or flash cards.

7. Nurses can overcome the language barrier by:
    1) Speaking clearly
    2) Using long, simplified explanations
    3) Following up on client's "OK" responses
    4) Not shouting

Correct Answer: 3
Topic: Language Barrier
Step of the Nursing Process: Implementation
Cognitive Level: Comprehension
Difficulty: Moderate
Rationale: It is important to verify that the client understands the communication. Saying "OK" does not necessarily mean understanding.

8. You are caring for a Hispanic client. You need to communicate with the family about the client's illness. Which family member should you contact?
    1) Oldest female family member
    2) Oldest male family member
    3) Oldest daughter of client
    4) Oldest son of client

Correct Answer: 2
Topic: Level of Family Involvement
Step of the Nursing Process: All Phases of the Nursing Process
Cognitive Level: Application

Difficulty: Easy
Rationale: There is a sex-linked hierarchy in the Hispanic culture. The oldest male is the final authority on family matters.

9. Mr. Garcia, a Mexican American, has a standing weekly appointment for monitoring of his blood pressure. His appointment is for 9:30 a.m., but he shows up at 12:00 noon. An appropriate nursing diagnosis applicable to this situation would be:
    1) Noncompliance related to missing appointment
    2) Impaired verbal communication related to cultural dissonance
    3) Impaired social interaction related to sociocultural dissonance
    4) Impaired role performance related to client's value system

Correct Answer: 3
Topic: Time Orientation
Step of the Nursing Process: Diagnosis
Cognitive Level: Analysis
Difficulty: Moderate
Rationale: Many Mexican Americans believe that time is flexible and that commitment to an appointment is not as important as attending to what is happening in the moment. Western health care culture, on the other hand, values exact time frames for appointments. This situation illustrates a dissonance between the two cultures. The client was not noncompliant in missing the appointment; it was part of his cultural viewpoint that the time frame was flexible.

10. You are having a conversation with Mr. Wong, an Asian client. Which is the best response for communicating with him about his discomfort?
    1) "Tell me how to make you more comfortable."
    2) "Describe your position of greatest relief."
    3) "I will return to give you a pain medication."
    4) "I will roll your bed down and place a pillow between your legs."

Correct Answer: 1
Topic: Language Barrier
Step of the Nursing Process: Assessment
Cognitive Level: Application
Difficulty: Moderate

Rationale: It is important to speak clearly and use simple words. This question allows the client the opportunity to talk about traditional cultural treatments as well.

11. You are assigned to give a bed bath to Josie, a client who cannot speak English. Which of the following communication strategies should you use?
    1) Nonverbal communication
    2) Official interpreter
    3) Family member as interpreter
    4) Other staff member who speaks the same language

Correct Answer: 3
Topic: Use of Interpreter
Step of the Nursing Process: Implementation
Cognitive Level: Application
Difficulty: Moderate
Rationale: A family member as interpreter would be the first choice because he or she would understand dialect and subtle nuances of the culture. Also, because the situation described is personal and sensitive, a family member as interpreter would be more comfortable for the client.

12. Nurse Jones is caring for her postpartum client, an African American. Nurse Jones knows to use:
    1) Ebonics strategies
    2) Only simple language strategies
    3) Folk healing strategies
    4) Trust development

Correct Answer: 4
Topic: Intercultural Communication
Step of the Nursing Process: All Phases of the Nursing Process
Cognitive Level: Application
Difficulty: Moderate
Rationale: Establishing trust is a critical element for success with African American clients. They are more willing to participate in treatment when they feel respected and treated as partners in their health care.

13. Which of the following statements is true?
    1) A Muslim client may refuse to take insulin if it has a beef base

    2) African American females are at greater risk for development of cancer
    3) Hispanic clients have difficulty talking with health care professionals
    4) Asian clients view preventive health care as a priority

Correct Answer: 3
Topic: Applications to Special Populations
Step of the Nursing Process: All Phases of the Nursing Process
Cognitive Level: Comprehension
Difficulty: Moderate
Rationale: Hispanic clients like to keep their problems within the family, and it is important to develop trust in the health care provider.

14. You are examining a 5-year-old Asian child in the emergency department and observe that he has welts on his body. Your first course of action is to:
    1) Report child abuse to the authorities
    2) Consult a traditional healer
    3) Question the family about cultural practices
    4) Ignore it as it is an imbalance between "yin and yang"

Correct Answer: 3
Topic: Application to Special Populations
Step of the Nursing Process: Assessment
Cognitive Level: Analysis
Difficulty: Moderate
Rationale: A process called "coining" is sometimes used by Asian healers. A coin is heated and rubbed on the body, thus producing welts. The nurse in this scenario needs to assess for this particular practice.

15. You are performing a physical examination on a Native American. As a professional nurse, you should complete the physical examination:
    1) as rapidly as possible
    2) as slowly as possible
    3) in stages
    4) with family member present

Correct Answer: 3
Topic: Native American Clients

Step of the Nursing Process: Assessment
Cognitive Level: Application
Difficulty: Moderate
Rationale: It is best to ask questions in short sessions rather than all at once.

Rationale: The poor in our society are powerless and have no control over meeting their basic needs for food, housing, clothing. They cannot trust that their efforts can make a difference, and they expect others to take responsibility to make things better.

16. Which of the following is a true statement in regard to the culture of poverty?
    1) Poor people are able to meet only their basic needs, as defined by Maslow
    2) They take personal responsibility for being where they are
    3) They don't care to expend the effort to produce change
    4) In our society, being poor means being powerless

Correct Answer: 4
Topic: Culture of Poverty
Step of the Nursing Process: All Phases of the Nursing Process
Cognitive Level: Knowledge
Difficulty: Moderate

17. Which of the following is *not* an important component in ethical considerations of the culturally unique client?
    1) Treatment in a nonjudgmental manner
    2) Being aware of personal biases
    3) Respect for human dignity
    4) Uniform treatment of each client

Correct Answer: 4
Topic: Ethical Considerations
Step of the Nursing Process: All Phases of the Nursing Process
Cognitive Level: Knowledge
Difficulty: Moderate
Rationale: Each client should be treated as culturally unique.

CHAPTER 12
Communicating in Groups

1. A group is defined as:
    1) A verbal exchange during a meeting of people
    2) People meeting on a scheduled basis to achieve a common goal
    3) Collaborative practice relationships
    4) A unique gathering of people to communicate about their diverse backgrounds

Correct Answer: 2
Topic: Communicating in Groups
Step of the Nursing Process: All Phases of the Nursing Process
Cognitive Level: Knowledge
Difficulty: Easy
Rationale: A group is not just a collection of people but a deliberate gathering who meet together over a period of time for a common cause, purpose, or goal.

2. As a nursing student, you are a member of which group?
    1) Focus group
    2) Educational group

    3) Primary group
    4) Secondary group

Correct Answer: 3
Topic: Communicating in Groups
Step of the Nursing Process: All Phases of the Nursing Process
Cognitive Level: Comprehension
Difficulty: Moderate
Rationale: Primary groups are linked to the values of an individual and are chosen because of a common interest.

3. Which of the following describes groupthink?
    1) A member of a corporate executive committee states, "You could be making a big mistake"
    2) Members of a corporate executive committee fail to inform the chairperson that some middle managers do not support the decision
    3) A corporate executive committee holds a press conference regarding a new product despite poor market survey results

4) A leader presents executive committee agenda items with little discussion by group members

Correct Answer: 2
Topic: Groupthink
Step of the Nursing Process: All Phases of the Nursing Process
Cognitive Level: Analysis
Difficulty: Hard
Rationale: Groupthink is cohesiveness carried to an extreme. Loyalty to the group is carried to an extreme, and members are afraid to express conflicting ideas. Critical thinking and realistic appraisal become lost.

4. Which of the following statements are true in relation to role functions?
   1) When task functions predominate, member satisfaction increase
   2) When maintenance functions predominate, goals are achieved
   3) Task functions include giving and seeking information
   4) Role functions equate to group role position

Correct Answer: 3
Topic: Role Function
Step of the Nursing Process: All Phases of the Nursing Process
Cognitive Level: Knowledge
Difficulty: Moderate
Rationale: Seeking or giving information or opinion is a task function.

5. As you lead a group meeting, you notice that Amy and Robert are talking. Which of the following represents the best intervention?
   1) State to group, "Have you noticed who is talking at this time?"
   2) Address Amy and Robert, "I would like you to stop talking."
   3) State to group member, George, "Would you repeat what you just said to Amy and Robert?"
   4) State to Amy and Robert, "Would you share your comments with the group?"

Correct Answer: 4
Topic: Communication in Groups
Step of the Nursing Process: Implementation
Cognitive Level: Application

Difficulty: Moderate
Rationale: Amy and Robert are using roles to meet self-needs at the expense of other members' needs and group values. This is a group issue; therefore the leader, in dealing with the issue, reflects it back to the group.

6. The group leader states, "Today we discussed some of the issues about taking medications, and each one of you developed a goal in relation to some of the problems you were experiencing. I think it was helpful that some of you were able to share your experiences with other group members." The leader is using the technique of:
   1) Harmonizing
   2) Summarizing
   3) Encouraging
   4) Compromising

Correct Answer: 2
Topic: Summarizing
Step of the Nursing Process: Implementation
Cognitive Level: Application
Difficulty: Moderate
Rationale: This is an example of summarizing. The leader links together common themes and the group's activities and makes a statement about the group dynamics.

7. You notice that Bill is quiet during meetings of a support group. What is the best intervention for involving Bill in the group process?
   1) Address group, "Have you noticed that Bill never talks?"
   2) Address group, "What can we do to involve Bill more?"
   3) Address Bill, "I would like to see you after the meeting."
   4) Address Bill, "Would you comment on what Steve just said?"

Correct Answer: 4
Topic: Communicating in Groups
Step of the Nursing Process: Implementation
Cognitive Level: Application
Difficulty: Moderate
Rationale: The focus is on group interaction, so the leader tries to involve Bill by asking his response to what another member said rather than by giving a personal response. This is intended to help Bill feel more comfortable.

8. A breast cancer support group is an example of:
   1) Closed group
   2) Open group
   3) Homogeneous group
   4) Heterogeneous group

Correct Answer: 3
Topic: Types of Group Membership
Step of the Nursing Process: Planning
Cognitive Level: Knowledge
Difficulty: Easy
Rationale: Homogeneous groups have a common denominator pertaining to all members, such as diagnosis.

9. You are starting up an Alzheimer's group for family members. During the first few sessions, you know that it is necessary that trust develop. An intervention to develop trust would be to:
   1) Discuss the role of power and influence in the group
   2) Do "warm-up" exercises in which members reveal some personal information
   3) Reveal some information about yourself
   4) Discuss the difficulty in feeling "trusting" of each other

Correct Answer: 3
Topic: Forming Stage of Group Development
Step of the Nursing Process: Implementation
Cognitive Level: Application
Difficulty: Moderate
Rationale: This intervention can role-model trusting behavior for the group during the forming stage of group process.

10. Grace, a group member, says meekly "John, I think you have good ideas, but do you really think this group is about that issue?" John, in turn, becomes defensive, saying, "I don't think we can accomplish anything in this group, I don't even like sitting in this stupid circle!" The leader knows that:
   1) This is not a normal part of group process, so the group should be closed
   2) The group is entering the performing stage of group process
   3) John should be confronted directly about his negativity
   4) Ask how other group members feel about what John is saying

Correct Answer: 4
Topic: Storming Stage of Group Development
Step of the Nursing Process: Implementation
Cognitive Level: Analysis
Difficulty: Moderate
Rationale: The leader recognizes that the group is in the storming stage of group development and that it is important that the leader remain nonreactive and redirect John's provocative remarks back to the group.

11. A long-standing group therapy meeting has been in process for one-half hour, when Mrs. Martin, a member, comes in. Another member, Mr. Hornstein, says, "I thought we agreed as a group to come on time." Mr. Hornstein's statement represents which of the following?
   1) Regulation
   2) Law
   3) Role
   4) Norm

Correct Answer: 4
Topic: Group Norms
Step of the Nursing Process: Implementation
Cognitive Level: Application
Difficulty: Moderate
Rationale: Group norms are behavioral standards set by the group to help the group achieve its goals.

12. During a support group meeting, Donald, in a teasing manner, has made several provocative remarks about your appearance and behavior as a group leader. Select your most appropriate response:
   1) "What do you think Donald is trying to tell us?"
   2) "Donald, see me after this meeting."
   3) "Donald, what you are saying is inappropriate."
   4) "Donald, you are excused from the group."

Correct Answer: 3
Topic: Communicating in Groups
Step of the Nursing Process: Implementation
Cognitive Level: Application
Difficulty: Moderate
Rationale: When members test boundaries through provocative, flattering, or insulting remarks, limits must be set promptly.

13. When any group reviews all the significant events that have occurred during their meetings, the group has reached which phase of development?
    1) Formative phase
    2) Engagement
    3) Active intervention
    4) Termination

Correct Answer: 4
Topic: Termination
Step of the Nursing Process: Evaluation
Cognitive Level: Knowledge
Difficulty: Easy
Rationale: The group experience is summarized during termination.

14. Joan has been asked to start a therapy group on her unit for clients with schizophrenia. To set up this group, Joan knows that:
    1) Food should not be offered because of the mess the clients will make
    2) Since it is easy for psychotic patients to become bored, the room should be switched periodically
    3) The leader should take a passive role to avoid scaring the clients
    4) Joan should choose a fellow staff member to help co-lead the group

Correct Answer: 4
Topic: Therapeutic Groups in Psychiatric Settings
Step of the Nursing Process: Planning
Cognitive Level: Application
Difficulty: Moderate
Rationale: Co-leadership is recommended with psychotic clients because the demands of leadership are very intense.

15. John, a member of a support group, has noticed that over the past few weeks the group has not been ending on time and that some members have been pairing off to discuss group issues. He brings this up with the group for discussion. This is an example of which maintenance function?
    1) Standard setting
    2) Consensus taking
    3) Seeking information
    4) Initiating discussion

Correct Answer: 1
Topic: Group Maintenance Tasks
Step of the Nursing Process: Implementation
Cognitive Level: Application
Difficulty: Moderate
Rationale: Standard setting calls for the group to reassess or confirm group norms.

16. Pedro, a group member, begins the discussion at a support group for individuals grieving the loss of a spouse. "I think the group should discuss how to handle children's feelings about the loss of a parent." Which of the following nonfunctional self-roles is represented in this situation?
    1) Aggressor
    2) Avoider
    3) Blocker
    4) Self-confessor

Correct Answer: 2
Topic: Nonfunctional Self-Roles
Step of the Nursing Process: Implementation
Cognitive Level: Application
Difficulty: Moderate
Rationale: Pedro is trying to avoid dealing with his loss by attempting to change the focus of the group.

17. Select the group behavior that best indicates that members are working effectively with each other:
    1) Members appear happy in their group interactions
    2) Members say and do what is expected and wanted by others
    3) Members show concern for the feelings of the group leader
    4) Members are able to focus on discussion of the range of concerns of all group members

Correct Answer: 4
Topic: Effective Groups
Step of the Nursing Process: Implementation
Cognitive Level: Application
Difficulty: Moderate
Rationale: In an effective group, open, goal-directed communication of feelings and ideas is encouraged. Controversy is viewed as healthy.

CHAPTER 13
Communicating with Families

1. A self-identified group whose association is characterized by special terms, including strong emotional ties and durability of members, describes:
   1) Family function
   2) Family process
   3) Family
   4) Family ecomap

Correct Answer: 3
Topic: Definition of Family
Step of the Nursing Process: All Phases of the Nursing Process
Cognitive Level: Comprehension
Difficulty: Easy
Rationale: This is the definition of a family.

2. The idea that each person in the family influences every other family member is called:
   1) Equifinality
   2) Closed boundaries
   3) Circular causality
   4) Entropy

Correct Answer: 3
Topic: Communicating with Families
Step of the Nursing Process: All Phases of the Nursing Process
Cognitive Level: Knowledge
Difficulty: Easy
Rationale: Circular causality asserts that a change in one part of the system creates a change in the whole system.

3. _____ theory is based on the assumption that a person's behavior is closely linked to his or her functioning in the family of origin.
   1) Duvall's
   2) Bowen's
   3) Calgary family systems
   4) Satir's

Correct Answer: 2
Topic: Theoretical Models
Step of the Nursing Process: Assessment
Cognitive Level: Knowledge
Difficulty: Easy
Rationale: Bowen's system theory links patterns of behavior to those in the multigenerational family.

4. Jane worries about what other people think of her. She needs acceptance and approval from others. You know that she is showing:
   1) Self-differentiation
   2) Emotional cutoff
   3) Poor self-differentiation
   4) Open boundaries

Correct Answer: 3
Topic: Self-Differentiation
Step of the Nursing Process: Assessment
Cognitive Level: Application
Difficulty: Moderate
Rationale: Poorly self-differentiated people depend on others for their self-identity. In contrast, self-differentiated people are able to think, feel, and act for themselves as separate individuals without being at the mercy and whims of others.

5. The dysfunctional child, family hero, and family scapegoat are examples of:
   1) Multigenerational transmission
   2) Family projection process
   3) Sibling position
   4) Triangulation

Correct Answer: 2
Topic: Bowen's System Theory
Step of the Nursing Process: Assessment
Cognitive Level: Knowledge
Difficulty: Easy
Rationale: When family tensions become too high, the family unconsciously projects its anxiety onto one of its own members.

6. Mary and Joe are discussing the day's events at dinner. Joe states, "I quit my job today." Mary becomes angry and responds, "How dare you do that without discussing it with me!" Joe states "I did discuss it with our friend June." Mary leaves the room. Identify the family behavior:
   1) Scapegoating
   2) Triangulation
   3) Placating
   4) Blaming

Correct Answer: 2
Topic: Triangulation
Step of the Nursing Process: Assessment

Cognitive Level: Application
Difficulty: Moderate
Rationale: Triangulation occurs when a third person is brought in to stabilize the tension between two members.

7. Which family theory uses developmental tasks as a framework?
   1) Bowen
   2) Duvall
   3) Satir
   4) McCullin

Correct Answer: 2
Topic: Family Theory
Step of the Nursing Process: Assessment
Cognitive Level: Knowledge
Difficulty: Easy
Rationale: Duvall's model looks at the family's developmental process of growth, aging, and change over its life span.

8. You are conducting a family meeting. John, the 17-year-old son, states "I wouldn't go out so much if my parents wouldn't stress me out." This is an example of:
   1) Placating
   2) Super-reasonableness
   3) Blaming
   4) Irrelevant response

Correct Answer: 3
Topic: Dysfunctional Ways of Communicating
Step of the Nursing Process: Assessment
Cognitive Level: Application
Difficulty: Easy
Rationale: Blaming is an example of attributing responsibility for problems to others.

9. The Adams family consists of Robert, a 28-year-old unemployed factory worker; Ann, Robert's 20-year-old wife, and Joan, their 2-month-old daughter. The Adamses have requested public assistance for food stamps. During your home visit, Ann states, "My daughter needs food because I feed her only watered-down milk with cereal." Robert states, "I cannot get a job." Ann states, "You don't even try." Which of the following is the most appropriate family coping model to use in this situation?

   1) A-B-C-X: The event interacts with resources and with the family's perception to produce a crisis
   2) Double A-B-C-X: A pile-up of demands, family system resources, and postbehavior crisis result
   3) ABCX with intended C: The family is willing to accept a less-than-perfect solution
   4) Family resilience: Key processes enable less-than-perfect solutions

Correct Answer: 1
Topic: Crisis Model of Family Coping
Step of the Nursing Process: Implementation
Cognitive Level: Application
Difficulty: Moderate
Rationale: The event, Robert's unemployment (A), interacts with the family's resources (B) and the family's perception of the event (C)—running out of food because Robert can't get a job—to produce the crisis; that is, the baby has no food (X).

10. You are a nurse performing the assessment of a family in crisis. Which of the following tools would you use to describe family life events and patterns?
    1) Ecomap
    2) Gendergram
    3) Family time lines
    4) Genogram

Correct Answer: 4
Topic: Assessment Tools
Step of the Nursing Process: Assessment
Cognitive Level: Application
Difficulty: Moderate
Rationale: A genogram is the most appropriate tool to use when identifying family patterns. A genogram records information about family members and their relationship for at least three generations.

11. You want to design a therapeutic task for the Jenkins family, whose middle son has just been charged with using marijuana. Which of the following should *not* be considered when selecting the task?
    1) The health care team's definition of the problem
    2) Language, beliefs, and strengths
    3) Response patterns of family members

4) Family treatment goals

Correct Answer: 1
Topic: Recognizing Families at Risk
Step of the Nursing Process: Planning
Cognitive Level: Application
Difficulty: Moderate
Rationale: The health care team's definition should not be considered; it is the family's definition that is important.

12. Amy Wong, RN, is interviewing the family of a client newly diagnosed with Alzheimer's disease. Amy wants to help the family members sort out their fears and identify strengths. Amy uses:
    1) Interventive questioning
    2) A genogram
    3) An ecomap
    4) Offering commendations

Correct Answer: 1
Topic: Supporting Family Coping
Step of the Nursing Process: Interventions
Cognitive Level: Application
Difficulty: Moderate
Rationale: Questioning is a nursing intervention to help families identify strengths and fears and to explore options.

13. You are interviewing the family of a client who is suffering from alcoholism. The communication technique you use is called circular questioning. The advantage of this technique is that it:
    1) Is used to examine relationships
    2) Aids the nurse in diagnosis
    3) Identifies the effect of the illness on the family
    4) Helps the nurse gain specific information

Correct Answer: 3
Topic: Circular Questioning
Step of the Nursing Process: Planning
Cognitive Level: Application
Difficulty: Moderate
Rationale: Circular questioning allows open discussion so that family members get to hear other members' concerns and can reflect on the meaning of their own concern.

14. You are interviewing the Brown family. You ask Jerry, the 14-year-old son, to respond to the question, "How has your mother's illness affected you?" Tom, Jerry's father, states, "He has been angry, irritable, not helping around the house, and missing school." You respond by:
    1) Responding to Tom and addressing him directly
    2) Addressing Jerry directly, not responding to Tom
    3) Repeating the question to Sheri, Jerry's 12-year-old sister
    4) Clarifying the behavior by questioning the mother

Correct Answer: 2
Topic: Giving Corrective Feedback
Step of the Nursing Process: Implementation
Cognitive Level: Application
Difficulty: Hard
Rationale: Corrective feedback is used in this situation when Tom, the father, speaks for his son. The nurse does not respond to Tom but addresses Jerry, the son, directly.

15. You are conducting the final meeting with the Jones family. You know that in terminating with the family, there are specific issues to address. Which of the following is an important consideration when terminating with the Jones
    1) The meeting should be kept very short and to the point
    2) Ensure that the family has your home number in case of emergencies
    3) Ensure that family needs have been met
    4) Ensure family awareness of progress toward goals

Correct Answer: 4
Topic: Termination
Step of the Nursing Process: Evaluation
Cognitive Level: Application
Difficulty: Moderate
Rationale: Progress toward goals is summarized so that the family is aware of what happened and what was gained.

16. Which of the following describes the dyad family unit?
    1) A father and mother with one or more children living together

2) First-, second-, and third-generation members not living together
3) Husband and wife living separately each with one child
4) Husband and wife living alone without children

Correct Answer: 4
Topic: Forms of Family Units
Step of the Nursing Process: Assessment
Cognitive Level: Knowledge
Difficulty: Moderate
Rationale: A dyad family is a couple living alone without children.

17. Which of the following is a true statement in comparing biological and blended families?
1) In biological families, rules are varied and complex
2) A blended family is born of loss
3) In biological families, there are multiple sets of rules
4) In blended families, traditions are shared

Correct Answer: 2
Topic: Blended/Biological Families
Step of the Nursing Process: Assessment
Cognitive Level: Knowledge
Difficulty: Easy
Rationale: There has been a loss of a biological parent or partner in a blended family.

CHAPTER 14
Resolving Conflict Between Nurse and Client

1. Your client, Mr. Smith, is shouting at you and demanding to see his physician. Although it is difficult, you know that the best response to use is:
1) Defensiveness
2) Empathy
3) Aggression
4) Assertiveness

Correct Answer: 2
Topic: Conflict
Step of the Nursing Process: Implementation
Cognitive Level: Application
Difficulty: Hard
Rationale: The nurse's best response is to remain calm and to empathize with what the client is experiencing.

2. Which of the following is true in relation to conflict?
1) Conflict is always negative
2) Conflict does not occur in every relationship
3) Conflict is not a natural part of human relationships
4) All conflict produces stress

Correct Answer: 4
Topic: Conflict
Step of the Nursing Process: All Phases of the Nursing Process
Cognitive Level: Knowledge

Difficulty: Moderate
Rationale: It is true that all conflict produces stress.

3. Which personal conflict management style do females tend to use?
1) Avoidance and compromise
2) Collaboration and competition
3) Avoidance and collaboration
4) Competition and compromise

Correct Answer: 1
Topic: Conflict Management Styles
Step of the Nursing Process: Assessment
Cognitive Level: Knowledge
Difficulty: Moderate
Rationale: Women have been socialized to react in ways that will assuage the other person's anger and tend to use accommodative styles such as compromise and avoidance.

4. The most positive personal conflict management style is:
1) Accommodation
2) Avoidance
3) Competition
4) Collaborative

Correct Answer: 4
Topic: Conflict
Step of the Nursing Process: Implementation

Cognitive Level: Knowledge
Difficulty: Moderate
Rationale: Collaborative is a solution-oriented response; it is a win-win situation.

5. You want to purchase a motorcycle for cheap, convenient transportation. You also want to have money for college tuition. The feeling you would most probably exhibit at this time would be:
   1) Overt conflict
   2) Felt conflict
   3) Interpersonal conflict
   4) Intrapersonal conflict
Correct Answer: 4
Topic: Conflict
Step of the Nursing Process: Assessment
Cognitive Level: Application
Difficulty: Moderate
Rationale: Intrapersonal conflict represents opposing feelings within an individual.

6. Which of the following describes assertiveness?
   1) Insisting on doing things your way
   2) Getting even
   3) Standing up for yourself
   4) Fighting back
Correct Answer: 3
Topic: Assertiveness
Step of the Nursing Process: All Phases of the Nursing Process
Cognitive Level: Knowledge
Difficulty: Easy
Rationale: Assertiveness allows people to stand up for their rights without putting the other person down.

7. Which of the following is true about assertiveness?
   1) Components include ability to say no and to ask for favors
   2) Assertiveness responses consist of "you" statements
   3) Assertiveness skills are inborn
   4) Assertiveness allows the person to dominate
Correct Answer: 1
Topic: Assertiveness

Step of the Nursing Process: All Phases of the Nursing Process
Cognitive Level: Knowledge
Difficulty: Moderate
Rationale: Components of assertion are the ability to say no, to ask for what you want appropriately, to express thoughts and feelings, and to initiate and terminate the interaction.

8. Which of the following is the therapeutic way to acknowledge your anger to a client?
   1) Remain silent and don't respond
   2) Use "I" message when you feel others are at fault
   3) Make a statement, for instance, "You make me angry"
   4) Turn your back and walk away
Correct Answer: 2
Topic: Assertiveness
Step of the Nursing Process: Implementation
Cognitive Level: Application
Difficulty: Moderate
Rationale: "I" messages are assertive statements that allow the sender to get the message across without suppressing the other person's rights.

9. For a nurse, it is acceptable to express strong feelings of anger to:
   1) The nurse's family
   2) Strangers
   3) The client
   4) The client's family
Correct Answer: 1
Topic: Conflict in the Nurse–Client Relationship
Step of the Nursing Process: All Phases of the Nursing Process
Cognitive Level: Comprehension
Difficulty: Moderate
Rationale: As nurses, we affect the behavior of our clients through actions. Expressing strong feelings of anger can have negative outcomes for the client.

10. A client states to you in a hostile voice, "I am sick of being poked at and stuck with needles. Go away and leave me alone." Which of the following is the best intervention?
   1) "I am not surprised that you wish to be left alone."

2) "I know you have had many examinations and treatments."
3) "You feel vulnerable and depressed as a result of all these treatments."
4) "OK, I will go away."

Correct Answer: 2
Topic: Conflict
Step of the Nursing Process: Implementation
Cognitive Level: Application
Difficulty: Moderate
Rationale: This is the most useful intervention. The client's anger is validated, and the situation is reframed in a more adaptive manner.

11. You find Mr. Greg, a client diagnosed with psychotic disorder, not otherwise specified, pacing and occasionally punching at the wall. Your first response should be to:
    1) Assertively tell him to stop that behavior
    2) Request that he write in his journal to calm down
    3) Speak in a loud voice to alert other staff members
    4) Ensure that there is plenty of physical space between you and the client

Correct Answer: 4
Topic: Client Intrapersonal Conflict
Step of the Nursing Process: Intervention
Cognitive Level: Application
Difficulty: Moderate
Rationale: It is important for safety reasons that the nurse not get too close to this client. Psychotic clients can be unpredictable, and at this point he would not be likely to respond positively to a suggestion to write in a journal. Speaking in a loud voice may escalate the situation, and he is already out of control.

12. After fasting from 10 p.m. the previous evening, your client Gladys Evans, finds out that her test has been canceled. She curses at you and states that you are incompetent. Your best response would be:
    1) "You have no right to say that to me. You are nasty"
    2) "I can understand your being upset, but I feel uncomfortable when you swear at me"
    3) "We need to learn to control our anger!"
    4) Leave room and refuse to return to answer the call light when she calls

Correct Answer: 2
Topic: "I" Statements
Step of the Nursing Process: Interventions
Cognitive Level: Application
Difficulty: Moderate
Rationale: This is an assertive statement that validates what the client is feeling but also lets the client know how her behavior has affected the nurse.

13. You are providing home health care to a client suffering from Alzheimer's disease who fell and broke his hip 3 weeks ago. You teach the family in the use of the walker. This represents which stage of the nurse-caregiver relationship?
    1) Worker-helper
    2) Worker-worker
    3) Manager-worker
    4) Nurse as nurse for family caregiver

Correct Answer: 2
Topic: Defusing Potential Conflicts When Providing Home Health Care
Step of the Nursing Process: Interventions
Cognitive Level: Application
Difficulty: Moderate
Rationale: During the worker-worker stage, the nurse teaches care skills to family members.

14. Your client, Mr. Graham, yells, "Take this mess away from here. How could anyone eat this food? What kind of a place are you running here?" You use your skills of assertiveness to promote change that is focused on:
    1) Feelings
    2) Attitudes
    3) Behaviors
    4) Motivation

Correct Answer: 3
Topic: Assertiveness
Step of the Nursing Process: Implementation
Cognitive Level: Application
Difficulty: Moderate
Rationale: Undesired behaviors are the focus for change.

15. Mrs. Green is a difficult client. You are discussing her care at a team conference. Which of the following is *not* a positive approach for dealing with a difficult client?

1) Promote trust by providing immediate feedback
2) Plan and set goals for the client with the assistance of the health care team
3) Use incentives and withdrawal of privileges
4) Explain all options along with outcomes

Correct Answer: 2

Topic: Approaches for Dealing with Difficult Clients
Step of the Nursing Process: Planning
Cognitive Level: Application
Difficulty: Moderate
Rationale: The client should be involved in her care with the focus on mutual goals set by the nurse and client.

CHAPTER 15
Health Promotion and Client Learning Needs

1. Which of the following statements about health teaching is true?
   1) The nurse assures the outcome of health teaching
   2) The client is responsible for the quality of the health teaching
   3) Only the client can assure the outcome of the heath teaching
   4) The outcomes match the effort put into the teaching

Correct Answer: 3
Topic: Self-Awareness
Step of the Nursing Process: Evaluation
Cognitive Level: Comprehension
Difficulty: Moderate
Rationale: The nurse is responsible for the quality of the teaching, but only the client can assure the outcome.

2. The concept of well-being consists of the ability to:
   1) Work at producing an income
   2) Perform activities of daily living
   3) Define it personally
   4) Partner with a health professional

Correct Answer: 3
Topic: Well-being
Step of the Nursing Process: All Phases of the Nursing Process
Cognitive Level: Knowledge
Difficulty: Easy
Rationale: Well-being is a subjective experience, always defined by the client.

3. Which of the following is an example of tertiary prevention?
   1) Stress management program

   2) Prenatal clinic
   3) Annual gynecology examination
   4) Diabetic meal planning class

Correct Answer: 4
Topic: Tertiary Prevention
Step of the Nursing Process: Implementation
Cognitive Level: Comprehension
Difficulty: Moderate
Rationale: Tertiary prevention is aimed at minimizing the handicapping effects of a disease.

4. Mary, a client recovering from her second myocardial infarction, refuses to give up smoking. She states "I've smoked so long now that there's no point quitting, as the damage is done." This statement is best understood in the context of which of the following?
   1) Social learning theory
   2) Pender's health promotion model
   3) The Transtheoretical Model of Change
   4) Healthy People 2010

Correct Answer: 2
Topic: Health Promotion
Step of the Nursing Process: All Phases of the Nursing Process
Cognitive Level: Application
Difficulty: Moderate
Rationale: According to Pender, a person's perception of benefits and barriers to health-promoting behaviors strengthen or weaken interest in participating in health-promoting behaviors.

5. Even though Mrs. Green's cholesterol level is elevated, she continues to eat red meat and fried foods. Which stage of change is Mrs. Green experiencing?

1) Determination
2) Action
3) Pre-contemplation
4) Contemplation

Correct Answer: 3
Topic: Stages of Change
Step of the Nursing Process: Assessment
Cognitive Level: Application
Difficulty: Moderate
Rationale: In the pre-contemplation stage, the individual does not think that there is a problem and is not considering change.

6. Robert, age 26, loves to eat and weighs 300 pounds. He is admitted to the hospital for a breathing problem associated with walking a short distance. Which of the following statements reflects Bandura's social theory?
   1) "Robert, your cardiac studies reveal an enlarged heart. This is a sign of cardiac problems"
   2) "Robert, I know you love to eat, but your current life style is not conducive to good health"
   3) "Robert, can you remember what it was like to get up and go to work every day? Your buddies miss you"
   4) "Robert, I am concerned about your continuing to eat large amounts because it affects your weight. I understand you lost your job as a security guard because you could not stay on your feet for long periods."

Correct Answer: 4
Topic: Bandura's Social Theory
Step of the Nursing Process: Implementation
Cognitive Level: Application
Difficulty: Hard
Rationale: The nurse can use his or her understanding of the different types of motivators to improve learning readiness. In this statement, the nurse is using physical motivators and social incentives.

7. You are supervising the administration of insulin to your client who has had insulin-dependent (type 1) diabetes for several years. You observe that he is doing some things incorrectly. It is important to remember that:

1) Learning is smooth and linear
2) The learning process is not affected by life events
3) The nurse needs to challenge learning patterns
4) Previous knowledge can be a barrier to learning

Correct Answer: 4
Topic: Factors Affecting Readiness to Learn
Step of the Nursing Process: Interventions
Cognitive Level: Application
Difficulty: Moderate
Rationale: Previous knowledge can present barriers and confusion for the client in learning new information.

8. Which of the following is the best intervention for a client who does not pay attention to others?
   1) Speak loudly and clearly
   2) Direct conversation toward concrete, familiar objects
   3) Personalize speech by using first name
   4) Use touch with speech

Correct Answer: 2
Topic: Factors Affecting Ability to Learn
Step of the Nursing Process: Implementation
Cognitive Level: Application
Difficulty: Moderate
Rationale: Visual aids help make the concepts "concrete" and allow the client to recognize familiar symbols and objects.

9. When teaching a health education class to teenagers about the importance of safe sex, it is important to remember that they:
   1) feel that women are responsible for taking precautions
   2) think that modern medicine has treatment for existing illness
   3) think that they are immortal
   4) think that illness happens to other people

Correct Answer: 3
Topic: Developmental Level
Step of the Nursing Process: Implementation
Cognitive Level: Application
Difficulty: Moderate
Rationale: Developmental level affects teaching strategies. Teenagers believe that they are immortal.

10. Which of the following teaching strategies is recommended for a client who is newly diagnosed with diabetes at age 75 and has a low literacy level?
    1) Relate teaching to client's immediate experience
    2) Give choices and multiple perspectives
    3) Use a multisensory approach in the lesson plan
    4) Encourage self-directed learning

Correct Answer: 3
Topic: Developmental Level
Step of the Nursing Process: Implementation
Cognitive Level: Application
Difficulty: Moderate
Rationale: Visual aids provide cues to help the client understand meanings. Planning formats that involve more than one sense help the client to learn.

11. You know that educational interventions must be tailored to the individual's developmental level. Which of the following statements is true in relation to developmental level?
    1) School-aged children are not interested in learning better ways to take care of themselves
    2) Adult learners learn best when the focus is theoretical
    3) Long formats assist with elderly client's learning needs
    4) Previous life experience should be incorporated into the teaching plan of adult learners

Correct Answer: 4
Topic: Developmental level
Step of the Nursing Process: Implementation
Cognitive Level: Application
Difficulty: Moderate
Rationale: Experience is a rich source that can be used to help with new learning experiences.

12. Jose needs to learn to administer his antiviral medication. Jose's English is limited. Your teaching plan encompasses:
    1) Including family members
    2) Reviewing major points
    3) Providing minimal information
    4) Answering questions honestly and factually

Correct Answer: 1

Topic: Culture
Step of the Nursing Process: Implementation
Cognitive Level: Application
Difficulty: Moderate
Rationale: The family should be included in developing the plan and implementing it and in the evaluation, or the plan may be sabotaged when the client goes home.

13. Pedro, age 30, is coming to the wound clinic for treatment of his leg ulcers. You note that healing is not occurring and an infection is present. What statement can you make to Pedro that would address his stage of change?
    1) "Your wound culture shows the presence of some infection. This is a deterioration from your last visit."
    2) "You have had these ulcers a long time. Can you remember what it was like to be free of them?"
    3) "What are you going to do to improve this situation?"
    4) "You are good at paying attention when I change the dressing. Is there anything else I can show you today?"

Correct Answer: 1
Topic: Stages of Change
Step of the Nursing Process: Implementation
Cognitive Level: Application
Difficulty: Hard
Rationale: Pedro is in the pre-contemplative stage of change. The intervention at this stage is to raise awareness of a health problem.

14. Jim has just completed his detoxification from alcohol. His wife left him, his job is in jeopardy, and his liver enzymes are elevated. He states, "Alcohol is ruining my life, I'll do anything it takes to quit drinking." The best intervention for the nurse is to:
    1) Give Jim information about a 28-day addiction rehabilitation center
    2) Give Jim a copy of his laboratory results
    3) Have Jim complete a cost-benefit worksheet of alcohol use
    4) Point out positive changes

Correct Answer: 1
Topic: Stage of Change
Step of the Nursing Process: Implementation
Cognitive Level: Application

Difficulty: Moderate
Rationale: Jim is in the determination stage of change. The approach at this stage is to assist the client in choosing the best course of action to resolve the problem.

15. Which of the following strategies in health education is recommended by the United States Preventive Services Task Force?
    1) Use a standard teaching format
    2) Eliminate established behaviors
    3) Provide general information
    4) Suggest small changes rather than large ones

Correct Answer: 4
Topic: Strategies in Health Education
Step of the Nursing Process: Implementation
Cognitive Level: Knowledge
Difficulty: Moderate
Rationale: Change occurs in small increments, depending on the stage of readiness to learn.

CHAPTER 16
Health Teaching in the Nurse–Client Relationship

1. Educational standards requiring health care agencies to provide systematic health education was established by:
    1) ANA
    2) Nurse Practice Acts
    3) JCAHO
    4) Medicare

Correct Answer: 3
Topic: Professional, Legal, and Ethical Mandates of Health Teaching
Step of the Nursing Process: Implementation
Cognitive Level: Knowledge
Difficulty: Moderate
Rationale: The Joint Commission on Accreditation of Hospital Organizations has set four standards related to health education.

2. Which of the following statements is true in relation to health teaching?
    1) It involves connecting two domains, cognitive and affective
    2) Health teaching must be incongruent with what is important to the client
    3) Behavioral change in the affective domain takes less time than learning in the cognitive domain
    4) Emotional factors affect the client's readiness to learn

Correct Answer: 4
Topic: Health Teaching
Step of the Nursing Process: Planning
Cognitive Level: Knowledge
Difficulty: Moderate

Rationale: Emotional factors, such as health beliefs and identified concerns, influence readiness to learn.

3. The outcome, "The client will be able to accurately draw up the correct dose of insulin," refers to health teaching in which domain?
    1) Changing attitudes
    2) Psychomotor
    3) Understanding content
    4) Promoting acceptance

Correct Answer: 2
Topic: Health Teaching Domains
Step of the Nursing Process: Implementation
Cognitive Level: Application
Difficulty: Moderate
Rationale: The psychomotor domain refers to learning a skill through "hands-on practice."

4. The teaching outcome, "The client will be able to identify three physical effects of alcohol abuse," refers to learning in which domain?
    1) Cognitive
    2) Affective
    3) Psychomotor
    4) Emotional

Correct Answer: 1
Topic: Health Teaching Domains
Step of the Nursing Process: Planning
Cognitive Level: Application
Difficulty: Moderate
Rationale: Teaching the cognitive domain targets understanding of the disease.

5. Which health education model can be used with diverse learners in a community-based setting?
    1) Skinner's behavioral approach
    2) The Premack Principle
    3) The Precede Model
    4) Client-centered health teaching

Correct Answer: 3
Topic: Theoretical Frameworks
Step of the Nursing Process: Implementation
Cognitive Level: Knowledge
Difficulty: Easy
Rationale: The Precede Model is used to develop community approaches to health teaching.

6. You are planning an education class for clients suffering from addiction. You know that a format that encourages empowerment is an important goal of health teaching. Which of the following is *not* an empowering strategy?
    1) Providing sufficient information
    2) Providing emotional support
    3) Setting mutual goals
    4) Using negative reinforcers

Correct Answer: 4
Topic: Empowerment
Step of the Nursing Process: Planning
Cognitive Level: Application
Difficulty: Moderate
Rationale: Negative reinforcement is used in the behavioral approach and is not an empowering strategy.

7. A strategy that helps a client restructure a problem is known as:
    1) Empowerment
    2) Reinforcement
    3) Critical thinking
    4) Shaping

Correct Answer: 3
Topic: Critical Thinking
Step of the Nursing Process: Implementation
Cognitive Level: Knowledge
Difficulty: Moderate
Rationale: Critical thinking facilitates learning by helping clients to restructure problems and to bring about change.

8. Which of the following represents a critical thinking approach to a teaching problem?
    1) Collaborating with the client in development of a teaching plan
    2) Using examples and analogies with client to solve learning problems
    3) Enabling clients to take as much responsibility as possible for their learning
    4) Role-modeling desired learning with client

Correct Answer: 2
Topic: Critical Thinking
Step of the Nursing Process: Implementation
Cognitive Level: Knowledge
Difficulty: Moderate
Rationale: Using examples and analogies are part of critical thinking to help the client generalize the problem-solving process.

9. Mary, an RN, is discussing nutrition with Gregg, an adolescent. Mary states, "If your food diary includes more fruits and vegetables, you will not be required to attend all of the dietary sessions." Which type of reinforcement is being used in this situation?
    1) Negative reinforcement
    2) Positive reinforcement
    3) Punishment
    4) Extinguishing

Correct Answer: 4
Topic: Reinforcement
Step of the Nursing Process: Implementation
Cognitive Level: Application
Difficulty: Moderate
Rationale: Behaviors are extinguished by ignoring their existence; that is, not eating a balanced diet is ignored, but if Gregg does eat fruits and vegetables, the nurse acknowledges it.

10. Your client, Dean, who is suffering from schizophrenia and cocaine abuse, has continued to isolate himself in his room, refusing to attend unit activities. In using the behavioral approach to learning, what is the first step you will take?
    1) Define specific consequences
    2) Describe the behavior requiring change
    3) Reframe the problem
    4) Identify tasks in sequential order

Correct Answer: 2
Topic: Implementing a Behavioral Approach

Step of the Nursing Process: Planning
Cognitive Level: Application
Difficulty: Moderate
Rationale: The first step is to carefully describe the concrete behavior requiring change.

11. Which of the following represents the most important aspect about timing for a teaching session?
    1) Scheduling the session to allow appropriate length of time
    2) Informing the client of what to expect at beginning of scheduled session
    3) Scheduling session at a time the client is ready
    4) Scheduling session at time of day convenient for both nurse and client

Correct Answer: 3
Topic: Timing
Step of the Nursing Process: Planning
Cognitive Level: Knowledge
Difficulty: Easy
Rationale: Timing is essential because learning takes place only when the learner is ready.

12. Mary has completed a diabetic teaching class regarding insulin administration. As her nurse, how do you provide the most appropriate feedback?
    1) "Mary, you had a tough time, but you will do better with practice"
    2) "Mary, you were able to accurately draw up the insulin. Now what you need to do is practice the needle insertion"
    3) "Mary, you seem to be having a tough time because it was your first class"
    4) "Mary, you seem to understand what I said. Is there anything else I can help you with?

Correct Answer: 2
Topic: Feedback
Step of the Nursing Process: Implementation
Cognitive Level: Application
Difficulty: Hard
Rationale: Feedback should be descriptive, not evaluative, should include both positive and negative elements.

13. Accurate documentation of client teaching is a critical component of quality care. Mr. Brown has been treated for alcoholism and is being discharged today. Which of the following is an accurate documentation on Mr. Brown's chart?
    1) The client was educated about the physical complications of alcoholism
    2) The client received information on diet and vitamin therapy
    3) The client was taught the signs and symptoms of alcohol withdrawal
    4) The client was able to identify five triggers for relapse and was assisted to develop a relapse prevention plan

Correct Answer: 4
Topic: Evaluation of Client Teaching
Step of the Nursing Process: Evaluation
Cognitive Level: Application
Difficulty: Moderate
Rationale: Health education documentation needs to be detailed, comprehensive, and objective. This documentation evaluates the learning in a concrete, measurable way.

14. You are teaching a family group about schizophrenia. Your format includes a 20-minute video, didactic portion, and discussion period. You know that:
    1) If you experience technical difficulties, try to fix them, then cancel the group
    2) A humorous opening grabs the audience's attention
    3) Minimal preparation is needed for this format
    4) Environment is not as important as with other formats

Correct Answer: 2
Topic: Group Presentations
Step of the Nursing Process: Planning
Cognitive Level: Application
Difficulty: Moderate
Rationale: A quote or humorous opening will capture the audience's attention.

15. You are preparing material for a diabetic teaching class. The most important aspect of preparing overhead transparencies for group teaching is use of:
    1) color to maintain interest
    2) large text so all participants can view the content

3) several transparencies to cover the lesson plan
4) copy of transparencies as a handout to reinforce learning

Correct Answer: 2
Topic: Using Visual Aids
Step of the Nursing Process: Implementation
Cognitive Level: Application
Difficulty: Easy
Rationale: Visual aids help reinforce the words, but it is important that the print be large enough for all clients to read. A font of 32 points is recommended and should include no more than four or five items per transparency.

16. Which of the following questions would you ask the client upon discharge?
    1) Whether he has any cultural issues
    2) His medical history and whether he has any allergies
    3) Who will assume responsibility for continuing care
    4) Whether he has any difficulties administering his insulin

Correct Answer: 3
Topic: Discharge Teaching
Step of the Nursing Process: Implementation
Cognitive Level: Comprehension
Difficulty: Moderate
Rationale: During discharge, the nurse asks focused questions to find out what is likely to happen when the client returns home.

17. Which of the following statements is true?
    1) Clients can reproduce teaching outcomes in the hospital better than in the home
    2) The nurse should arrive at the client's home unannounced to get an accurate picture of the client's situation
    3) Part of the teaching assessment includes appraisal of the home environment
    4) The nurse is a guest in the client's home and should wash her hands where the family does, for example, the kitchen sink

Correct Answer: 3
Topic: Health Teaching in the Home
Step of the Nursing Process: Implementation
Cognitive Level: Knowledge
Difficulty: Moderate

Rationale: Appraisal of home environment, family supports, and resources are part of the teaching assessment.

18. Mr. Miller, age 75, is hospitalized as a result of a fall. He states, "I want to return home because I like to be independent." The nurse notes that Mr. Miller lives alone and will be required to attend physical therapy three times a week. Which nursing diagnosis is the relevant home health teaching diagnosis?
    1) Anxiety
    2) Ineffective coping
    3) Self-care deficit
    4) Impaired home maintenance

Correct Answer: 3
Topic: Nursing Diagnosis Amenable to Health Teaching
Step of the Nursing Process: Diagnosis
Cognitive Level: Application
Difficulty: Moderate
Rationale: Mr. Miller lives alone and requires physical therapy related to his fall. He will require assistance to care for himself.

19. Which of the following is an effective teaching objective? The client will be able to:
    1) Ambulate short distances
    2) Learn self-insulin administration within 3 weeks
    3) Understand his diabetes and its implications for his lifestyle
    4) Perform foot care correctly after three teaching sessions

Correct Answer: 4
Topic: Effective Goals and Objectives
Step of the Nursing Process: Planning
Cognitive Level: Comprehension
Difficulty: Moderate
Rationale: This objective is action-oriented, specific, achievable, and measurable.

20. Mrs. Henry requires health teaching for exercises related to arthritis in her shoulder. During your assessment, Mrs. Henry tells you she is a "hands-on" learner. What teaching resource would you recommended for Mrs. Henry? An exercise:

1) book
2) video
3) schedule with physical therapist
4) audiotape

Correct Answer: 3
Topic: Learning Styles

Step of the Nursing Process: Planning
Cognitive Level: Application
Difficulty: Easy
Rationale: The kinesic learner learns best with hands-on involvement.

CHAPTER 17

Communicating with Clients Experiencing Communication Deficits

1. Which of the following is true in relation to communication deficits?
    1) Communication deficits occur only as a result of physical disabilities
    2) Communication deficits can arise from sensory deprivation
    3) Individuals who are equally impaired are equally disabled
    4) The primary nursing goal is to minimize the client's independence

Correct Answer: 2
Topic: Communication Deficits
Step of the Nursing Process: All Phases of the Nursing Process
Cognitive Level: Knowledge
Difficulty: Moderate
Rationale: Communication deficits can occur in intensive care units related to temporary immobility and environmental limitations.

2. Your client, Mr. Harold, refuses to attend the team meeting. He tells you that there is no point in going because he doesn't get anything out of it. You suspect that he is suffering from hearing loss. You know that:
    1) He will readily acknowledge that this is the problem if asked
    2) He may try to hide his deficits by withdrawing from relationships
    3) Decreased hearing ability is not related to conversational style
    4) Older adults have better consonant discrimination

Correct Answer: 2
Topic: Hearing Loss
Step of the Nursing Process: Assessment
Cognitive Level: Application

Difficulty: Moderate
Rationale: Deprived of a primary means of receiving signals, the client may try to hide his deficit and withdraw from relationships.

3. Aphasia is a:
    1) Neurological deficit
    2) Cognitive deficit
    3) Sensory deficit
    4) Mental deficit

Correct Answer: 1
Topic: Communicating with the Aphasic Client
Step of the Nursing Process: All Phases of the Nursing Process
Cognitive Level: Knowledge
Difficulty: Easy
Rationale: Aphasia is defined as a neurological linguistic deficit.

4. When communicating with Jane, a client with chronic schizophrenia, it is important to recognize:
    1) The sensory channels in psychotic clients are not intact
    2) Clients with autism and depression have the most difficulties communicating
    3) Clients with schizophrenia are usually hyperverbal
    4) Psychotic clients may isolate themselves and may suffer from impaired coping and low self-esteem

Correct Answer: 4
Topic: Serious Mental Illness
Step of the Nursing Process: All Phases of the Nursing Process
Cognitive Level: Application
Difficulty: Moderate

Rationale: As a result of the client's inability to receive or express language signals, the client may suffer from social isolation, impaired coping, and low self-esteem.

5. Which of the following describes what happens to the client who experiences environmental deprivation, such as a stay within the intensive care unit?
    1) Clients cannot process and respond appropriately to sensory input due to physical immobility
    2) Clients cannot decode the meaning of messages due to physical immobility
    3) Clients cannot respond appropriately to changes in the environment because of physical immobility
    4) Clients experience changes in cognitive equilibrium because of the nature of the unit and their physical immobility

Correct Answer: 4
Topic: Environmental Deprivation
Step of the Nursing Process: All Phases of the Nursing Process
Cognitive Level: Knowledge
Difficulty: Moderate
Rationale: Temporary reversible changes in cognitive equilibrium occur because there are few organizing structures to anchor the client.

6. When the nurse is caring for a client with hearing loss, which of the following interventions is indicated?
    1) Speaking louder
    2) Making gestures using hands
    3) Speaking in a normal manner
    4) Making tactile contact

Correct Answer: 2
Topic: Communicating with a Client with Hearing Loss
Step of the Nursing Process: Implementation
Cognitive Level: Knowledge
Difficulty: Moderate
Rationale: The use of gestures and facial expressions reinforce the verbal content. The nurse should speak in a moderate, even tone and should articulate words clearly.

7. Which of the following is associated with blindness?
    1) Depression
    2) Paranoia
    3) Withdrawal from relationships
    4) Frustration

Correct Answer: 2
Topic: Communicating with Blind Clients
Step of the Nursing Process: Assessment
Cognitive Level: Knowledge
Difficulty: Moderate
Rationale: For the blind client, the world is full of shadows and lacking in details. Visual impairment has been shown to be associated with a high occurrence of paranoia.

8. Which of the following clients with a communication deficit requires the use of touch during a therapeutic encounter?
    1) Blind clients
    2) Clients with a hearing loss
    3) Mentally ill clients
    4) Clients experiencing environmental deprivation

Correct Answer: 1
Topic: Communicating with Clients Experiencing Communication Deficits
Step of the Nursing Process: Implementation
Cognitive Level: Knowledge
Difficulty: Easy
Rationale: The social isolation experienced by blind clients is profound, and the need for contact is important.

9. When the nurse is caring for a blind client, the most important thing to remember is to:
    1) Announce her arrival to the client
    2) Explain her actions to the client
    3) Use Braille materials with the client
    4) Provide the client with information regarding resources for the blind

Correct Answer: 2
Topic: Communicating with Blind Clients
Step of the Nursing Process: Interventions
Cognitive Level: Knowledge
Difficulty: Moderate
Rationale: Nurses need to use words to supply additional information to counterbalance missing visual cues.

10. Mrs. Davidson, age 55, is recovering from a stroke. When you try to communicate with her, she nods her head when you speak and responds using a few words that are coherent to you. Which type of aphasia does Mrs. Davidson exhibit?
    1) Expressive aphasia
    2) Receptive aphasia
    3) Global aphasia
    4) Cognitive aphasia

Correct Answer: 1
Topic: Communicating with Aphasic Clients
Step of the Nursing Process: All Phases of the Nursing Process
Cognitive Level: Application
Difficulty: Moderate
Rationale: Expressive aphasia refers to an inability to find words or associate ideas with accurate word symbols.

11. Mr. Bates is a client who has experienced global aphasia secondary to a stroke. Which of the following interventions are most appropriate for this client?
    1) Explaining what you are doing while you are providing care
    2) Consulting with the family about the best individualized intervention
    3) Providing a radio tuned to a station familiar to the client
    4) Spending long periods of time talking with the client to provide stimulation

Correct Answer: 3
Topic: Global Aphasia
Step of the Nursing Process: Interventions
Cognitive Level: Analysis
Difficulty: Hard
Rationale: The radio provides connections to a social environment without exerting pressure on the client to talk and provides mental stimulation in a nontaxing way.

12. Joanne is a psychotic college student who has been observed standing in the main hallway for the past 3 days. She has not interacted with anyone. As a nursing student, how would you begin an interpersonal communication with Joanne?
    1) Ask Joanne if she will let you examine her ears

2) Consult with staff nurses regarding the correct intervention
3) Approach Joanne, make eye contact, and ask how she feels
4) Acknowledge Joanne's presence each time you are within a close distance

Correct Answer: 3
Topic: Communicating with Clients with Serious Mental Illness
Step of the Nursing Process: Interventions
Cognitive Level: Application
Difficulty: Moderate
Rationale: The nurse needs to use simple, concrete sentences and maintain eye contact while speaking in a calm voice.

13. Mrs. Evans is in the intensive care unit following complications of surgery. A family member reports to you that a nurse at Mrs. Evans' bedside said, "I wouldn't want to live in her condition." What did this nurse not realize about Mrs. Evans' capabilities?
    1) The client can read lips
    2) She can hear what the nurse says
    3) She can respond to statements via written communication
    4) She can be sensitive to the nurse's nonverbal behavior

Correct Answer: 2
Topic: Nonverbal Behavior
Step of the Nursing Process: All Phases of the Nursing Process
Cognitive Level: Application
Difficulty: Moderate
Rationale: Hearing is the last sense to go. The nurse should not say anything she would not want the client to hear.

14. Your client, Grace Smith, does not respond verbally to you. As a nurse in the intensive care unit, you should:
    1) Frequently change her position for physiological benefit only
    2) Continue to talk to the client
    3) Not explain procedures because the client will not understand
    4) Create a less stimulating environment

Correct Answer: 2
Topic: Environmental Deprivation
Step of the Nursing Process: Interventions

Cognitive Level: Application
Difficulty: Moderate
Rationale: Even if the client is unwilling or unable to talk, the nurse should continue to communicate in a one-way mode.

15. You are attempting to communicate a procedure to your Spanish-speaking client, Maria. A strategy that you could use to facilitate understanding would be to:
    1) Speak loudly
    2) Have her child interpret
    3) Use visual aids such as pictures
    4) Become bilingual

Correct Answer: 3
Topic: Communication Deficits Due to Foreign Language
Step of the Nursing Process: Interventions
Cognitive Level: Application
Difficulty: Moderate
Rationale: Pictures and photographs can be used to facilitate communication.

16. Your client, Mr. Jones, is deaf and legally blind in his right eye. He has just had cataract surgery on his left eye. You know that:
    1) You should hold his arm and lead him to the bathroom
    2) Verbal speech is useless in this situation
    3) Develop signs and signals to communicate
    4) Do not touch the client, as this will startle him

Correct Answer: 3
Topic: Helping the Deaf-Blind Client
Step of the Nursing Process: Interventions
Cognitive Level: Application
Difficulty: Moderate
Rationale: Develop and use signs and signals to identify yourself and to give directions to the client.

17. Your client, Jim, is disoriented and is exhibiting psychotic symptoms. You suspect intensive care unit psychosis. What is a strategy that would not be useful in this situation?
    1) Display pictures from home
    2) Place a clock and calendar within view
    3) Dim the lights and leave the client alone
    4) Reassure the client that cognitive psychological disturbances are common

Correct Answer: 3
Topic: Communicating with Clients in the Intensive Care Unit
Step of the Nursing Process: Interventions
Cognitive Level: Application
Difficulty: Moderate
Rationale: Dimming the lights and leaving the client isolated might increase psychosis and fear.

CHAPTER 18

Communicating with Children

1. Tools needed by caregivers to provide effective and ethical care are:
    1) Cognitive, societal, and educational
    2) Educational, cultural, and interpersonal
    3) Cognitive, interpersonal, and attitudinal
    4) Attitudinal, cultural, and societal

Correct Answer: 3
Topic: Communicating with Children
Step of the Nursing Process: All Phases of the Nursing Process
Cognitive Level: Knowledge
Difficulty: Easy
Rationale: Tools needed by caregivers to provide effective and ethical care are cognitive, interpersonal, and attitudinal. For each of these domains, the child's socioeconomic status and cultural background must be considered.

2. According to Piaget, which of the following cognitive stages of development is Johnny, age 4, experiencing?
    1) Concrete operational
    2) Formal operations
    3) Preoperational
    4) Sensory-motor

Correct Answer: 3
Topic: Cognitive Stages of Development
Step of the Nursing Process: All Phases of the Nursing Process
Cognitive Level: Knowledge

Difficulty: Easy
Rationale: The preoperational stage relates to the preschool child.

3. When communicating with Brian, age 5, who is admitted to the hospital for cardiac surgery, which is the best means to describe his impending operation?
    1) Use a teddy bear to indicate where the heart is located; say it is sick and the doctor will fix it
    2) Explain what surgery will be like, and answer questions honestly
    3) Role-play the surgery with reassuring facial expressions
    4) Read a story describing cardiac surgery using a child as lead character

Correct Answer: 1
Topic: Communicating with Children
Step of the Nursing Process: Implementation
Cognitive Level: Analysis
Difficulty: Hard
Rationale: At the preschool stage, verbal explanations should be accomplished by the use of concrete, touchable objects.

4. Factors affecting the child's response to illness include:
    1) Acuity of illness, family's ability to cope
    2) Family's financial status, child's cognitive ability
    3) Chronicity of illness, family's ability to cope
    4) The parent's educational level, chronicity of illness

Correct Answer: 3
Topic: Child's Response to Illness
Step of the Nursing Process: Assessment
Cognitive Level: Comprehension
Difficulty: Moderate
Rationale: Factors that affect the child's response include chronicity of illness, the impact on lifestyle, the child's cognitive understanding of the illness, and the family's ability to cope with the illness.

5. When the nurse is assessing a child's reaction to illness, it is important to:

1) Observe the interaction between parent and child
2) Recognize that chronological age matches cognitive level
3) Realize that children are more comfortable with female health care providers
4) Recognize that the child's behavior will be age-appropriate

Correct Answer: 1
Topic: Assessing a Child's Reaction to Illness
Step of the Nursing Process: Assessment
Cognitive Level: Application
Difficulty: Moderate
Rationale: Assessing a child's reaction to illness involves observing interactions with parents and behavioral responses to others.

6. Bobby, a 4-year-old boy, has been hospitalized for treatment of pneumonia. He has had two episodes of bed-wetting. The nurse should:
    1) Refer Bobby to a urologist
    2) Obtain a urine sample and send it to the laboratory
    3) Reassure the parents that bed-wetting is common
    4) Restrict fluids after dinner

Correct Answer: 3
Topic: Regression as a Form of Childhood Communication
Step of the Nursing Process: Implementation
Cognitive Level: Analysis
Difficulty: Moderate
Rationale: Bed-wetting in this example is a form of regression. It is important to reassure the parents that this is a common response to the stress of illness.

7. Joan, a pediatric nurse, is explaining about how children cope with hospitalization. Which of the following statements by Joan is correct?
    1) The quiet, compliant child who never complains is comfortable on the unit
    2) The child who screams and cries is terrified of being in the hospital
    3) The 2-year-old asking for a bedtime bottle is showing regression
    4) The child who screams and cries may be less frightened than the quiet child who never complains

Correct Answer: 4

Topic: Regression
Step of the Nursing Process: Assessment
Cognitive Level: Application
Difficulty: Hard
Rationale: The nurse needs to obtain detailed information about the usual responses of the family and child.

8. When communicating with hospitalized infants and toddlers, the nurse knows that:
    1) She should use long sentences with sooth-ing words
    2) She cannot communicate with a preverbal infant
    3) Moving to the child's eye level and main-taining eye contact is important
    4) She should pick up an 18-month-old infant immediately

Correct Answer: 3
Topic: Communicating with Infants
Step of the Nursing Process: Implementation
Cognitive Level: Comprehension
Difficulty: Moderate
Rationale: A face-to-face position, maintaining eye contact and reassuring facial expressions assist with interactions with infants.

9. During the preoperational period, children:
    1) Ask numerous questions to clarify messages
    2) Can process auditory information quickly
    3) Can clearly distinguish between fantasy and reality
    4) Misunderstand messages

Correct Answer: 4
Topic: Preoperational Stage
Step of the Nursing Process: All Phases of the Nursing Process
Cognitive Level: Comprehension
Difficulty: Moderate
Rationale: Messages can be easily misunderstood by preoperational children because they do not ask for clarification and they cannot process auditory information quickly. They cannot make a clear distinction between fantasy and reality.

10. Following hip surgery, Jenna, a 4-year-old, is found crying and has been refusing to eat. The best communication strategy for the pediatric nurse to use is:

1) Sit at the bedside and hold the client's hand
2) Tell the client she is not being punished
3) Get the client some clay, crayons, and paper
4) Encourage the client to visualize her feelings

Correct Answer: 3
Topic: Play as a Communication Strategy
Step of the Nursing Process: Interventions
Cognitive Level: Application
Difficulty: Moderate
Rationale: Play can be used to help children express their feelings and to role-play coping strategies. Preschoolers lack the vocabulary to express thought and feelings. Play is a primary tool for assessing perceptions, anxieties, and fears.

11. Andy, a 15-year-old, has been sent to the school nurse's office. The principal reports that Andy is having trouble controlling his anger. Which of the following interventions should the school nurse use?
    1) "Andy, tell me what the principal means when he says you are out of control?"
    2) "Andy, let's develop a plan of action to control your behavior"
    3) "Andy, it is tough for you to get along with the other kids in your class"
    4) "Andy, are you willing to take some time to discuss what it is like for you during these incidents? I will not tell the principal what you tell me, within certain limita-tions."

Correct Answer: 4
Topic: Communicating with Adolescents
Step of the Nursing Process: Interventions
Cognitive Level: Analysis
Difficulty: Hard
Rationale: Assessment of the adolescent should occur in a private setting. Discussion should be confidential if the nurse wants to obtain informa-tion about substance use and sexual activity. The limits of maintaining confidentiality must be explained, for example, if the client states that he feels suicidal. The nurse in this situation is indicat-ing that she will listen to what the experience is like for the client.

12. Which of the following is true in relation to the stress of having an ill child?

1) Coping with the uncertainty of the outcome is the most stressful factor for parents
2) Financial and marital stress causes the most distress for parents
3) The level of stress is consistent across cultures
4) The parent's inability to comfort the child is more stressful than factors connected with the illness

Correct Answer: 4
Topic: Interacting with Parents
Step of the Nursing Process: All Phases of the Nursing Process
Cognitive Level: Knowledge
Difficulty: Moderate
Rationale: The loss of the ability to comfort the child and to alleviate pain is more stressful to parents than factors connected with the illness, including the uncertainty of the outcome.

13. When admitting 16-year-old Tom, the nurse knows she should keep in mind which of the following?
    1) To use the "three wishes question" to assess cognitive level
    2) When a teen asks a direct question, he does not really want the answer
    3) Teens recognize that life is a roller coaster ride with ups and downs
    4) Teens are able to self-assess their own competency

Correct Answer: 1
Topic: Assessing Teens
Step of the Nursing Process: Assessment
Cognitive Level: Application
Difficulty: Moderate
Rationale: By asking a teen to name three wishes he would like to have in 5 years, the nurse can assess his cognitive level.

14. The nurse conveys respect to the child by:
    1) Being a "buddy" to the client
    2) Protecting the child from the truth about procedure or illness
    3) Using the concept of mutuality
    4) Keeping his or her emotions in check

Correct Answer: 3
Topic: Conveying Respect
Step of the Nursing Process: All Phases of the Nursing Process

Cognitive Level: Application
Difficulty: Moderate
Rationale: The concept of mutuality promotes respect and helps foster positive outcomes.

15. You are working the evening shift on a pediatric unit. Diane is a 2-year-old whose parents have just gone home for the evening. She is standing at the edge of the crib and crying, Which of the following interventions will you use?
    1) "Diane, Mommy and Daddy will return tomorrow"
    2) Hug Diane, and start playing with her
    3) "Diane, I came to get you ready for sleep"
    4) Hug Diane and state, "I am here because you miss Mommy and Daddy"

Correct Answer: 2
Topic: Communicating with Children
Step of the Nursing Process: Interventions
Cognitive Level: Analysis
Difficulty: Hard
Rationale: To deal with separation anxiety, hug and rock the child and play games.

16. When communicating with school-aged children, it is important to:
    1) Speak to them at eye level
    2) Involve their parents
    3) Be aware of their privacy needs
    4) Use touch

Correct Answer: 3
Topic: Communicating with Children
Step of the Nursing Process: Interventions
Cognitive Level: Knowledge
Difficulty: Moderate
Rationale: School-aged children have an increased need for privacy. Respect privacy, knock on the door before entering, and tell them when and why you will return to their room.

17. The best way to deal with a toddler experiencing separation anxiety is to:
    1) Accept the child's crying and screaming as normal
    2) Position yourself across the room so as not to escalate the situation
    3) Attempt to suppress the child's anger to avoid upsetting the other clients

4) Give the child plenty of time to be alone

Correct Answer: 1
Topic: Separation Anxiety
Step of the Nursing Process: Interventions
Cognitive Level: Knowledge
Difficulty: Moderate
Rationale: Accept the child's behavior as a healthy expression of separation anxiety.

18. Andrea, age 14, is being treated for a skin condition that affects her face and arms. She states, "I look like a freak." Which of the following is a nursing diagnosis for Andrea's situation?
    1) Body image disturbance
    2) Ineffective coping
    3) Anxiety
    4) Threat to body integrity

Correct Answer: 1
Topic: Communicating with Adolescents
Step of the Nursing Process: Diagnosis
Cognitive Level: Application
Difficulty: Moderate
Rationale: Andrea has a disturbance in body image related to her skin condition, as evidenced by her statement, "I look like a freak."

19. When administering consequences for unacceptable behavior, the nurse should remember that consequences are:
    1) Applied after a detailed verbal exchange with the client
    2) Person-centered, not situation-centered
    3) Applied in a matter-of-fact manner

4) Applied at a time negotiated between nurse and client

Correct Answer: 3
Topic: Consequences for Unacceptable Behavior
Step of the Nursing Process: Implementation
Cognitive Level: Knowledge
Difficulty: Moderate
Rationale: Consequences should be applied in a matter-of-fact manner immediately following the unacceptable behavior and without a lengthy discussion.

20. Marie, a 9-year-old, has been admitted to the hospital because of an accident during her gymnastics session. She complains of not feeling her legs. Marie's parents ask you, "What is going to happen to our daughter? Will she walk again?" Your response is:
    1) "I'm sure everything will be OK. She is in good hands"
    2) "The best thing you can do for Marie is to act as if everything is all right"
    3) "You will have to ask the doctor; he is in surgery right now"
    4) "You must have several fears and concerns. We will let you know the test results as soon as they are available"

Correct Answer: 4
Topic: Interacting with Parents of Ill Children
Step of the Nursing Process: Interventions
Cognitive Level: Analysis
Difficulty: Hard
Rationale: It is important to reassure parents that it is all right to be scared and to keep the parents continually informed about the child's progress.

CHAPTER 19

Communicating with Older Adults

1. The assessment of the older adult should focus on:
    1) Chronological age
    2) Functional level
    3) Relationship needs
    4) Social functioning

Correct Answer: 2
Topic: Assessment of the Older Adult
Step of the Nursing Process: Assessment
Cognitive Level: Knowledge

Difficulty: Easy
Rationale: Functional level is a more accurate indication of client needs. Functional abilities can range from vigorous and independent to frail and dependent regardless of chronological age.

2. Mr. and Mrs. Barnes are an elderly couple who were traveling across the country in their mobile home, when Mrs. Barnes experienced

acute abdominal pain and had to be hospitalized. Mr. Barnes states to you, "I don't know what I would do if she doesn't make it." Mrs. Barnes states, "We must continue this trip, because it may be my last one." Which nursing diagnosis is appropriate for this situation?
1) Ineffective individual coping by Mr. Barnes
2) Ineffective family coping
3) Knowledge deficit
4) Alteration in role expectation

Correct Answer: 2
Topic: Communicating with Older Adults
Step of the Nursing Process: Diagnosis
Cognitive Level: Analysis
Difficulty: Moderate
Rationale: The problem in this situation is the failure of the couple to communicate their concern to each other.

3. Mr. Adams, age 85, tells you, "My life has been a waste." This statement demonstrates which aspect of psychosocial development?
1) Ego integrity
2) Ego despair
3) Lack of generatively
4) Isolation

Correct Answer: 2
Topic: Theoretical Frameworks
Step of the Nursing Process: Assessment
Cognitive Level: Application
Difficulty: Moderate
Rationale: Ego despair is defined as a failure to accept one's life as meaningful.

4. You are conducting a goal-setting group on your unit. When it comes to Clara Jones turn, she states, "I feel old. I just feel so old and that I have nothing in common with anyone here." In planning interventions for Clara, it is important to:
1) Find other clients on the unit that she can identify with
2) Help her to identify strengths that she has used in the past
3) Allow family members to visit more frequently
4) Have her work on a craft in recreational therapy

Correct Answer: 2

Topic: Psychosocial and Environmental Changes
Step of the Nursing Process: Planning
Cognitive Level: Application
Difficulty: Hard
Rationale: The strengths of the client form the basis for planning and intervention.

5. You have identified loneliness as a problem for Gladys, your 83-year-old client. This problem is associated with which level of Maslow's hierarchy of needs?
1) Biological integrity
2) Belonging
3) Self-actualization
4) Self-esteem

Correct Answer: 2
Topic: Theoretical Frameworks
Step of the Nursing Process: Assessment
Cognitive Level: Application
Difficulty: Moderate
Rationale: Loneliness is associated with Maslow's third level on the hierarchy; belonging (e.g., having friends or affiliating with groups).

6. It is critical to assess hearing loss in the elderly because:
1) Hearing loss has a direct impact on communication
2) Deafness causes hair loss
3) There is an initial inability to hear low-frequency consonants
4) Older adults can hear at only 90 words per minute

Correct Answer: 1
Topic: Assessing Sensory Deficits
Step of the Nursing Process: Assessment
Cognitive Level: Knowledge
Difficulty: Easy
Rationale: Sensory deficits, including hearing loss, have a direct and significant effect on communication.

7. You have assessed significant hearing loss in your 70-year-old client, Jim Grant. You are planning interventions to assist him. An appropriate intervention would be to:
1) Introduce yourself first
2) Shout into his good ear
3) Teach Mr. Grant sign language

4) Check his hearing aid batteries

Correct Answer: 4

Topic: Interventions to Use with Hearing Changes

Step of the Nursing Process: Planning

Cognitive Level: Application

Difficulty: Moderate

Rationale: The elderly client may not realize that his batteries need replacement, or he may lack the manual dexterity to replace them.

8. Mrs. Jones, your elderly client, is visually impaired. You have just completed her care plan. Which of the following interventions are appropriate for Mrs. Jones?
    1) Stand away from the client when communicating to avoid obstructing the view of the immediate environment
    2) Touch the client before you speak to let him or her know that you are there
    3) Verbally explain all written information unless the client is wearing her reading glasses
    4) Verbally describe what is on her meal tray and where each item is located

Correct Answer: 4

Topic: Therapeutic Strategies to Use with the Visually Impaired

Step of the Nursing Process: Implementation

Cognitive Level: Application

Difficulty: Moderate

Rationale: Verbal explanations are important even if the client does not request help and appears to be looking at her tray.

9. You are assessing Albert Green's need for support services. He is an 85-year-old man who was hospitalized after falling on the sidewalk. He lives alone. He seems reluctant to accept assistance. You know that this is likely due to his fear of:
    1) Not being able to pay for services
    2) Putting a financial burden on his family
    3) Loss of independence
    4) Loss of privacy

Correct Answer: 3

Topic: Using a Proactive Approach

Step of the Nursing Process: Assessment

Cognitive Level: Application

Difficulty: Moderate

Rationale: Older adults may minimize difficulties and refuse services because of their fear of loss of independent living. They often associate accepting help as the first step toward a nursing home.

10. You are making a home visit to Mr. and Mrs. Andrews. You note that she frequently shifts the conversation to reminisce. Which of the following communication techniques would be most effective with her?
    1) Restating
    2) Changing the subject
    3) Giving information
    4) Asking exploring questions

Correct Answer: 4

Topic: Reminiscing

Step of the Nursing Process: Intervention

Cognitive Level: Application

Difficulty: Moderate

Rationale: Asking exploring questions will give you an opportunity to gain insight into the person.

11. Mrs. Martin is a 74-year-old woman. You introduce yourself as Miss Gordon. Mrs. Martin says, "Do you know where the bathroom is? This is not my home. Please Angie, get me out of here. My parents will be wondering where I am." Select the relevant nursing diagnosis for Mrs. Martin.
    1) Impaired sensory input
    2) Impaired verbal communication
    3) Alteration in thought process
    4) Knowledge deficit

Correct Answer: 3

Topic: Communicating with Older Adults

Step of the Nursing Process: Diagnosis

Cognitive Level: Analysis

Difficulty: Moderate

Rationale: Mrs. Martin is disoriented to time and place. There is no evidence of impaired sensory input or knowledge deficit, and she can communicate verbally. It is her thought processes that are impaired.

12. The loss of the ability to take purposeful action even when muscles, senses, and vocabulary seem intact is known as:
    1) Presbycusis
    2) Obstinance

3) Apraxia
4) Echolalia

Correct Answer: 3
Topic: Communicating with the Cognitively Impaired Adult
Step of the Nursing Process: Assessment
Cognitive Level: Knowledge
Difficulty: Moderate
Rationale: Apraxia causes a person to appear to register on a command but then to act in a manner that suggests little understanding.

13. You are caring for Mrs. Greg, a client who has a moderate cognitive disability. You know that when developing a relationship with her it is important to know that:
    1) Recent memory is retained longer than remote memory
    2) Elderly clients like to give material gifts
    3) Reminiscing about the past can cause distress
    4) Reminiscing about the past can improve verbal communication

Correct Answer: 4
Topic: Reminiscence
Step of the Nursing Process: Interventions
Cognitive Level: Application
Difficulty: Moderate
Rationale: Mentally impaired persons become more verbal when they are allowed to reminisce.

14. Which of the following is the best action when caring for a disoriented client?
    1) Speak in simple sentences
    2) Explain what you are doing
    3) Look at client when speaking
    4) Personalize social amenities

Correct Answer: 1
Topic: Communicating on Strategies with the Cognitively Impaired Client
Step of the Nursing Process: Implementation
Cognitive Level: Knowledge
Difficulty: Moderate
Rationale: By speaking in simple sentences, the nurse enables the older adult to use his or her remaining capabilities.

15. Mrs. Ames is an elderly client who calls you sister Ann, even though you have introduced

yourself as Mr. Wong. Before you ask how she is, the best response to Mrs. Ames is:
1) Tell her who you are
2) Ask her if she wears glasses
3) Ask Mrs. Ames to explain where she is
4) Ask Mrs. Ames to repeat what she said

Correct Answer: 1
Topic: Communicating with Older Adults
Step of the Nursing Process: Implementation
Cognitive Level: Application
Difficulty: Hard
Rationale: Repetition is useful in focusing the older adult's attention. Restating and using the same words and sequence help the conversation continue.

16. When communicating with cognitively impaired elderly clients, the nurse should understand the use of touch. Which of the following is true in relation to using touch with the elderly?
    1) Touch increases their agitation and confusion
    2) Touch is calming
    3) The use of touch must be determined on an individual basis
    4) Touch the client's face to establish rapport

Correct Answer: 3
Topic: Use of Touch
Step of the Nursing Process: Interventions
Cognitive Level: Knowledge
Difficulty: Moderate
Rationale: The use of touch must be appropriate and determined on an individual basis.

17. You want to promote autonomy and independence of your cognitively impaired elderly client, Mrs. Brant, in the performance of activities of daily living. The most beneficial instructions to your client would be:
    1) "Let's brush our teeth now, dear."
    2) "I want you to brush your teeth."
    3) "Do you want to brush your teeth?"
    4) "Mrs. Brant, take the lid off the toothpaste. Now put the brush under the water."

Correct Answer: 4
Topic: Repetition and Instructions
Step of the Nursing Process: Interventions
Cognitive Level: Analysis
Difficulty: Moderate

Rationale: Breaking down the instructions into smaller steps may make the activity possible and may reinforce self-esteem.

18. Catastrophic reactions can occur in the cognitively impaired elderly. An appropriate way of dealing with this type of reaction is to:
    1) Directly confront the client
    2) Ask the client to act more civilized
    3) Tell the client that he is acting like a baby having a temper tantrum
    4) Use distraction

Correct Answer: 4
Topic: Use of Distraction
Step of the Nursing Process: Interventions
Cognitive Level: Knowledge
Difficulty: Moderate
Rationale: The nurse should use distraction to move the client away from the offending stimuli.

19. You are interviewing Mr. and Mrs. Hart, an elderly couple, at home. Mr. Hart asks to speak to you alone. He tells you that Mrs. Hart has become forgetful lately and that yesterday he received an overdue tax bill. He asks, "Should I take over this responsibility?" What would you say to Mr. Hart?
    1) "Old people get forgetful at times"
    2) "Tell Mrs. Hart that you will help with the bill paying"

    3) "Tell Mrs. Hart that you will assume the responsibility now"
    4) You don't know what to suggest. This is a family matter

Correct Answer: 2
Topic: Implementation
Step of the Nursing Process: Implementation
Cognitive Level: Analysis
Difficulty: Hard
Rationale: By encouraging spousal support, you are supporting Mrs. Hart's independence and helping her to keep her dignity even though she has become forgetful.

20. When performing a mental status examination on an elderly client, you discover that he is illiterate and has only a third grade education. How would you assess cognition?
    1) Have him spell "world" backwards
    2) Have him spell "world" forwards
    3) Ask him to perform serial seven's
    4) Have him tell you the days of the week backwards

Correct Answer: 4
Topic: Mental Status Testing of the Older Adult
Step of the Nursing Process: Assessment
Cognitive Level: Application
Difficulty: Moderate
Rationale: Naming the days of the week is a good alternative if the client has never learned to spell.

CHAPTER 20

Communicating with Clients in Stressful Situations

1. What type of stress increases the level of thyroxine?
   1) Eustress phase
   2) Alarm phase
   3) Resistance phase
   4) Exhaustion phase

Correct Answer: 2
Topic: General Adaptation Syndrome
Step of the Nursing Process: All Phases of the Nursing Process
Cognitive Level: Knowledge
Difficulty: Moderate
Rationale: During the alarm phase, the level of thyroxine increases, which increases the metabolic rate.

2. Which of the following is true about how males and females differ in their reaction to stress?
   1) Men act out their stress as depressive behavior
   2) Women act out their stress as depressive behavior
   3) Women act out their stress as denial behavior
   4) Women act out their stress as aggression

Correct Answer: 2
Topic: Basic Concepts Related to Stress
Step of the Nursing Process: All Phases of the Nursing Process

Cognitive Level: Knowledge
Difficulty: Moderate
Rationale: Women internalize stress and may experience depression, whereas men are more likely to respond with denial or anger.

3. Which of the following is true in relation to stress?
   1) Men and women respond to stress in the same fashion
   2) Culture does not affect the stress experience
   3) Stress is always a negative experience
   4) Stress can be experienced as a response to positive circumstances
Correct Answer: 4
Topic: Stress
Step of the Nursing Process: All Phases of the Nursing Process
Cognitive Level: Knowledge
Difficulty: Moderate
Rationale: People can experience stress in response to a positive event, such as a promotion or the birth of a child.

4. You are conducting a family assessment in which alcoholism is suspected. When assessing 5-year-old Jimmy for the effects of stress, you know that:
   1) He will tell you if something is wrong
   2) His complaints of a tummy ache must be related to something he ate
   3) Quiet, withdrawn behavior can result from stress in a child
   4) Loss of appetite must be related to a physiological cause
Correct Answer: 3
Topic: Special Issues for Children
Step of the Nursing Process: Assessment
Cognitive Level: Application
Difficulty: Moderate
Rationale: Stress in the child can present as withdrawn or acting-out behavior.

5. The stress that an individual experiences in response to completing a project with a deadline is an example of:
   1) Stress
   2) Eustress

   3) Stressor
   4) Distress
Correct Answer: 2
Topic: Theoretical Models of Stress
Step of the Nursing Process: All Phases of the Nursing Process
Cognitive Level: Application
Difficulty: Moderate
Rationale: Eustress is a mild level of stress that acts as a positive stress response.

6. The stress model that describes a patterned response to environmental demands is known as:
   1) Cannon's model of stress as a physiologic response
   2) Selye's General Adaptation Syndrome
   3) Holmes and Rahe's model of stress as a stimulus
   4) Lazarus and Folkman's Transactional Model of Stress
Correct Answer: 2
Topic: Theoretical Models of Stress
Step of the Nursing Process: All Phases of the Nursing Process
Cognitive Level: Knowledge
Difficulty: Moderate
Rationale: According to Selye, a patterned response occurs to stress in response to either a physical or psychological stressor.

7. Which of the following is true in relation to primary and secondary appraisal of stressors?
   1) Primary appraisal consists of a person's perception of coping skills
   2) Primary and secondary appraisals are discrete
   3) Primary appraisal is a subjective experience
   4) Primary appraisal is an objective experience
Correct Answer: 3
Topic: Transactional Model of Stress
Step of the Nursing Process: All Phases of the Nursing Process
Cognitive Level: Knowledge
Difficulty: Moderate
Rationale: Primary appraisal of a stressful situation is a subjective experience influenced by a variety of factors.

8. Mr. Adams, the husband of your client, Joan, who has just received a terminal diagnosis, is yelling at you and calling you incompetent in caring for his wife. When you are dealing with a hostile family member, it is important that you:
    1) Threaten to call security
    2) Defend yourself and the care you provide
    3) Realize that stressed people say things that they don't mean but like to keep hidden
    4) Do not take the anger personally

Correct Answer: 4
Topic: Hostility
Step of the Nursing Process: Implementation
Cognitive Level: Application
Difficulty: Moderate
Rationale: Do not take the anger personally, but realize that this is a temporary emotional response displaced onto you.

9. Which of the following statements is true in relation to anxiety?
    1) Anxiety has a direct, identifiable source of discomfort
    2) Anxiety is experienced as a single emotion
    3) Anxiety is always expressed directly
    4) The inability to recall information is a symptom of anxiety

Correct Answer: 4
Topic: Anxiety
Step of the Nursing Process: Assessment
Cognitive Level: Knowledge
Difficulty: Moderate
Rationale: Psychological symptoms of anxiety include inability to recall information, blocked speech, and fear of losing control.

10. Which of the following represents the most effective intervention when dealing with a hostile family member?
    1) Tell the family member that his expectations are unrealistic
    2) Ask the family member to go to the coffee shop for a break
    3) Refer the family member to the administrator
    4) Listen carefully to the family member

Correct Answer: 4
Topic: Hostility
Step of the Nursing Process: Interventions

Cognitive Level: Application
Difficulty: Moderate
Rationale: Listening calmly is helpful in dealing with a hostile client or family member.

11. Mr. Adams becomes angry with you. Which of the following is the best way to handle the situation?
    1) "I hear your anger; what is happening here?"
    2) "I hear your anger, but I have feelings too."
    3) "I will not be caring for you again."
    4) "I think you'd better get control of yourself."

Correct Answer: 1
Topic: Dealing with Hostility
Step of the Nursing Process: Implementation
Cognitive Level: Application
Difficulty: Moderate
Rationale: The first part of the statement acknowledges the anger, the second part asks for more information. The nurse is not agreeing with the client or becoming defensive as in 2), 3), and 4).

12. Mrs. Roberts visits her mother, who is experiencing the terminal stage of cancer, and discovers bruises on her mother's arms. Mrs. Roberts states, "I don't understand why you can't take better care of my mother." Which of the following is the best response?
    1) "I think you should know that your mother pulled out her tubes."
    2) "Lets make a plan for improving her care."
    3) "I don't have to accept your criticism."
    4) "I think the nursing care is good, but your mother is confused at times."

Correct Answer: 4
Topic: Hostility
Step of the Nursing Process: Implementation
Cognitive Level: Application
Difficulty: Hard
Rationale: This statement encourages the family member to enter into a partnership. This takes the focus off nonproductive blaming and helps refocus on problem-solving.

13. Which type of coping strategy allows the individual to take direct action?
    1) Ego defense mechanism
    2) Short-term ego defense

3) Ego-enhancing strategy
4) Threat distortion

Correct Answer: 3
Topic: Coping Strategies
Step of the Nursing Process: Assessment
Cognitive Level: Knowledge
Difficulty: Moderate
Rationale: Ego-enhancing strategies include obtaining information, seeking practical advice, and taking direct action.

14. Doug, a 10-year-old child, has been uncooperative with the health care team, refusing treatment and bed baths. Determine how you would communicate with Doug:
    1) "Doug, what is wrong?"
    2) "Doug, I will give you a reward for allowing me to give you a bath."
    3) "Doug, I will leave the bathing equipment at your bedside and return later to help you finish it."
    4) "Doug, do you know what is happening to you?"

Correct Answer: 4
Topic: Special Issues for Children
Step of the Nursing Process: Interventions
Cognitive Level: Application
Difficulty: Moderate
Rationale: Asking children what they know about their illness and how they think they are doing encourages them to voice fears and concerns.

15. Mrs. Evans, age 82, suffers from chronic pain associated with terminal cancer. As you communicate with her, what is your expectation of her view of illness?
    1) Fear of dying
    2) Fear of pain
    3) Mourning of social death
    4) Fear of the unknown

Correct Answer: 3
Topic: Special Issues for Frail Elderly
Step of the Nursing Process: All Phases of the Nursing Process
Cognitive Level: Application
Difficulty: Moderate
Rationale: Instead of fearing physical death, the frail elderly fear a prolonged, meaningless existence with the loss of all that matters. They often long for death.

16. Mrs. Burke, age 85, has been diagnosed with terminal lung cancer. Her health record indicates that the family does not want Mrs. Burke to know her diagnosis. Mrs. Burke asks you, "Am I going to die?" Which of the following is the best response?
    1) "What prompted that question, Mrs. Burke?"
    2) "Mrs. Burke, I will ask your physician to discuss this matter with you."
    3) "Let's take each day as it comes, Mrs. Burke."
    4) "Mrs. Burke, you are asking me a question that you need to discuss with your family."

Correct Answer: 1
Topic: Hidden Stressors
Step of the Nursing Process: Interventions
Cognitive Level: Analysis
Difficulty: Hard
Rationale: Before you answer, it is useful to ask the client what prompted the question to gather information about the client's level of knowledge. This also allows you to focus on the client's unique concerns.

17. Which of the following is a coping task that must be addressed in health care settings?
    1) Developing different perspectives
    2) Modifying stressful situations through direct action
    3) Sustaining a positive self-image
    4) Reducing toxic waste

Correct Answer: 3
Topic: Diagnosis
Step of the Nursing Process: Diagnosis
Cognitive Level: Knowledge
Difficulty: Moderate
Rationale: Sustaining a positive self-image is one of the five coping tasks identified by Lazarus and Folkman.

18. Tory has been working as a critical care nurse for the past five years. Lately he has not been able to sleep well and has been staying past the end of his shift to complete his work. He has not been taking a lunch break. He spends his time off worrying about the clients he has cared for. Tory is suffering from:
    1) Physical stress
    2) Burnout

3) Psychological stress
4) Lack of time management skills
Correct Answer: 2
Topic: Effects of Stress on the Nurse
Step of the Nursing Process: All Phases of the Nursing Process
Cognitive Level: Application
Difficulty: Moderate
Rationale: Burnout is a term used to describe physical, emotional, and spiritual exhaustion among caregivers.

19. Henry has been dismissed from college. He talks about which classes he enjoyed this semester and those scheduled for next semester. Which of the following mechanism does this situation represent?
    1) Denial
    2) Intellectualization
    3) Repression
    4) Sublimation
Correct Answer: 3

Topic: Ego Defense Mechanisms
Step of the Nursing Process: Assessment
Cognitive Level: Application
Difficulty: Moderate
Rationale: Repression is the unconscious forgetting of parts or all of an experience.

20. Which of the following interventions would be classified as secondary prevention for stress?
    1) Classify stressor
    2) Mobilize resources
    3) Educate client and family
    4) Coordinate resources
Correct Answer: 2
Topic: Using the Nursing Process in Stressful Situations
Step of the Nursing Process: Interventions
Cognitive Level: Knowledge
Difficulty: Moderate
Rationale: Mobilizing resources is classified as a secondary prevention intervention.

CHAPTER 21

Communicating with Clients in Crisis

1. Edith, age 35, is admitted to the hospital for removal of her right ovary. She recently lost her son in an automobile accident. Which type of crisis is she experiencing?
   1) Developmental crisis
   2) Situational crisis
   3) Developmental and psychological crisis
   4) Situational and developmental crisis
Correct Answer: 4
Topic: Types of Crises
Step of the Nursing Process: All Phases of the Nursing Process
Cognitive Level: Application
Difficulty: Moderate
Rationale: Developmental crisis occur in connection with maturational changes. A situational crisis represents an external event that occurs randomly.

2. Interpersonal challenges that occur during transitional crisis points in the life cycle is a concept of which theoretical crisis framework?
   1) Kaplan's model of preventive psychiatry

   2) Erikson's theory of developmental psychosocial crises
   3) Aguilera and Messick's nursing crises intervention model
   4) Crisis theory
Correct Answer: 2
Topic: Theoretical Frameworks
Step of the Nursing Process: All Phases of the Nursing Process
Cognitive Level: Knowledge
Difficulty: Moderate
Rationale: Erikson's theory provides a basis for understanding the role of psychosocial crises at every life stage.

3. Which of the following is an abnormal response to a crisis?
   1) Emotional imbalance
   2) Mental illness
   3) Failure of coping strategies
   4) "Leaden paralysis"
Correct Answer: 4

Topic: Clinical behaviors of the crisis state
Step of the Nursing Process: Assessment
Cognitive Level: Knowledge
Difficulty: Moderate
Rationale: A crisis state is a normal response to an abnormal situation. Physical symptoms include feelings of "leaden paralysis."

4. During the recoil period of the crisis state:
    1) Behaviors appear normal
    2) Clients can experience déjà vu
    3) Clients reestablish identity
    4) Substance abuse

Correct Answer: 1
Topic: Crisis State
Step of the Nursing Process: Assessment
Cognitive Level: Knowledge
Difficulty: Moderate
Rationale: Client behaviors can appear normal to outsiders.

5. Joan, age 20, was raped by an acquaintance a week ago. She has come to the woman's health center for follow-up. "I keep reliving the rape, and it frightens me." Your response is:
    1) "Joan, you need to focus on the present."
    2) "Tell me more about this nightmare."
    3) "You are experiencing a normal reaction to rape."
    4) "Joan, would you like to attend a support group for victims of rape?"

Correct Answer: 3
Topic: Crisis Intervention
Step of the Nursing Process: Implementation
Cognitive Level: Application
Difficulty: Moderate
Rationale: The crisis victim can experience nightmares, phobic reactions, and flashbacks of the traumatic event. These are all normal responses to the event.

6. Which of the following statements describes crisis intervention?
    1) A long-term treatment to improve coping skills
    2) A strategy that focuses on future problem-solving skills
    3) A way to promote a level of functioning that exceeds the pre-crisis level

    4) A strategy designed to result in an adaptive outcome

Correct Answer: 4
Topic: Crisis Intervention
Step of the Nursing Process: Implementation
Cognitive Level: Knowledge
Difficulty: Hard
Rationale: Crisis intervention is designed to promote an adaptive outcome.

7. Listening to the client is a strategy to be used during which step in the three-step process model of intervention?
    1) Exploring the problem
    2) Applying the model
    3) Engaging the client
    4) Developing alternatives

Correct Answer: 3
Topic: Crisis Intervention Model
Step of the Nursing Process: Interventions
Cognitive Level: Knowledge
Difficulty: Moderate
Rationale: In the early stages of crisis, people need to be listened to rather than receive information.

8. You have identified that your client in crisis is experiencing a sense of hopelessness. Which focusing strategy likely assisted you in the identification of hopelessness?
    1) Identifying central themes
    2) Providing truth in information
    3) Clarifying distortions
    4) Normalizing feelings

Correct Answer: 1
Topic: Crisis Intervention
Step of the Nursing Process: Interventions
Cognitive Level: Application
Difficulty: Moderate
Rationale: Identifying central themes is a focusing strategy to identify such issues as powerlessness, shame, and hopelessness.

9. You are meeting with the Jones family in the waiting room outside the intensive care unit. The father, Bruce Jones, is unconscious and is not expected to recover. You know to expect which of the following emotional symptoms in the family?

1) Relief, happiness, and anxiety
2) Anxiety, anger, and relief
3) Anxiety, anger, and shock
4) Acceptance, grief, and hopelessness

Correct Answer: 3
Topic: Families in Crisis
Step of the Nursing Process: Assessment
Cognitive Level: Application
Difficulty: Moderate
Rationale: Emotional symptoms of a family in crisis include anxiety, anger, shock, denial, guilt, grief, and hopelessness.

10. In dealing with a family in crisis, the nurse needs to remember:
    1) That functional families do not experience crises
    2) That family members experience crises in a similar manner
    3) To give an explanation to the family, not to the ill client
    4) To observe the family's physical state

Correct Answer: 4
Topic: Families in Crisis
Step of the Nursing Process: Assessment
Cognitive Level: Knowledge
Difficulty: Moderate
Rationale: Observation of the family's physical state is important because the family may need encouragement to take time out.

11. Which phase of the community response to disaster occurs when the community pulls together?
    1) Reconstruction phase
    2) Honeymoon phase
    3) Heroic phase
    4) Disillusionment phase

Correct Answer: 2
Topic: Community Response Patterns
Step of the Nursing Process: Interventions
Cognitive Level: Knowledge
Difficulty: Moderate
Rationale: The honeymoon phase occurs when the community pulls together.

12. Clients become violent when they:
    1) Feel helpless
    2) Feel threatened

3) Feel frustrated
4) Feel out of control

Correct Answer: 4
Topic: Violence
Step of the Nursing Process: Assessment
Cognitive Level: Knowledge
Difficulty: Moderate
Rationale: Violence is associated with power and control. The perpetrator feels powerless and out of control in a maladaptive attempt to restore emotional balance.

13. Which of the following is not a contributing factor to violence?
    1) Psychosis
    2) Childhood abuse
    3) Level of education
    4) Mental retardation

Correct Answer: 3
Topic: Violence
Step of the Nursing Process: Assessment
Cognitive Level: Knowledge
Difficulty: Moderate
Rationale: An individual's level of education is not a risk factor for violence.

14. Mrs. Cary, a recent widow, lives alone and only comes to clinic when she needs follow-up for her irregular heartbeat. This time Mrs. Cary states, "It doesn't matter. I will soon be with my husband." Your response is:
    1) "Can you tell me more about joining your husband?"
    2) "Your husband is dead, and you have so much to live for."
    3) "Your heartbeat was good today. The medication seems to be working."
    4) "Have you talked to your children recently about how you're doing?"

Correct Answer: 1
Topic: Suicide
Step of the Nursing Process: Assessment
Cognitive Level: Analysis
Difficulty: Moderate
Rationale: This question is designed to clarify what the client means and to assess level of risk.

15. Your client, Henry, is expressing thoughts of hopelessness and has had past episodes of

depression and one past suicide attempt. In assessing suicide risk, you know that:
1) People who talk about suicide do not kill themselves
2) Decreased suicide risk is indicated by increased mood
3) If a client is really experiencing suicidal ideation, he will not admit it
4) Distorted thoughts about the suicide attempt increase risk

Correct Answer: 4
Topic: Suicide
Step of the Nursing Process: Assessment
Cognitive Level: Application
Difficulty: Moderate
Rationale: Distorted feelings or thoughts increase the risk of suicide.

16. You are attempting to assess a client in the emergency department. His behavior is escalating, and you have just received a report on his toxicology screen that shows positive results for PCP. The most appropriate nursing action at this time is to:
1) Encourage ventilation
2) Demonstrate acceptance
3) Reassure the client
4) Take control

Correct Answer: 4
Topic: Interventions
Step of the Nursing Process: Implementation
Cognitive Level: Application
Difficulty: Moderate
Rationale: During the escalation period, taking control while maintaining a safe distance is the most appropriate action.

17. You are interviewing a client in crisis. You want to find out about social supports. You ask:
1) "What are your hobbies?"
2) "How do you spend your spare time?"
3) "Do you have any close friends?"
4) "How much do you spend a week on entertainment?"

Correct Answer: 3
Topic: Crisis Intervention
Step of the Nursing Process: Assessment
Cognitive Level: Application
Difficulty: Moderate

Rationale: Social support from family and friends can provide a sense of security, can offer encouragement, and can provide practical alternatives in a crisis situation.

18. Your client, Jim, who has a history of drug use and depression, has just lost his job and has found out that his mother has terminal cancer. With your knowledge of crisis intervention, you know that:
1) Individuals who have dealt with previous crises have a more difficult time dealing with new ones
2) The client's network will help the client resolve his crisis
3) Drug use and psychiatric illness makes a person more vulnerable
4) The client's network will hinder the client in resolving the crisis

Correct Answer: 3
Topic: Crisis Intervention
Step of the Nursing Process: Assessment
Cognitive Level: Application
Difficulty: Moderate
Rationale: Major psychiatric illness and drug use make a person more vulnerable to the effects of a crisis situation.

19. Which of the following is an indicator of potential violence?
1) Hyperalertness
2) Flat affect
3) Staring
4) Confusion

Correct Answer: 4
Topic: Violence
Step of the Nursing Process: Assessment
Cognitive Level: Knowledge
Difficulty: Moderate
Rationale: The nurse should assess mental status before attempting interventions. Confusion is an indicator of potential violence.

20. Robert, a client well known to the unit for a past history of substance abuse and violence, is observed pacing and speaking to other clients in a menacing way. What should your initial intervention be?

1) Encourage him to stop pacing and to sit down
2) Escort him to the dayroom to participate in unit activities
3) Call him by name using a low, calm tone of voice
4) Assign a male nurse to handle the situation

Correct Answer: 3
Topic: Treatment of Violent Clients
Step of the Nursing Process: Implementation
Cognitive Level: Application
Difficulty: Moderate
Rationale: Calling him by name and using a low, calm tone of voice help to defuse tension.

21. Gracie is a 17-year-old client who has been admitted to the psychiatric unit for a conduct

disorder. She was admitted with superficial scratches to both wrists and does not agree not to harm herself while on the unit. What level of supervision does this behavior warrant?
1) Observation every 30 minutes
2) Close observation every 5 to 10 minutes
3) A 1:1 restriction
4) Seclusion

Correct Answer: 2
Topic: Suicide
Step of the Nursing Process: Implementation
Cognitive Level: Application
Difficulty: Moderate
Rationale: Close observation is warranted because the client is unable to agree not to attempt suicide and has made a recent gesture.

CHAPTER 22
Communicating with Other Health Professionals

1. Using the skills of teacher, counselor, and leader to protect and support client's rights is known as:
1) Empowerment
2) Self-awareness
3) Advocacy
4) Lobbying

Correct Answer: 3
Topic: Advocacy
Step of the Nursing Process: All Phases of the Nursing Process
Cognitive Level: Knowledge
Difficulty: Moderate
Rationale: Client advocacy is a professional role that requires self-awareness and empowers clients.

2. When performing the advocate role of nursing, you provide care:
1) To clients
2) For clients
3) With clients
4) That takes charge of clients

Correct Answer: 3
Topic: Advocacy
Step of the Nursing Process: Implementation
Cognitive Level: Comprehension
Difficulty: Moderate

Rationale: The advocacy role requires the nurse to view the client as an equal partner in health care.

3. As a nurse, you refer a client recovering from breast cancer to a support group. Which type of advocacy is reflected in this situation?
1) Anticipatory guidance
2) Role-modeling
3) Educational support
4) Primary prevention

Correct Answer: 3
Topic: Types of Advocacy
Step of the Nursing Process: Implementation
Cognitive Level: Application
Difficulty: Moderate
Rationale: By referring the client to a community resource, the nurse is providing educational support to the client.

4. Ellen, a 45-year-old married woman, is admitted to hospital for rectal bleeding. Colon surgery is performed, and chemotherapy is recommended. Ellen refuses chemotherapy, she says, "because it will only make me feel worse and I will lose my hair." Your response is:

1) "Chemotherapy is recommended because of evidence of some spread of cancer."
2) "You have the right to a second opinion."
3) "You have the opportunity to change your mind."
4) "You have the right to determine your treatment plan."

Correct Answer: 4
Topic: Advocacy
Step of the Nursing Process: Implementation
Cognitive Level: Analysis
Difficulty: Hard
Rationale: Client advocacy recognizes the client's inherent right to make decisions. The nurse is respectful of client's choices even if they are not what the nurse would recommend.

5. Steps in the advocacy process include:
   1) Assess, diagnose, evaluate
   2) Assess, plan, implement
   3) Diagnose, implement, collaborate
   4) Protect, implement, diagnose

Correct Answer: 2
Topic: Steps in the Advocacy Process
Step of the Nursing Process: All Phases of the Nursing Process
Cognitive Level: Knowledge
Difficulty: Easy
Rationale: Steps in the advocacy process include assess, plan, implement, protect, evaluate, and collaborate.

6. In your role as a nurse, collaboration means two or more professionals:
   1) provide services to the client separately
   2) work with the client to provide services
   3) provide services to the client jointly
   4) work with the client separately to provide services

Correct Answer: 2
Topic: Collaboration
Step of the Nursing Process: Implementation
Cognitive Level: Comprehension
Difficulty: Moderate
Rationale: Collaboration means working simultaneously with one another and with the client.

7. Jamie, an unlicensed assistive person, is working with you on the night shift. You delegate to Jamie the changing of beds of clients who are incontinent. When you make your 6 a.m. rounds, you encounter a client who complains that she had to sleep in a wet bed all night. Which principle of delegation is violated in this situation?
   1) Oversee tasks that are delegated
   2) Evaluate tasks that are delegated
   3) Know the tasks that Jamie is capable of performing
   4) Know Jamie's willingness to perform delegated tasks

Correct Answer: 4
Topic: Delegation
Step of the Nursing Process: Implementation
Cognitive Level: Analysis
Difficulty: Hard
Rationale: In delegating, the nurse must know the knowledge level of the unlicensed assistive personnel, must assess the readiness for delegation, must delegate appropriately, must oversee the task, and must evaluate the outcomes.

8. Which of the following statements is true about conflict?
   1) Conflict is detrimental to productivity
   2) It is necessary to deal with all interpersonal conflicts
   3) The focus of conflict strategies is on the status relations of the health care providers
   4) A different type of relationship can be developed using conflict management techniques

Correct Answer: 4
Topic: Conflict
Step of the Nursing Process: All Phases of the Nursing Process
Cognitive Level: Comprehension
Difficulty: Moderate
Rationale: The primary goal in dealing with workplace conflict is to find a mutually acceptable win-win strategy.

9. Contributing factors in physician-nurse conflict include:
   1) Assertive nurses
   2) Well-educated nurses
   3) Physicians' attitudes

4) Changes in society

Correct Answer: 3
Topic: Physician-Nurse conflict
Step of the Nursing Process: All Phases of the Nursing Process
Cognitive Level: Comprehension
Difficulty: Easy
Rationale: Physicians' attitudes that a nurse is not a professional partner but is an accessory and that the physician is the only legitimate authority contribute to conflict.

10. You meet with your clinical instructor and obtain your final grade, a "C." You are disappointed because you expected a "B." Your instructor tells you that you did not always apply theory to practice using the most appropriate reference materials. Which of the following responses represents the ability to accept constructive criticism?
    1) "I have always been a 'B' student, and I think I deserve a 'B'"
    2) "I expected a 'B' grade. May we discuss this further at a later time?"
    3) "Will you review the evaluation form with me?"
    4) "How would you suggest I improve my clinical research?"

Correct Answer: 4
Topic: Constructive Criticism
Step of the Nursing Process: All Phases of the Nursing Process
Cognitive Level: Analysis
Difficulty: Moderate
Rationale: This response indicates that the student has listened carefully and has paraphrased the criticism. She has avoided becoming defensive, as in 1), 2), and 3), and wants to develop a plan to deal with the criticism.

11. Mike makes a derogatory statement to you in front of a client. You confront him about his verbal behavior. Which of the following is the best statement to defuse the situation?
    1) Say to Mike the next day, "Did you know that your behavior affects my job satisfaction?"
    2) At the end of the shift, say, "I felt embarrassed in front of Mr. Adams when you criticized my care."

3) "Mike, I did not appreciate the behavior you just displayed in there."
4) Gain your composure and state, "Mike, I am a good nurse, so don't criticize me again in front of a client."

Correct Answer: 3
Topic: Responding to Putdowns
Step of the Nursing Process: All Phases of the Nursing Process
Cognitive Level: Application
Difficulty: Moderate
Rationale: Once a putdown is recognized, the nurse needs to respond immediately in an assertive manner.

12. You are feeling anxious around a colleague and realize this is a result of conflicting values. You consider seeking peer negotiation because you are aware that:
    1) Friction can turn relationships from competitive to collaborative
    2) It is appropriate to seek peer negotiation when personal conflict occurs
    3) Concrete, observable facts related to the issue should be the focus
    4) Sharing feelings about a conflict increases the intensity

Correct Answer: 3
Topic: Peer Negotiation
Step of the Nursing Process: All Phases of the Nursing Process
Cognitive Level: Application
Difficulty: Moderate
Rationale: Personal feelings should not be discussed during peer negotiation. You should stick to discussing concrete, observable facts.

13. Professional group productivity and member satisfaction are best achieved by which of the following leadership styles?
    1) Authoritarian
    2) Democratic
    3) Laissez-faire
    4) Autocratic

Correct Answer: 2
Topic: Leadership Styles
Step of the Nursing Process: All Phases of the Nursing Process
Cognitive Level: Knowledge
Difficulty: Easy

Rationale: Member satisfaction is highest in groups with a democratic leader. This leader encourages open expression of ideas, which increases productivity.

14. You have volunteered to be part of a workgroup whose purpose is to look at ways to prevent medication errors. You know that:
    1) Group process is not important in a task group
    2) Teamwork enhances the probability of goal achievement
    3) The goals should be set by management
    4) The leader assumes responsibility for the overall group functioning

Correct Answer: 2
Topic: Member Responsibilities
Step of the Nursing Process: All Phases of the Nursing Process
Cognitive Level: Application
Difficulty: Moderate
Rationale: A group format benefits problem resolution by generating new ideas.

15. You are a member of a workgroup to update policies and procedures and to computerize them. Your general responsibilities as a workgroup member include:
    1) Examining problems subjectively
    2) Helping to develop a single solution
    3) Sitting quietly and not interrupting
    4) Coming prepared to all meetings

Correct Answer: 4
Topic: Member Responsibilities
Step of the Nursing Process: All Phases of the Nursing Process
Cognitive Level: Application
Difficulty: moderate
Rationale: A workgroup member must take personal responsibility as a member and come prepared for all sessions.

16. Group member responsibilities are outlined clearly and understood by all during which stage of group development?
    1) Norming
    2) Storming
    3) Forming
    4) Performing

Correct Answer: 1
Topic: Task Identification
Step of the Nursing Process: All Phases of the Nursing Process
Cognitive Level: Knowledge
Difficulty: Moderate
Rationale: Member responsibilities such as maintaining confidentiality and regular attendance are outlined during the norming stage.

17. Which of the following is *not* a right in nursing practice?
    1) The right to a reasonable workload
    2) The right to an equitable wage
    3) The right to get what you want
    4) The right to make mistakes and to be responsible for them

Correct Answer: 3
Topic: Chenevert's Rights in Nursing Practice
Step of the Nursing Process: All phases in the Nursing Process
Cognitive Level: Knowledge
Difficulty: Easy
Rationale: You have the right to ask for what you want as long as it does not interfere with the rights of others.

18. After working 12 hours on a busy medical unit, your supervisor asks you to work another 12-hour shift. You say no. In doing this, you are exercising your right to:
    1) Ask for what you want
    2) Assume a reasonable workload
    3) Refuse an unreasonable request
    4) Give and receive information

Correct Answer: 3
Topic: Chenevert's Rights in Nursing Practice
Step of the Nursing Process: All Phases of the Nursing Process
Cognitive Level: Application
Difficulty: Moderate
Rationale: You have the right to refuse unreasonable requests without making excuses or feeling guilty.

19. "The dress code in this facility does not include wearing blue jeans while on duty." This statement is an example of using which step in giving constructive criticism?
    1) Expressing empathy

2) Describing the behavior
3) Stating expectations
4) Listing consequences

Correct Answer: 3
Topic: Giving Constructive Criticism
Step of the Nursing Process: All Phases of the Nursing Process

Cognitive Level: Knowledge
Difficulty: Easy
Rationale: This statement would be used in the third step of giving constructive feedback, in which behavioral expectations are clearly stated.

CHAPTER 23

Documentation in the Age of Computers

1. Which of the following purposes of documentation is specific to computerized technology?
   1) Provides a record of care
   2) Helps establish benchmark for care
   3) Substantiates quality of care
   4) Provides evidence for reimbursement

Correct Answer: 2
Topic: Computerized Documentation
Step of the Nursing Process: All Phases of the Nursing Process
Cognitive Level: Comprehension
Difficulty: Moderate
Rationale: Computerized documentation allows for the aggregation of patient care information to establish benchmarks for care and care pathways.

2. The need for all agencies to computerize has been accelerated as a result of:
   1) Faster access to laboratory test results
   2) Easier retrieval for billing and reimbursement
   3) Increased deaths from medication errors
   4) The need to support telehealth

Correct Answer: 3
Topic: Computerized Documentation
Step of the Nursing Process: All Phases of the Nursing Process
Cognitive Level: Knowledge
Difficulty: Moderate
Rationale: The need for all agencies to computerize has been accelerated by the Institute of Medicine report on deaths from medication errors.

3. One major advantage of computer-assisted documentation is:
   1) Flow sheets of client data
   2) Portability of health record
   3) Summary list of client needs

   4) Intake and output forms

Correct Answer: 2
Topic: Computerized Documentation
Step of the Nursing Process: All Phases of the Nursing Process
Cognitive Level: Knowledge
Difficulty: Moderate
Rationale: The computerized patient record (CPR) can be stored in a data warehouse that is accessible to all care providers.

4. Which of the following is not a disadvantage of computerized technology?
   1) Cost
   2) Confidentiality
   3) Incompatibility
   4) Reduction of errors

Correct Answer: 4
Topic: Computerized Technology
Step of the Nursing Process: All Phases of the Nursing Process
Cognitive Level: Knowledge
Difficulty: Moderate
Rationale: Reduction of errors caused by illegible handwriting is an advantage of computerized technology.

5. Which of the following is a disadvantage of computerized charting?
   1) Lack of uniform language
   2) Improved access to health record
   3) Standardized charting
   4) Preset codable activities

Correct Answer: 3
Topic: Computerized Charting
Step of the Nursing Process: All Phases of the Nursing Process
Cognitive Level: Knowledge

Difficulty: Moderate
Rationale: Nurses are concerned that the use of standardized charting will lose the richness of individualized care.

6. Roy, age 35, is recovering from an appendectomy. Which of the following coding systems would you use for documenting changing of his postoperative abdominal dressing?
    1) Current procedural terminology
    2) Diagnostic related groups
    3) Nursing Interventions Classification (NIC)
    4) North American Nursing Diagnosis Association (NANDA)

Correct Answer: 3
Topic: Coding Systems
Step of the Nursing Process: Interventions
Cognitive Level: Application
Difficulty: Moderate
Rationale: The nursing intervention classification organizes nursing interventions under domains.

7. Which classification system can be used readily with the nursing diagnosis Immobility related to a stroke?
    1) The Omaha system of client problems
    2) Clinical pathways
    3) Nursing Interventions Classification (NIC)
    4) International Classification of Disease

Correct Answer: 3
Topic: Classification Systems
Step of the Nursing Process: Diagnosis
Cognitive Level: Analysis
Difficulty: Moderate
Rationale: The nursing intervention classification organizes nursing interventions under domains.

8. It is 3 days after Ted's gallbladder surgery as a result of gallstones. *Domain:* Physiological. *Class:* Fluid and electrolyte balance. *Activity:* Check intravenous fluid rate intake every hour. Which of the following nursing coding systems is represented in this situation?
    1) North American Nursing Diagnosis Association (NANDA)
    2) Nursing Interventions Classification (NIC)
    3) Nursing Outcomes Classification (NOC)
    4) The Omaha system of client problems

Correct Answer: 2

Topic: Classification Systems
Step of the Nursing Process: Interventions
Cognitive Level: Analysis
Difficulty: Hard
Rationale: Nursing intervention classification identifies nursing interventions that are classified under domains and classes.

9. Which of the following components of the nursing minimum data set gives direction for activities of therapeutic nursing actions?
    1) Nursing diagnosis
    2) Nursing interventions
    3) Nursing outcomes
    4) Nursing intensity of care

Correct Answer: 1
Topic: Nursing Minimum Data Set
Step of the Nursing Process: Diagnosis
Cognitive Level: Knowledge
Difficulty: Moderate
Rationale: The nursing minimum data set can be used to describe utilization and nursing care needs and allocating resources according to nursing diagnosis.

10. Which type of charting reveals a nurse's critical thinking processes?
    1) Charting by exception
    2) SOAP charting
    3) Flow sheets
    4) Narrative charting

Correct Answer: 2
Topic: Charting
Step of the Nursing Process: All Phases of the Nursing Process
Cognitive Level: Analysis
Difficulty: Hard
Rationale: This four-step method of documentation lists subjective (S), objective (O), analysis of the problem (A), and the plans (P) for the client.

11. Federal Medical Record Privacy Regulations are known as:
    1) ICD-9
    2) HIPAA
    3) PDA
    4) Nightingale tracker system

Correct Answer: 2
Topic: Confidentiality and Privacy
Step of the Nursing Process: All Phases of the Nursing Process

Cognitive Level: Knowledge
Difficulty: Easy
Rationale: HIPAA, the Health Insurance Portability and Accountability Act, protects the client's medical record confidentiality.

12. Which of the following is a guideline for using passwords?
    1) Select passwords that consist of uppercase letters
    2) Use birthdays and telephone numbers
    3) Reuse passwords to avoid forgetting them
    4) Use different passwords for different accounts

Correct Answer: 4
Topic: Ethical, Regulatory, and Professional Standards
Step of the Nursing Process: All Phases of the Nursing Process
Cognitive Level: Knowledge
Difficulty: Moderate
Rationale: The use of uppercase letters helps keep passwords secret so that unauthorized persons cannot access clinical information.

13. You have been asked to fax the report of a magnetic resonance image (MRI) of your client to the physician's office. After pressing the "Send" key, you realize that the fax was misdirected. The first thing you should do is:
    1) Notify the client
    2) Send the MRI report to the correct location
    3) Contact the receiver
    4) Do nothing, because there was a confidentiality statement on the cover sheet

Correct Answer: 3
Topic: Guidelines for Faxing Medical Records
Step of the Nursing Process: All Phases of the Nursing Process
Cognitive Level: Application
Difficulty: Moderate
Rationale: Contact the receiver and request that the report be returned or destroyed.

14. Review the charting sample and determine which documentation error occurred:
    1000: Hygienic care given
    1100: Complaint of leg pain
    1300: Appetite good, resting comfortably

1) Failure to record complete, pertinent health information
2) Failure to record drug information and administration
3) Not recording all nursing actions
4) Failure to record outcome of an intervention

Correct Answer: 2
Topic: Documentation
Step of the Nursing Process: All Phases of the Nursing Process
Cognitive Level: Application
Difficulty: Moderate
Rationale: The nurse has not documented the administration of an analgesic medication.

15. Your client, Andy, age 14, has diabetes, yet is found eating a cheeseburger, french fries, and a large milkshake. When questioned, he states, "What's wrong with this diet?" Which of the following is an appropriate nursing diagnosis?
    1) Insulin-dependent diabetes mellitus
    2) Impaired health teaching
    3) Knowledge deficit related to nutritional status, as evidenced by diet
    4) Impaired nutritional status, as evidenced by diet

Correct Answer: 3
Topic: Nursing Diagnosis
Step of the Nursing Process: Diagnosis
Cognitive Level: Analysis
Difficulty: Moderate
Rationale: Andy's problem is his lack of knowledge about his diabetes nutrition, as evidenced by his high-calorie diet.

16. Which of the following is a nursing outcome in relation to pain?
    1) Promotion of rest
    2) Chronic pain
    3) Recognition of pain onset
    4) Pain management

Correct Answer: 3
Topic: Nursing Outcomes
Step of the Nursing Process: Planning
Cognitive Level: Application
Difficulty: Moderate
Rationale: Recognizing the onset of pain is an outcome that will allow the client to seek pain intervention early to prevent pain increase.

NOTES

NOTES

NOTES

NOTES

NOTES

NOTES

NOTES

NOTES

NOTES

NOTES

NOTES

NOTES

NOTES

NOTES